797,885 Books

are available to read at

Forgotten Books

www.ForgottenBooks.com

Forgotten Books' App
Available for mobile, tablet & eReader

ISBN 978-1-331-62187-4
PIBN 10214178

This book is a reproduction of an important historical work. Forgotten Books uses state-of-the-art technology to digitally reconstruct the work, preserving the original format whilst repairing imperfections present in the aged copy. In rare cases, an imperfection in the original, such as a blemish or missing page, may be replicated in our edition. We do, however, repair the vast majority of imperfections successfully; any imperfections that remain are intentionally left to preserve the state of such historical works.

Forgotten Books is a registered trademark of FB &c Ltd.
Copyright © 2015 FB &c Ltd.
FB &c Ltd, Dalton House, 60 Windsor Avenue, London, SW19 2RR.
Company number 08720141. Registered in England and Wales.

For support please visit www.forgottenbooks.com

1 MONTH OF FREE READING

at

www.ForgottenBooks.com

By purchasing this book you are eligible for one month membership to ForgottenBooks.com, giving you unlimited access to our entire collection of over 700,000 titles via our web site and mobile apps.

To claim your free month visit:
www.forgottenbooks.com/free214178

* Offer is valid for 45 days from date of purchase. Terms and conditions apply.

English
Français
Deutsche
Italiano
Español
Português

www.forgottenbooks.com

Mythology Photography **Fiction**
Fishing Christianity **Art** Cooking
Essays Buddhism Freemasonry
Medicine **Biology** Music **Ancient Egypt** Evolution Carpentry Physics
Dance Geology **Mathematics** Fitness
Shakespeare **Folklore** Yoga Marketing
Confidence Immortality Biographies
Poetry **Psychology** Witchcraft
Electronics Chemistry History **Law**
Accounting **Philosophy** Anthropology
Alchemy Drama Quantum Mechanics
Atheism Sexual Health **Ancient History**
Entrepreneurship Languages Sport
Paleontology Needlework Islam
Metaphysics Investment Archaeology
Parenting Statistics Criminology
Motivational

Marshal Foch and General Pershing at Chaumont, France, American General Headquarters

King Albert of Belgium, who decorated several of our men of the 37th Division for bravery in action

President W. O. Thompson

Dean Edward Orton, Jr.

Lieut. Col. Ralph D. Mershon

Major George L. Converse

These gentlemen shaped and promoted the National Defense Act

HISTORY OF
THE OHIO STATE UNIVERSITY

VOLUME IV

THE UNIVERSITY
IN THE GREAT WAR

PART I

WARTIME ON THE CAMPUS

By

WILBUR H. SIEBERT
Research Professor in History

With a Chapter by
PROFESSOR CARL WITTKE

Illustrated

THE OHIO STATE UNIVERSITY PRESS
COLUMBUS
1934

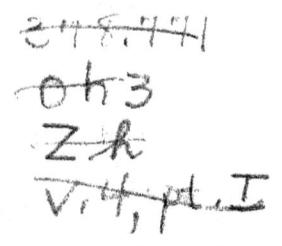

COPYRIGHT, 1935
BY THE OHIO STATE UNIVERSITY

INSCRIBED TO
THOSE MEN AND WOMEN
WHOSE RECORDS IN THESE VOLUMES
ARE A SOURCE OF PRIDE
TO THE UNIVERSITY AND THE STATE

PREFACE

The notable part played by the University, its teachers and administrators, and its sons and daughters, in the Great War is recounted as far as possible in this work, which comprises three parts; namely, Part I, In War Time on the Campus; Part II, Ohio State Men and Women in Service; and Part III, Our Men in Military and Naval Service.

The materials for Part I, which have entered into the preparation of the present volume, were gathered from the records of the Board of Trustees, the University and College Faculties, the printed *Reports* of President W. O. Thompson, the full and detailed communications generously furnished by the heads and other members of practically all departments of the institution, as also by the fraternities, sororities, and those organizations, whether permanent or temporary, that engaged in war work, and from the student and other University publications of the period under review. A section dealing with these publications during the time of hostilities has been kindly supplied by Professor Carl Wittke, and a much longer section on "Our Men on the Battle Fronts," which appears in Part II, has with equal kindness been prepared by Professor Edgar H. McNeal.

The University and the State of Ohio are indebted to these gentlemen and to all others who by their aid have made possible the preparation of this work.

The author of most of the chapters contained in Parts I and II, who was also the final compiler of "Our Roll of Honor," "The List of Decorations and Citations," and the several lists of service records, acknowledges with grateful thanks all help received, especially the personal interest shown by President George W. Rightmire in the progress of the undertaking and the provision by him of needed clerical assistance.

Such mistakes as appear in these volumes, and it would indeed be curious if mistakes have not crept in despite all efforts to prevent it, must be attributed to the undersigned alone.

May, 1929.   WILBUR H. SIEBERT, '88.

CONTENTS

Chapter		Page
I	The University, the National Defense Act, and the Exodus for Service..	1
II	United States Military Schools on the Campus..........	17
III	War Drives at the University..........................	41
IV	Red Cross Activities..................................	51
V	War Work of the Religious Organizations...............	67
VI	The Ohio Union in Wartime...........................	77
VII	Campus Publications During the War..................	83
VIII	Athletics During the War.............................	107
IX	The Sororities and Fraternities During 1917 and 1918....	113
X	The College of Agriculture and the Food Problem........	131
XI	Various Services of the College of Arts, Philosophy, and Science	147
XII	The College of Commerce and Journalism in Wartime....	171
XIII	The College of Dentistry, the Dental Clinic, and Military Service	183
XIV	The Psychological and Other Services of the College of Education..	189
XV	The College of Engineering and Technical War Service...	197
XVI	The Problems of the Graduate School...................	243
XVII	The Services of the College of Homeopathic Medicine.....	247
XVIII	The Temporary Closing of the College of Law and Its Later Service	251
XIX	The Services of the College of Medicine.................	255
XX	Men of the College of Pharmacy in Medical, Sanitary, and Hospital Units	273
XXI	Services of the College of Veterinary Medicine...........	275
XXII	The Aftermath of the War in the University............	285

ILLUSTRATIONS

Frontispiece

Marshal Foch and General Pershing at Chaumont, France, American General Headquarters

King Albert of Belgium, who decorated several of our men of the 37th Division for bravery in action

President W. O. Thompson, Dean Edward Orton, Jr., Major George L. Converse, Col. Ralph D. Mershon

Facing page

The Academic Board, United States Army School of Military Aeronautics	16
Landing Field on the Campus, west of Neil Avenue Extension	16
A class in range-finding and shell spotting	17
A class in machine-gun practice	17
Taking off from the University Landing Field in wartime	40
Trustee Charles F. Kettering arriving after a flight from Dayton, Ohio	40
Professor W. A. Knight and a class in airplanes, after examining Trustee Kettering's flying machine	41
Barracks for the Army School of Military Aeronautics, built near Woodruff Avenue in wartime	41
Mrs. W. O. Thompson and ten other ladies finishing the service flag	58
The service flag displayed on the front of the Library	59
T. M. Magruder and his ambulance on the road at Maison Rouge, near the Chemin des Dames, September, 1917	76
T. M. Magruder (in center) and his ambulance just south of Beauvais, France, April, 1918	76
Columbus, Ohio, Red Cross Hospital Unit No. 5 at the Naval Operating Base, Hampton Roads, Virginia, April 17, 1919	77
Interior of part of Hayes Hall, which was used as barracks	106
Cadets engaging in one form of recreation	106
The Military Hospital where two hundred influenza patients were treated in the autumn of 1918	107
A class in surveying, Army School of Military Aeronautics	107
A class in trap-shooting, Army School of Military Aeronautics	170
Professor H. C. Lord conducting a class in aids to flight	170

ILLUSTRATIONS

Graduating exercises of a unit of the Army School of Military Aeronautics	171
A University wartime parade passing the State House, Columbus, Ohio	171
Officers of the Laboratory and Inspection Division, Edgewood Arsenal, Maryland, under Major W. L. Evans	214
The Chlorine Plant at Edgewood Arsenal	214
Airplane view of the toxic-gas buildings at Edgewood	215
Tear-gas Plant at Edgewood, designed and erected by Major O. R. Sweeney	215
Mustard-gas Manufactory at Edgewood, designed and erected under the direction of Major Dana J. Demorest	274
Chemical Laboratory at Edgewood for research and control work, presided over by Major W. L. Evans	274
Apparatus for the manufacture of carbon monoxide gas at Edgewood, designed in part by Major Demorest	275
Tanks of phosgene gas ready for shipment	275
President Thompson and Ohio State men at Fort Benjamin Harrison, Indiana, on May 27, 1917	293
The 166th Infantry, 42d (Rainbow) Division, being received at the Union Station on Saturday, May 10, 1919	294
The 166th Infantry marching down High Street	294

WARTIME ON THE CAMPUS

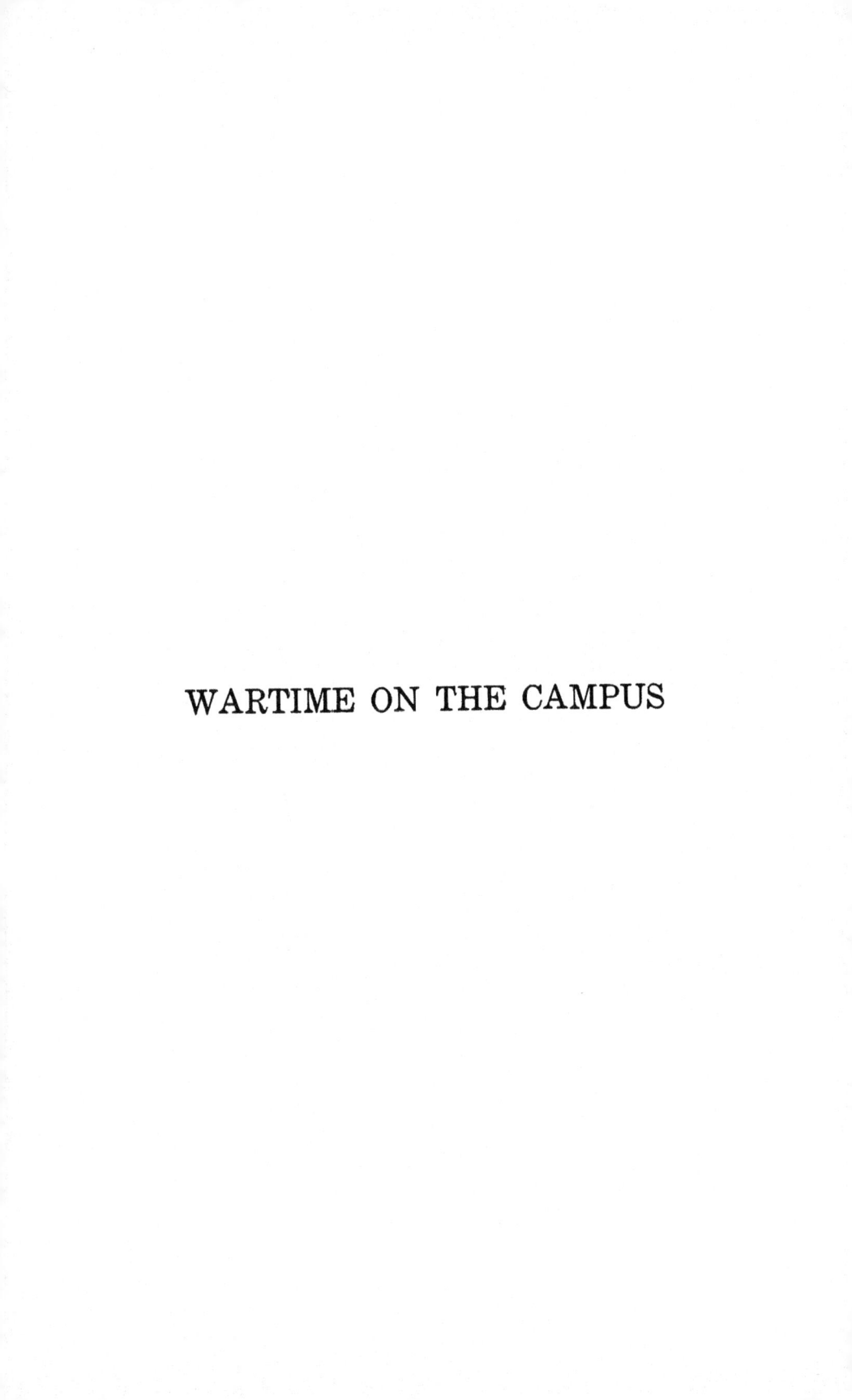

CHAPTER I

THE UNIVERSITY, THE NATIONAL DEFENSE ACT, AND THE EXODUS FOR SERVICE

It is not generally known that President W. O. Thompson and certain graduates and members of the Ohio State University Faculty had an important share in the framing of the National Defense Act of June 3, 1916. The credit for the collegiate features of that act belongs to Ohio State through the active interest in military education and the wise management of Professor Edward Orton, dean of the College of Engineering; Captain George L. Converse, who for some years previous to the Great War had insisted that in an emergency the Government would have to look to the colleges for military officers; President Thompson, who cooperated with these men, and Mr. Ralph D. Mershon '90, who promoted their ideas among the members of Congress.

In November, 1913, Dean Orton read a paper on "The Status of the Military Department of the Land-Grant Colleges" before the Association of Agricultural Colleges and Experiment Stations in Washington, at which the engineering colleges of the land-grant institutions were also represented. Dean Orton pointed out in his paper the need of some mechanism by which students who had graduated from the military departments of the 48 land-grant colleges could become eligible for service in the United States Army through an officers' reserve corps. General Leonard Wood was present, with several officers of his staff, and not only discussed the paper, but also secured permission subsequently to print and circulate it among Army officers on school duty and among the presidents of the colleges and academies giving military instruction.

Already the Ohio State University battalion numbered about 1,500 men, and the time of its commandant was being largely consumed in administrative routine. In order to afford Captain Converse more leisure for developing military instruction at the University, Messrs. Mershon and Orton generously provided the money for employing two student assistants in the regiment. In September, 1914, the Board of Trustees took up the matter and appropriated $1,000 for the payment of a second officer, and the War Department detailed Lieutenant T. D. Thorpe (retired) to fill the new position. This appointment made possible the differentiation between the first- and second-year work in military instruction. The second-year work was made more advanced, including small maneuvers, tactical marches and demonstrations, and officers' classes in mapping and military theory. Lieutenant Thorpe's service lasted until June, 1916, when the detail of officers on the active list of the Army became possible under the newly passed National Defense Act.

Meanwhile, questionnaires had been sent to the land-grant colleges, and they were found to be in general accord with the fundamental ideas advanced in Dean Orton's paper of 1913. Accordingly, President Thompson, with the aid of his associates and in conference with representatives of the Association of Military Schools (private schools and academies) and the War College Committee on Education, drew up a bill on behalf of the land-grant institutions. This bill provided (a) for a much larger allotment of officers for instructional work than in the past; (b) for the creation of a Reserve Officers' Training Corps of which the military departments of the colleges were to be units, and (c) for the establishment of an Officers' Reserve Corps, to which the graduates of the training corps would be eligible, certain inducements being offered to them to go into it. President Thompson secured the introduction of this bill in the fall of 1915 simultaneously in the Senate and House as the Pomerene Bill (S. B. 3946) and the Gard Bill (H. B. 10845).

As other bills for Army reorganization were also being introduced, it became necessary to bring to the attention of congressmen the merits of the Pomerene-Gard measure. Mr. Mershon was at the time president of the American Institute of Electrical Engineers, and, with the aid of his associates at the University, prepared the letters of information and appeal which he printed and sent at his own expense to the membership of all the great engineering societies of the country. These engineers, besides many influential manufacturers among their acquaintances, took up the matter with the congressmen from their districts, and thus aroused a considerable sentiment for the Pomerene-Gard bill.

In May, 1916, the four Ohio State supporters of this bill went to Washington and succeeded in getting its provisions incorporated in the National Defense Act, which was passed on June 3. In the following September the War Department issued General Orders No. 49, containing the "regulations and instructions governing the establishment, administration, and maintenance of the Reserve Officers' Training Corps at educational institutions," under Section 40 of the Defense Act. This section authorized the President of the United States to establish and maintain a senior division of the Reserve Officers' Training Corps at State universities and other State educational institutions required to provide instruction in military science and tactics under the law of Congress establishing the land-grant colleges, with the object of preparing students "to perform intelligently the duties of commissioned officers in the military forces of the United States."

Needless to say, a unit of the R. O. T. C. was established at the University in the fall of 1916. However, the War Department was then involved in the Mexican Punitive Expedition, and provisions to carry into effect certain features of the law were not made; hence military instruction on the campus remained on substantially the old basis, except that the commandant was now assisted by a detail of two commissioned officers, Captain J. D. Tilford and Lieutenant R. G. Sherrard, and five noncommissioned officers. The principal effect of this increase of officers was to improve the quality of the military instruction. The declaration of war against the German Government, April 6, 1917, again delayed the work of organizing the Reserve Officers' Training Corps, as specified in the act of June 3, 1916.

OHIO STATE UNIVERSITY MOBILIZES

On May 7, 1915, the *Lusitania* was torpedoed and sunk off the Irish coast, after warnings from the German embassy to Americans not to sail on the ship. It was said that she carried neither cannon nor explosives, but that did not save the lives of over 1,000 passengers, of whom more than 100 were Americans. In the course of the next year the German Government gave a solemn pledge to the United States that ships would not be sunk thereafter without warning. Nevertheless, on February 1, 1917, this pledge was countermanded and the old practice was revived. The State Department had already made public the Zimmerman Note, in which a German official offered our southwestern States to Mexico if she would join Germany and Japan in hostilities against us. German agents and sympathizers in America had been busy in fomenting a revolution in Ireland, placing bombs upon ships, blowing up buildings, and promoting strikes. On February 3, 1917, President Wilson dismissed the German ambassador and severed diplomatic relations. On the 26th he recommended armed neutrality, and a fortnight later he ordered American merchant vessels to be armed. The Russian Revolution in March so endangered the cause of democracy that the President urged Congress, April 2, to declare war on the German Imperial Government, whose recent course, he said, was "nothing less than war against the Government and people of the United States." Four days later Congress issued the declaration.

Already on March 31 the Ohio State University had taken steps to mobilize her sons. Professor Orton and Captain Converse had prepared a circular letter, or call, to be sent to all commissioned officers of the University regiment since 1890, urging them to offer their services to the Government through the Officers' Reserve Corps. This letter was submitted to the

Faculty, April 2, and approved by that body, as it was also approved by the Board of Trustees and the president of the Alumni Association, Mr. George Smart. Between 400 and 500 copies of this letter were mailed out, bearing the signature of Captain Converse, and were followed by a similar letter addressed to about 4,000 graduates and former students who had received military instruction as privates in the University regiment. The address list of all these men, together with information as to their education and military training, was sent to the War Department, with the suggestion that application blanks for commissions or for entrance to training camps be forwarded to them. It is gratifying to record that a large proportion of these men responded to the call of the University and promptly entered the service in some capacity.

It was also on April 2 and 3 that the Faculty and Trustees joined in authorizing President Thompson to send a message to the White House, expressing their entire confidence in Mr. Wilson's leadership of the nation and messages of the same import to our representatives and senators in Congress. Dr. Thompson's letter pledged the loyal support of both Trustees and Faculty to the Chief Executive and placed at his command the resources of the University in research laboratories and in men.

Meantime, a communication was drafted and sent to the president and commandant of every land-grant college and State university, telling of the call issued to the sons of Ohio State and suggesting similar action on their part, in order that the Government might have the service of as many as possible of the 300,000 graduates and former students of these institutions who had received military training and were of military age.

Not only did the University take steps to mobilize its graduates and former students for military purposes; it also mobilized numbers of the undergraduates in order to increase food production in 1917. In the early part of April of this year President Thompson, who was then chairman of the executive committee of the Association of Agricultural Colleges and Experiment Stations, appealed to these institutions to do their utmost to improve the food situation. His appeal stated that in 1915 ten bushels of wheat *per capita* were produced in the United States; in 1916, six bushels *per capita*, while we consumed six and one-third bushels *per capita* and exported two and one-half bushels *per capita* in this year. He added that in 1917 world conditions were such as to bring the wheat supply in reserve to a low level, and that the crop prospects in important wheat-producing areas were not good. He declared that the colleges should recognize that the supreme duty of the hour was to produce food supplies enough to maintain our own people and provide a surplus for other nations. He pointed out that immediate action was necessary, on account of the rapid advance of the planting season.

After considering this appeal, the Agricultural Faculty of the Ohio State University recommended, April 14, that all the colleges of the University excuse for the remainder of the academic year all students who would pledge themselves to engage in agricultural service from May 1 to August 31, 1917. The recommendation of the College of Agriculture was laid before the Administrative Council, and the University Faculty was called together in special session, April 17. It was voted, in view of the food emergency confronting the country and the whole world, to excuse from class work those students who were needed on their home farms, or would go into other agricultural service approved by the dean of the College of Agriculture, on condition of signing a pledge to devote their energy and efforts to such service. On returning with a signed statement from their employer testifying to their faithful performance of their duty, they were to receive full credit for their scheduled courses, in case their records had previously been satisfactory. Seniors fulfilling these conditions were to be awarded their degrees at Commencement. Within a month after the announcement of this action about 1,200 students withdrew from the University, most of them to engage in farm work, while some departed to enter military or naval service. The Faculty also approved the immediate release of eight seniors of high standing from the College of Medicine, these men having passed the Government naval examination for temporary assignment to the United States Naval Medical College at Washington in preparation for regular service. These and many other seniors were graduated *in absentia* at Commencement, June 5, 1917.

The mobilization of the undergraduates did not stop with the Faculty action in mid-April. About a month later Governor James M. Cox, deeply impressed by the foreboding reports of the war he had received in Washington, called the presidents of the state-supported universities and normal schools in conference and then issued an executive order for the purpose of sending as many as possible of the male students remaining at these institutions into the productive industries. This order was, of course, adopted by the Faculty, and the undergraduates concerned were dismissed, May 15, 1917, excepting members of the graduating class, premedical, engineering, pharmacy, dentistry, and veterinary students, who were exempted in accordance with the policy of the Federal Government. The dismissal carried with it the express understanding that those involved would receive credit for the rest of the semester, according to their standing at the time. In the case of those whose ratings were below the pass mark, opportunity was to be afforded to take an examination on their return.

Four hundred and forty-four men withdrew on May 15. This brought the total number of withdrawals for Government service since the entrance of the United States into the war up to 1,560. During this period the College of Arts, Philosophy, and Science lost 645 of its students, leaving about 770. In the College of Agriculture 385 remained out of an enrollment of 963. The College of Commerce and Journalism lost 51 of its 79 students, and the College of Education only 49 from its enrollment of 457. Approximately 2,900 students remained in the University; but it was estimated that 700 more would take their departure before the present rush of withdrawals was ended, leaving about 1,000 men and 1,200 women still in the institution.

On May 10 the Faculty had empowered the President to excuse seniors who were serving their country from attending the Commencement exercises, and the Board of Trustees remitted the diploma fees of these absent ones, many of whom were already undergoing training at Fort Benjamin Harrison or other camps. Commencement Day fell on June 5, which happened to be the date designated by President Wilson's proclamation requiring registration for military service of all men between the ages of 21 and 31 years. As the registration hours extended from 7 o'clock in the morning until 9 at night, the seniors in attendance were not prevented from taking part in the campus exercises, especially as the proclamation contained a clause making it possible for the University students to register in Columbus instead of returning to their own communities. Few others than seniors and juniors were under the necessity of registering.

After Commencement in June, 1917, members of the teaching staff began preparing to go into public service of one kind or another. At their meeting of July 3 the Trustees gave the President full power to arrange with instructors of all grades for leaves of absence and to make any necessary adjustment of salary. On July 24 the Board granted only one leave, but on September 4 it granted 25, nearly three-fifths of these being members of the Medical Faculty. Among the 25, however, were Professor Orton of the College of Engineering and Dean William McPherson of the Graduate School. At this time the Trustees adopted the policy of paying teachers entering public service the difference between the amount paid by the Government and the salary received from the University. On October 2 Dean Eugene F. McCampbell of the College of Medicine and Dean David S. White of the College of Veterinary Medicine were granted indefinite leaves of absence, others following until the total number reached 95. This number does not include those members of the Executive Staff and of the Division of Operation and Maintenance who were absent in service. There were 11 of these, including President Thompson and Secretary Carl E. Steeb. Two members of the Department of German were debarred from the campus as aliens by federal action in the fall of 1917, and another was given a year's leave of absence with the understanding that he was not to return. These three men were the only persons among the 412 members of the teaching staff whose sentiments were under suspicion, and two of these were subjects of the German Empire.

Not only was the University seriously affected in its work by the withdrawal of numbers of students and teachers; it was also confronted by the coal shortage. Early in July, 1917, the Trustees were informed that of the 39 operators and dealers who had been asked to submit bids covering the coming year, but one had responded; and his price would involve the University in an aggregate expense of at least $79,000 for the year's supply, whereas the appropriation for coal was only $35,000. On the advice of the State budget commissioner the Board decided to buy fuel in the open market until such time as the coal market adjusted itself. The situation had certainly not improved by the beginning of the Christmas recess, and President Thompson found it necessary to announce, December 19, that during the holidays the temperature of all buildings, except those devoted to administration, would be reduced to 45 degrees, and to urge that all societies and organizations hold their meetings during daylight hours, in order that the buildings might be closed at 6:30 o'clock, P. M. With the opening of the new year the Monday closing order of the federal fuel administrator was in operation, but, as a military post, the University was exempt from this order. Professor F. A. Ray, who was absent on leave during the second half of this year, devoted his energies to increasing the coal output and assisting the fuel administration. However, the institution was obliged to close for a few days on account of its inability to obtain fuel.

Another problem which the Board of Trustees and its agents had to deal with was the School of Military Aeronautics, the history of which is given in the following chapter. The only phase of the subject that need concern us here is the provision that was made for housing and feeding the detachments or squadrons of men who had been arriving each week since May 21, 1917, for training in aviation. At first the cadets were quartered in part of Hayes Hall and obtained their meals in the dining-room of Ohio Union. They attended classes and lectures partly in Hayes Hall and partly in Robinson Laboratory. By July their number had increased to 130 and gave promise of reaching very soon the maximum of 200, the number specified in the contract which the Trustees had signed with the War Department. Early in July, therefore, the Trustees directed President Thompson and Secretary Carl E. Steeb to have plans and estimates prepared at once for an Aeronautical Laboratory, a Machine-gun Range, and Barracks and a latrine of sufficient size to accommodate at least 200 aviators and their officers, and for additions to the dining-room and the refrigeration and storage room of the Union. Late in the same month the Trustees had a conference with Governor James M. Cox, who readily approved their projects as war measures. On September 10 the Emergency Board of the State took the same view of the matter and appropriated $80,000—the amount asked—for the proposed buildings. Without formal advertising, the bids were received two weeks later. That the University authorities were none too soon in their action is proved by the fact that the War Department decided at this time to call on the institution to undertake the training of 500 cadets, if necessary. Fortunately during the remaining months of the year 1917, that is, from August to December, inclusive, the number of cadets on the ground at any one time averaged a little less than 240. This situation was met without special difficulty by dismissing the regular classes in physical education and transforming the Gymnasium and Page Hall into dormitories for the military students, the upper floors of Hayes Hall being still used for the same purpose.

 The erection of Barracks of frame construction was begun early in August, and the additions to Ohio Union were soon under way. Early in March, 1918, the Trustees ordered the building of a small, well-planned, frame Hospital with a capacity of 20 beds, in addition to the Aeronautical Laboratory and Machine-gun Range. Work on these structures was begun at once. By this time there were four military schools in operation on the campus, the aggregate number of whose cadets had passed considerably beyond 800. All of these structures and annexes were completed in time for use by the schools, and they are permanent additions of value to the University plant. But already in April the number of cadets dropped by nearly 140; it dropped more than 100 in May; nearly 100 more in June; approximately 70 more in July, and about the same number again in August; and at the end of this month the last surviving military school on the campus, that of aviation, was closed by order of the War Department.

The allowance of $80,000 granted by the State Emergency Board did not, of course, cover the cost of the new buildings and additions ordered by the Trustees. In his report to the Governor of the State, President Thompson gives the additional items of wartime expenditure as follows: "The Trustees appropriated from the Endowment Fund, $11,209.62; the balance of the money used for improvements and changes on the campus came from the tuition receipts provided by the Government. Additional land at a cost of $41,320 was purchased in order to provide facilities for landing airplanes. The Ohio Union was enlarged at a cost of $11,883.97. The construction of the Barracks cost $50,310.06; the Aviation Laboratory cost $41,325.61; the Gun Range cost $754.80; the hospital near the Barracks cost $21,512. Other smaller items of expense were incurred in changes made necessary in buildings in order that they might be adapted for military purposes. Some of these improvements, like the purchase of land, erection of the Aviation Laboratory, the Barracks, and other facilities, will be of use to the University for years to come." In view of the experience of some other universities in undertaking to build extensively and at high cost to meet the war emergency just as the conflict was about to end, one can find nothing to criticize in the conservative action taken by the President and Trustees of the University and by the State authorities in the way of wartime expenditures on the campus. Their wisdom lay in considering in times of stress not only the exigency of the moment, but also the future needs of a large and growing institution.

In the autumn of 1916 the enrollment of students in the University as a whole was 5,084, while for the second half-year it was 4,675—a loss of more than 400. Most of this loss was in the larger colleges, as follows: the College of Agriculture, 95; the College of Arts, 84; the College of Education, 60; and the College of Engineering, 108. The smaller colleges, including the Graduate School, sustained losses of from three to 20 students, except the College of Commerce and Journalism alone, which gained five. These losses show clearly that our students were responding to the unsettled conditions in the country and were ready to enter service in case the demand should be made by the Government.

In view of the hundreds of withdrawals during the second half-year of 1916-17, especially in April and May, the enrollment in the summer session of 1917 was better than could have been expected. It amounted to 890, which was, in round numbers, 330 less than that of the summer session of 1916.

The registration in the autumn of 1917 was also surprising. It was 4,187, although this was nearly 1,000 less than twelve months before. Under normal conditions there would have been an increase of about 15 per cent. In February, 1918, the beginning of the second half-year, the number of students had fallen to 3,447, or 740 less than in the previous autumn. As in the spring of 1917, so also in that of 1918 the demand for labor on the farms and in war industries was so urgent that numbers of students withdrew from all the colleges to take employment, besides the hundreds who went into the Army, Navy, and Marine Corps, or to the officers' training camps. On April 1, 1918, the College of Agriculture excused those of its students who were in good standing, with a half-year's credit on condition of their entering agricultural service.

A number withdrew on these terms and others later in the year to help at home or go into military or naval service. By June, 1918, 222 men from the Arts College had enlisted in the Army and 47 in the Navy. Three of the latter and 48 of the former who had nearly completed their course were graduated in June. A few other Arts men left for service with the Y.M.C.A., or Red Cross, or to take up other war work. During the first half-year of 1917-18 the Graduate School lost 55 by withdrawal, including 17 holders of scholarships and fellowships. Hence the Graduate Council decided that during the war they would not recommend for such appointments any more candidates who were subject to call for military service.

During this year 149 students left the College of Engineering to enter some branch of service. Under the Selective Service Act 63 men were enrolled in the Engineer Enlisted Reserve Corps on the campus, thereby obtaining a reclassification that permitted them to finish their course before enlisting. Twelve of the fourth-year electrical students became cadets in the Signal Enlisted Reserve Corps by passing a wireless course prescribed by the War Department. A similar arrangement in the Dental and Medical Colleges on the campus kept most of their older students from leaving. They were on the "recognized" list of such institutions as were approved by Surgeon General Gorgas, according to a law passed by Congress in October, 1917. Eighty-three of our dental students, some of the men in our two medical schools, and 45 of our veterinary students were able to take advantage of this arrangement. Of these men, however, those whose grades fell below a certain standard were ordered into active service. Those who graduated were sent to officers' training camps, where they became professional assistants, or in many cases received commissions as officers. Some former students returned to the Colleges of Dentistry and Medicine, enrolled in the reserve corps, and graduated before entering active service.

By June, 1918, the University and College Faculties and the Administrative and Maintenance Divisions had been deprived of the services for a longer or shorter period of more than a hundred men, including President Thompson, Mr. Carl E. Steeb, secretary of the Board of Trustees, and several of the deans. The President's *Report* gives the following lists:

Faculty Men in Uniform

F. Elwood Allen	Alan E. Flowers	Edward Orton, Jr.
Clarence E. Andrews	Jonathan Forman	Walter T. Peirce
George F. Arps	Jacob A. Foust	Thomas G. Phillips
Hugh G. Beatty	Elijah J. Gordon	Charles I. Reed
Halbert B. Blakey	Fred B. Grosvenor	Harry F. Reichard
Gilbert W. Brehm	Arthur M. Hauer	Louis Reif
Allando A. Case	Wilmer C. Harris	Wilbert C. Ronan
Erwin O. Christensen	Samuel Hindman	Frank E. Sanborn
George L. Converse	Carl C. Hugger	George B. Schaeffer
Homer C. Corry	Ralph A. Knouff	Paul B. Sears
Dwight M. DeLong	Theodore F. Kotz	John W. Sheetz
Dana J. Demorest	Fonsa A. Lambert	Frank C. Starr
Verne A. Dodd	Edward C. Ludwig	Carl E. Steeb
Brooks D. Drain	Edmund S. Manson, Jr.	Alexander M. Steinfeld
Samuel D. Edelman	Eugene F. McCampbell	William N. Taylor
Philip H. Elwood, Jr.	William McPherson	David S. White
William Lloyd Evans	John W. Means	Phillip Wilson
George B. Faulder	Russell L. Mundhenk	T. Rees Williams
Fred Fletcher	John H. Nichols	

Faculty Men and Women in Civilian Service

John J. Adams	James E. Hagerty	Thomas D. Phillips
Frederic C. Blake	Thomas H. Haines	Rudolph Pintner
Cecil E. Boord	Matthew B. Hammond	Charles W. Reeder
James W. Bridges	Thomas M. Hills	Clyde O. Ruggles
Clyde Brooks	Charles F. Kelly	Earle C. Smith
Roy A. Brown	William A. Knight	Henry R. Spencer
J. Ernest Carman	William T. Magruder	Joseph R. Taylor
Alfred D. Cole	Franklin W. Marquis	William O. Thompson
Shirley J. Coon	Roderick D. McKenzie	George W. Trautman
Edwin A. Cottrell	Florence Meyer	Alonzo H. Tuttle
Berthold A. Eisenlohr	Cecil C. North	Henry F. Walradt
Thomas E. French	Carl E. Parry	Edna N. White
George Gephart	Robert G. Paterson	James R. Withrow

Men in Service from the Division of Operation and Maintenance

Thomas Allen	Emerson R. Davis	John Long
Andrew Armstrong	Charles M. Dunbar	Lee E. Vigor
Frank Corra	Ernest Long	

These lists have been greatly extended in the latter part of this work, which gives the records of the military and civilian service rendered by members of the Faculties, the Division of Administration, and the Division of Operation and Maintenance of this University.

The summer session of 1918 had an enrollment of 909 students, which was a gain of slightly less than a score over that of the summer session of the previous year. Four addresses were given before the convocation of the summer students in 1918, three of which were on war topics. The Rev. E. F. Chauncey spoke on "War Savings Stamps," Dr. E. A. Peterson on "Physical Education and the War," and Professor B. L. Bowen on "French Influences in America."

The signing of the Armistice on November 11, 1918, brought immense relief and unrestrained joy to the University, as it did to the country at large. It was already too late for the cessation of hostilities to produce an immediate increase in student enrollment, but that was to come in the autumn of 1919, as is shown by the following figures:

September, 1918	February, 1919	September, 1919
4,349	3,467	6,609

The Academic Board, U. S. Army School of Military Aeronautics

Landing Field on the Campus, west of Neil Avenue Extension

A class in range-finding and shell-spotting

A class in machine-gun practice

CHAPTER II

UNITED STATES MILITARY SCHOOLS ON THE CAMPUS

In the spring of 1917 the War Department decided to establish Schools of Military Aeronautics at six universities, namely, California, Cornell, Illinois, Massachusetts Institute of Technology, Texas, and Ohio State. The need for these schools was pressing, for there were already 2,500 applicants for enlistment in the Aviation Corps, besides the 600 who had been accepted. On May 2, 1917, the Department of Military Science and Tactics at the University received official notice of the decision to open these schools. Each of the chosen institutions was directed to send three representatives for a brief training course to the Royal Aviation School at Toronto, Canada, and President Thompson appointed for this purpose Professor William T. Magruder of the Department of Mechanical Engineering, Professor Henry C. Lord of the Department of Astronomy, and Professor William A. Knight of the Department of Industrial Arts. These gentlemen—the first members of the civilian academic staff of the new school—left for Toronto, May 5, and were back again by the middle of the same month with the necessary information in regard to the technical instruction to be given in the aviation ground school. On the day of their return President Thompson departed for Washington to complete arrangements for the opening and operation of the school.

Both the curriculum and organization of this school, as of those at the other universities, were determined by the Signal Corps at Washington, the chief signal officer sending the requisite instructions to the Academic Board, which was the administrative committee in charge of the school at Ohio State. The Academic Board comprised the military staff and the heads of departments of the civil academic staff. From the beginning of the school until December 1, 1917, Dr. W. O. Thompson was the president of the board. He then appointed Professor F. C. Blake of the Department of Physics as his successor. The principal military officers on the board were the commandant, the adjutant, and the supply officer. Major George L. Converse served as the commandant until the assignment of Captain George Stratemeyer, a graduate of West Point and of the Army School of Aeronautics at San Diego, Calif., at the close of May, 1917. Captain Stratemeyer was succeeded, June 15, 1918, by Major George R. Harrison, also a graduate of the United States Military Academy, who had been on duty in the Philippine and Hawiian Islands and on the Mexican Border. He had then served in the training camp at Fort Niagara, N. Y., where he had become a major in the Signal Corps, thence being sent to Selfridge Field, Mt. Clemens, Mich., next to Washington, D. C., and finally to Ohio State. The commandant and his staff gave the military instruction to the aviation cadets or pilots, while the scientific and technical instruction was in the hands of the following departments: (1) Signalling and Radio, (2) Gunnery, (3) Aids to Flight, (4) Airplanes, (5) Engines, and (6) Aerial Observation.

The total number of civilian instructors in the departments just named during the continuation of the School of Aeronautics and the other co-existant military schools was about one hundred. This number represents the original appointees and the later ones who replaced those who resigned from time to time to go into active service. Not a few of these instructors were more or less advanced students in the College of Engineering. About one-fourth of the total number was made up of University instructors, the distribution by departments being as follows:

Mr. Roy A. Brown of the Electrical Engineering Department, head of Signalling and Radio; Professor William A. Knight of the Department of Industrial Arts, head of the instruction in Gunnery and also in Airplanes; Dr. James H.

Snook of the Department of Veterinary Medicine, instructor in Gunnery; Professor Henry C. Lord, Mr. Jerry H. Service, Lieutenant Lloyd T. Stankard, and Samuel B. Folk, all of the Department of Astronomy, instructors in Aids to Flight; Professor William T. Magruder, Karl W. Stinson, Assistant Professor Aubrey T. Brown, Woodward A. Warrick, John W. Prinkey, Roland H. Wasson, and Theodore T. Theiss, all of the Department of Mechanical Engineering, instructors in Engines; Professor Thomas M. Hills and Kenneth C. Cottingham of the Department of Geology and Wilbert C. Ronan of the Department of Architecture, instructors in Aerial Observation; Professors Alonzo H. Tuttle, George W. Rightmire, Clarence D. Laylin, Homer C. Corry, and Joseph W. Madden of the Law School, instructors in Military Law; Professor Emery R. Hayhurst of the Department of Public Health and Sanitation, instructor in Hygiene; Professor Frank R. Castleman, Henry C. Olsen, and Ossian C. Bird of the Department of Physical Education, instructors in Supervised Recreation; and Mr. Charles W. Reeder of the University Library, instructor in War-Department Correspondence Files. Of the 25 men named above more than half belonged to the instructional staff of the Engineering College. The College of Law furnished five; the College of Arts, Philosophy, and Science, two; and the College of Veterinary Medicine, the College of Medicine, and the Library, one each.

The School of Aeronautics opened May 21, 1917, when the first "squadron" or group of 16 cadets reported. They were quartered in Hayes Hall and took their meals in the diningroom of the Ohio Union. For the next three weeks they underwent an intensive military training, their daily program consisting of one-half hour of calisthenics before breakfast, an hour of infantry drill soon after the morning meal, followed by an hour of manual at arms and feet movements, then intermission until dinner. At 2 o'clock they attended a class in United States Army regulations and went to drill at 3. From 4 to 5:30 came another intermission and then supper. The study period began at 7:30 and lasted three hours. This intensive military instruction was supplemented by a daily lecture on some military topic and by daily practice in the use of the machine gun and in wireless telegraphy. At the end of the first three weeks the squadron entered upon five weeks of theoretical and technical instruction in military aeronautics, that is, in signalling, gunnery, airplanes, engines, and aerial observation, while continuing in military training, both practical and theoretical, although in diminished amount. Their practical military training comprised infantry drill, guard duty, physical training, and first aid; while their theoretical work included lectures, demonstrations, and the study of texts. The principal subjects they studied were: (1) military courtesy, *esprit de corps,* and morale; (2) the organization and administration of the United States and modern European armies; (3) army regulations, and (4) military law.

In addition to these military studies, the cadets were expected to learn signalling with such proficiency as to send and receive at least eight words per minute, while becoming acquainted with the principles of radio and the parts of a simple wireless instrument. In gunnery the pilots had to become familiar with the mechanism and parts of machine guns, especially of the Lewis and Marlin aircraft guns, and were drilled in the correct sequence and methods of removing and replacing parts and in correcting faulty action. They were practiced in short-range shooting, a machine-gun range being at length constructed for this work. Aerial tactics involved the consideration of plane maneuvers to avoid or to gain advantage over an enemy plane. In this connection attention was given to the dive, loop the loop, zoom, Immelman turn, and roll. Later in the course aerial tactics was eliminated from the course and given only at the flying fields. Under the head of bombs and bombing various types of bombs were studied, including their mechanical features and the physical and chemical properties of explosives. The discussion of bomb dropping and the formation of a bombing raid was accompanied by practice in trap shooting, about 200,000 rounds of ammunition and an equal number of clay targets being used. The work of the Gunnery Department was carried on very largely in the Shops Building until the Aeronautical Laboratory was finished, when a part of it was transferred to that structure.

The course in aids to flight comprised one lecture a week on astronomy, three on meteorology, two on instruments and compasses, two on theory of flight, and two on photography. This outline of subjects was modified by the authorities in Washington from time to time, astronomy and photography being omitted altogether, while the other subjects were changed in amount. Professor Lord's problem in presenting these subjects was to select those features of each which would be serviceable to the aviator and to render them as simple and impressive as possible. As very little help was received from Washington, he was compelled to rely chiefly on his own ingenuity. A number of models were invented and built in the Astronomical Observatory, without the aid of a preliminary drawing. A table for locating the brighter stars was printed and given to each cadet, and lantern slides of the constellations were made by pricking holes in sheets of paper at points traced from a star map to show only the identification stars. By placing such a sheet between two panes of glass a constellation could be projected on the screen with better results than by using a slide taken from an actual photograph of the sky. At night the important stars visible were also pointed out to the cadets.

To illustrate the somewhat difficult subject, theory of flight, the following pieces of apparatus were devised and built by Professor Lord: one to illustrate wind resistance; two pieces to show lift and how it varies with the angle of attack; a piece to demonstrate lift, drift and head resistance; and a piece to illustrate suction on the top of the plane. These models awakened a great deal of interest and helped materially to clear up the subject. They were illustrated by photographs in a report prepared at the request of the commanding officer at McCook Field, Dayton, O., a copy of which was sent to the War Department. These photographs, together with one illustrating eddies and another illustrating the adjusting of a ship's compass for sub-permanent magnetism, were also inserted in an earlier report. Copies of most of these photographs were sent out by the War Department to other Schools of Military Aeronautics. As an additional aid in teaching the theory of flight use was made of lantern slides reproduced from such books as Loening's *Military Aeroplanes* and Duchene's *Mechanics of the Aeroplane.*

The subject of meteorology is one concerning which there is a mass of accumulated data, thus rendering the problem of selection a difficult one. What to teach about instruments and compasses was equally difficult, on account of the lack of official instructions. For the purpose of gaining light on these matters Professor Lord made a journey to the East, visiting the Blue Hill Observatory in Massachusetts, where he obtained many valuable suggestions from Professor Alexander G. McAdie, and making stops to gather information from the Sperry Gyroscope Company at Brooklyn and the Curtiss Aeroplane and Motor Corporation at Buffalo. This trip, which was undertaken before the opening of the School of Aeronautics, was made possible through the generosity of Mr. Emerson McMillin of New York City. The chief instructor of the aviation school at Toronto, Canada, paid Professor Lord the compliment, in October, 1917, of asking for his lectures on meteorology, which were gladly furnished him, together with a number of lantern slides. Later on the instruction in meteorology was assigned to Mr. J. H. Service, an instructor in the Department of Astronomy at the time, whose work was satisfactory in the highest degree.

An outline of the course on instruments and compasses was prepared under Professor Lord's supervision by Lieutenant Lloyd T. Stankard, assistant in the department, and afterwards morale officer at Camp Taylor, Ky., a copy being supplied to the commandant at the McCook Field, Dayton, O., by his request and another being sent to the Schools Division in Washington. Some of the excellent material used in this course was introduced into the *Manual on Instruments* issued by the Air Information, Signal Corps, at Washington, and was acknowledged by letter. In the preface of another manual, which was published by the Airplane Engineering Department, McCook Field, and is entitled *Applied Aeronautics, The Airplane*, Professor Lord is given credit for certain sections in the first chapter on the theory of flight, as well as jointly with Lieutenant Stankard for a large part of the chapters on instruments, while Professor W. A. Knight is credited with information furnished in regard to rigging and alignment of planes.

In the course on airplanes the various types of planes were studied, as also the proper adjustment of the rigging and the care and repair of machines. Laboratory work was conducted in Robinson Laboratory, where two full-rigged planes were at hand, one a Curtiss training plane and the other a standard, besides all the parts of a dissembled machine. Later, when the Aeronautical Laboratory was built, most of the airplane work was transferred to that building. There a full line of tools and work benches for 40 men was available, besides a large room for lecture and demonstration purposes. Under Professor W. A. Knight's direction, Messrs. R. A. Tobin, Daniel Maloney, and C. R. Upp were largely responsible for developing the courses of study, putting the airplane laboratory in order, and rendering other valuable assistance to the department, which required the services of four other instructors and two mechanics. The Department of Gunnery, of which Professor Knight was also the head, included Messrs. L. W. Birch, W. M. Holmes, and L. L. Matson as instructors. They were all members of the class of '17 in Electrical Engineering and received the commendation of their superior officer for their energy, resourcefulness, and their success in constructing working models, demonstration charts, and sighting devices, as well as for their own contributions in the development of the work. To facilitate the instruction two divisions of gunnery were formed. One of these was designated the Lewis general division and was placed under the charge of Mr. Birch as head instructor, the other being known as the

Marlin general division, with Mr. Matson as the head instructor. The total number of instructors for the two divisions was 16. Each cadet received five hours of instruction a week, the average number of cadets each week being about three hundred and twenty.

The course on engines required a knowledge of the principles of internal combustion, of aeronautical motors, and of the care of engines. Laboratory work played an important part in the study of the subject. As head of this department Professor W. T. Magruder had under his supervision 14 instructors.

Included under the title of aerial observation were such subjects as map reading, reconnaissance, artillery observation, and shell spotting on a miniature artillery range. The work in shell spotting gave opportunity for the application of knowledge gained by the cadets not only in aerial observation but also in other courses of the ground school, especially in radio. The cadets were seated in balconies or crows' nests, in imitation of airplanes, whence they looked down on a miniature, scenic battlefield painted on a semi-transparent fabric, under which the flashes of small electric lamps represented shell bursts. Several of these ranges were constructed by Professor T. M. Hills, with the aid of the instructors and assistants in the Geology Department and of Professor Charles S. Chubb of the Department of Architecture. The last of these miniature ranges was so devised as to rotate slowly, thereby imparting to the observers aloft the impression that they were flying in circles over the battlefield. The cadets were required to report by wireless where shells were exploding on the ground below. The instruction by means of this realistic range was highly commended in a bulletin sent out by the War Department to all ground schools, with the result that inspectors from the other schools came to examine the Ohio State University range and in two instances to ask the Department of Aerial Observation here to construct miniature artillery ranges for them.

The first pilot squadron completed the eight weeks' curriculum outlined above and graduated, July 16, 1917. Meantime, each week brought a new squadron of cadets, the first six or eight squadrons being all college men; and each week after July 16 saw a squadron graduate and leave for the Wilbur Wright Flying Field at Dayton, O., for instruction in the art of flying. Up to Christmas 32 squadrons of aviation cadets were received at the University. At that time such of them as had not graduated were sent to the ground schools at the Universities of Illinois and California. During the next two months the School of Military Aeronautics was in abeyance on the campus. For about three weeks, that is, from December 23 to January 12, the University would have been entirely without cadets had it not been for the opening of the School for Aero-Squadron Engineer Officers late in the previous October; and there were but 29 men in this school during the period named. But with the starting of a School for Aero-Squadron Adjutants on January 12, the number of cadets soon rose to nearly 350. Before the end of February airplane pilots were again being sent to the University, and the School of Aeronautics was revived. It continued in existence during the next six months, or until August 31, when it was closed permanently. During this interval the school received its squadron of cadets each week, the total number being 27 squadrons.

On March 1, 1918, the program of studies in military aeronautics, which had been originally planned and, until Christmas of the preceding year, carried out as an eight-weeks' course, was lengthened to 12 weeks. Under this new plan 498 hours of work were required to complete the program, 190 hours being assigned to military subjects, including drill military lectures, and inspection; 43 hours to signalling; 52 to gunnery; 55 to airplanes; 59 to engines; 39 to aerial tactics, and 60 to supervised recreation and sports. The total number of men trained in the School of Military Aeronautics during both periods of its operation was 1,291.

Although the time of the aviation cadets was largely occupied with their instruction and training, many of the men testifying that they had never worked so hard in their lives, a little more than one-sixth of their scheduled hours was reserved for supervised recreation and sports, as already mentioned above. This arrangement was favorable to the playing of military and baseball games and the holding of track meets, which were at times interspersed with other forms of entertainment. Toward the middle of July, 1918, for example, games were played between the aviation school nine and teams from Lancaster and Dayton, the latter made up of pilots in training at Wilbur Wright Flying Field. On July 21 the cadets participated in a "community sing" that was held on the athletic field of the University under the auspices of the Columbus War Camp Community Service. A part of the entertainment was provided by 500 young women of the Patriotic League, who at a signal fell into place to form a living flag. A few days later the aviation squadrons held a track meet in which, besides the usual events, there were some special ones, such as trapshooting, grenade-throwing, and a human-burden race. The winner in this meet was Squadron 49, Squadrons 52 and 51 taking second and third places, respectively. Not long after the meet a musical program was given in the Chapel by several vocal soloists, a novelty violinist, a dancer from one of the squadrons, and a "jazz band" of cadets. The pilots were present in large numbers and greatly enjoyed the vaudeville performance.

On August 16 the School of Military Aeronautics held a review in honor of the British and American aviators who visited Columbus in their machines for the purpose of demonstrating aerial maneuvers and promoting the sale of war-savings stamps. Groups of aviation students added zest to the life of their fellow-cadets on the campus by indulging in journalism. They were permitted to prepare and publish two souvenir magazines of the school, one of these being the *Esprit de Corps*, published by Squadron 8 of the Adjutants' School, which made its appearance on March 28, 1918, and the other, *The Pilot*, which was more elaborate than its predecessor and was circulated on August 18, 1918.

THE SCHOOL FOR AERO-SQUADRON ENGINEER OFFICERS

On October 19, 1917, the second of the United States military schools was opened at the University, when a squadron of seven cadets arrived for training as aero-squadron engineer officers. They entered upon an eight weeks' curriculum prescribed by the War Department, and graduated December 15. The second squadron did not appear until November 23. It numbered 19 members and finished the course on January 19, 1918. The third squadron, consisting of 10 men, began its studies on December 1 and graduated a week later than the second squadron. Thus, the School for Engineer Officers lasted only a little more than three months and was attended by but 36 cadets.

THE SCHOOL FOR AERO-SQUADRON ADJUTANTS

The third of the United States military schools opened at the University on January 12, 1918, with the arrival of the first squadron of men for training as aero-squadron adjutants. The explanation of the starting of this school is to be found in the abandonment of the aviation officers' school at Kelley Field, San Antonio, Tex., late in the previous month. The function of the school at Kelley Field had been to train three kinds of aero-squadron officers, namely, adjutants, engineer officers, and supply officers. With the closing of the Texas school, the instruction of the several classes of cadets it had been training was assigned to different institutions, Georgia School of Technology becoming a military school for supply officers; Massachusetts Institute of Technology, one for engineer officers, and Ohio State University, the school for aero-squadron adjutants. The curriculum for the new school on the campus, which was now the only one of the kind in the United States, was furnished by the War Department and covered a period of eight weeks. Each week of the course formed a separate unit, the men being promoted at the end of the week to the next higher squadron if their work was satisfactory. As in the case of all these wartime military schools at the University and elsewhere, a new squadron was received each week, and one was graduated each week until July 13, the total number of adjutants' squadrons being 19. As the cadets who came in from Texas at the beginning had already had six weeks of training at Kelley Field, they were able to complete their training at the end of a fortnight and were graduated then. It is deserving of mention also that many of the cadets had received officers' commissions at some training camp before being assigned to the school here. In fact, not a few of them, including several captains and one major, had seen regular army service for from five to twenty years before entering the School for Aero-Squadron Adjutants.

The program of instruction in the Adjutants' School was planned for a series of eight squadrons, each one more advanced than the preceding by one week's work. The program was an intensive military one, which called for 314 hours of work to complete it. More than one-third of this time was spent in military drill. The study in army regulations and army service occupied 48 hours; army paper work and war-correspondence files, 42 hours; interior guard duty, law, court martial and hygiene, 37 hours; and technical studies, including theory of flight, airplans, gunnery, engine laboratory, and motor transport to the extent of 38 hours, filled out the course. The average number of hours of work per week was 39 and a fraction. During the first five months the course was changed five times by the War Department. The whole number of men who took this training at the University was 887.

THE SCHOOL FOR BALLOON-SQUADRON ADJUTANTS

The last of the four military schools at the University began on March 13 and closed on August 3, 1918, being in session a little more than four and one-half months, a month more than the Engineer Officers' School. Like the School for Aero-Squadron Adjutants, this School for Balloon Officers was the only one of its kind in the United States. The men sent to it had already received their balloon training at Fort Omaha, Neb., or in Texas, which was now supplemented by a seven weeks' course to prepare them for officers' work. The curriculum was similar to that of the other adjutants' school, being arranged on the basis of promotion at the end of each week's work. By the seventh week the cadet who accomplished the tasks set before him became a member of the most-advanced squadron. Out of the 278½ hours required to complete the curriculum, 108½ hours were devoted to military drill, 48 to army regulations and field service, 42 to army paper and correspondence files, 41 to the study of officers' duties, 37 to interior guard duty, law, court martial, and hygiene, and 11 to technical studies. The number of men trained in the balloon officers' school was 219 (11 squadrons). The following tabulation shows (1) the time at which each of the four military schools began and closed, (2) the periods during which they were in operation, and (3) the average daily number of men in the schools month by month:

Aviation Pilots—Began May 21, 1917, closed December 23, 1917. Resumed February 23, 1918, closed August 31, 1918.

Engineer Officers—Began October 19, 1917, closed June 26, 1918.

Aero-Squadron Adjutants—Began January 12, 1918, closed July 13, 1918.

Balloon Adjutants—Began March 13, 1918, closed August 3, 1918.

Average daily number, 1917—May, 16; June, 60; July, 130; August, 221; September, 236; October, 231; November, 265; December, 238; 1918—January, 347; February, 725; March, 832; April, 695; May, 595; June, 490; July 419; August, 346.

The total number of men trained in the four military schools at the University was 2,397. While the four schools were in operation many squadrons were receiving instructions at the same time. By order of President Thompson the needs of these squadrons for classrooms and laboratories took precedence over the needs of the regular University classes, many of which were moved from their accustomed quarters to make room for the military classes. During the winter of 1918 the registrar, Miss Edith D. Cockins, who has charge of the assignment of classrooms, was confronted with the difficult task of supplying rooms for military classes to the extent of 300 hours per week.

The instructors in the School of Military Aeronautics were assigned largely from the teaching staff of the University. The instructors in the other schools were mostly army officers detailed by the War Department; although certain subjects in the School for Engineer Officers, and such studies as theory of flight, airplanes, gunnery, and engine laboratory in the curriculum of the School for Aero-Squadron Adjutants, and machine guns and map reading in that of the School for Balloon-Squadron Adjutants were taught by University instructors. It should be added that military law in the two adjutants' schools was taught by members of the Law Faculty.

The four military schools as they were established one after another were subject to the dual control of the military staff and the civil academic staff, both of which were represented on the Academic Board. This dual control was in general hard to manipulate not only at the University here, but also at the other institutions where military schools existed. The give and take that was demanded between the military officers and the civilian instructors, and especially between the commandant and the president of the Academic Board, was not easy of accomplishment; but it may be said, nevertheless, that cordiality of relationship existed at all times between the commanding officer and the University. The military schools at the Ohio State University were particularly fortunate in their successive commandants, especially in the person of Major J. E. Chaney, whose service lasted from November, 1917, until the middle of June, 1918.

THE STUDENTS' ARMY TRAINING CORPS

On May 8, 1918, the secretary of war issued the preliminary announcement of the Government's intention to organize units of a Students' Army Training Corps in approved colleges and universities of the country. Thousands of college men of military age were already in the great game of war, many with commissions, and were giving an excellent account of themselves. The National Defense Act of June 3, 1916, had provided for the establishment of units of the Reserve Officers' Training Corps in selected institutions of learning, and the promotion of the Students' Army Training Corps was an effort to apply the same policy by using the facilities of the colleges in the intensive training of cadets for admission to officers' and non-commissioned officers' training camps and to technical war work. The aim of the new plan was to hasten the mobilization of American troops by getting men into training earlier than if they awaited their call under the Selective Service Law. The method devised to accomplish this object was that of keeping the S. A. T. C. cadets under observation and test in the colleges in order to determine their qualifications as officer candidates and technical experts.

Under date of August 28, 1918, the War Department issued a statement to the colleges and universities, which said that the man-power bill then pending in Congress definitely bound the country to the policy of consecrating its entire energy to the winning of the war as quickly as possible; that the bill fixed the age limits from 18 to 45 years, inclusive; that the new military program, as outlined by the secretary of war, called for the increase of the Army by more than 2,000,000 men by July 1, 1919, and that, since students were not to be made a deferred or favored class, they would practically all be assigned to active service in the field by June, 1919.

On August 30 and 31, 1918, Colonel Rees submitted the plan for converting the colleges and universities into an integral part of the Army to an assembly of college presidents and deans from the Mississippi Valley at Fort Sheridan, Ill., for acceptance or rejection. It was recognized by all in attendance that the scheme would impose a great responsibility upon the colleges, which were asked to devote their chief energy and educational power to the phases of training desired by the

Government; but, nevertheless, the plan was unanimously approved.

The act of Congress of August 31, 1918, referred to above as the man-power bill, extended the Selective Service Law to include all young men between the ages of 18 and 20 who were physically fit for service. The cooperation of the War Department and the colleges was placed under the Committee of Education and Special Training, and this committee drew up the programs to be pursued by those who should join the Students' Army Training Corps.

The Government advised those who intended to enter college in the fall to do so, after registering with their local boards. Those who entered institutions where a unit of the S.A.T.C. was to be established could enlist in the college unit and choose the course of training which they wished to pursue. Under this arrangement the corps was raised by voluntary induction under the Selective Service Law, the cadets becoming regularly enlisted men, uniformed, housed, and subsisted at the expense of the Government while undergoing training and receiving the pay of private soldiers, that is, $30 a month. Many of the cadets assumed that they would be able to pursue their academic studies and were, consequently, greatly disappointed when they found this to be impossible. The plan called for a training of one term of three months for men 20 years of age, two terms for those of 19 years, and three terms for those of 18 years. This classification of cadets by ages was unsound pedagogically and proved to be one of the bad features of the Students' Army Training Corps. It should be noted also that no decision had been made as to how the retiring thirds would be recruited, or what would happen at the end of the three terms.

Shortly after the Government announced its purpose to organize the Students' Army Training Corps, the Trustees of the Ohio State University applied to the War Department for the discontinuance of the School of Military Aeronautics in August, 1918, in order to make room for the corps. On September 1 Acting President John J. Adams submitted to the

Trustees a contract, according to which the University was to provide special academic instruction approved by the War Department, proper housing and meals for 1,200 student-soldiers, drill grounds, and offices for the military administration, and was to cooperate closely with the War Department. On its part the Government agreed to provide military instruction for the cadets, besides uniforms and other personal equipment, cots, blankets and mattresses, and to pay the institution in accordance with the terms set down in the contract. The new school was to open on October 1, 1918, and last through the following nine months. This agreement was approved at once by the Board of Trustees.

When the University opened, September 17, 1918, the corridors of University Hall were packed with young people eager to enroll, and the path from the broad walk in front of the Library up to the entrance of the "main building" was filled with a double row of youths patiently awaiting their turn. The statistics reported to the Faculty on November 11 showed a total enrollment of 6,364, of whom 3,349 were regular students, 2,113 of this number being men and 1,236 women. The S. A. T. C. cadets numbered 1,965, and there was a Naval Unit of 50. The distribution of the cadets by colleges was as follows: Agriculture, 208; Arts, Philosophy, and Science, 634; Engineering, 810; Dentistry, 82; Medicine, 80; Veterinary Medicine, 71; Education, 24; Pharmacy, 22; Commerce and Journalism, 16; Homeopathic Medicine, also 16; Applied Optics, 7; Graduate School, 3; and Arts-Education, 2. Later inductions brought the total enrollment in the Students' Army Training Corps up to 2,017 and that of the Naval Unit up to 91.

At the time of the opening of the University instructions were received from the Committee on Education and Special Training at Washington that cadets would be permitted to carry regular academic subjects, besides their military drill and a limited amount of instruction in military subjects. All students were therefore assigned regular academic programs in the various colleges. Late in September the courses of study and training for the Students' Army Training Corps prepared by the Committee of Education and Special Training were received from Washington. These courses made it clear at last that the corps was to be a military school under the control of the War Department. Thus, in so far as the cadets were concerned, the University was to be on a war basis, while it was to remain on a peace basis for the other students. In other words, the University was to attempt to fill the double rôle of being at one and the same time a civilian institution and a military academy under separate managements.

In keeping with the terms of the contract with the Federal Government, the official induction of the S.A.T.C. was made on October 1, 1918, and the student-soldiers were sworn in as rapidly as possible. Major Norris S. Oliver was assigned as commandant and Captain Jay S. Cunningham as adjutant. There were 31 other officers assigned for actual military instruction, as well as a staff of medical officers and contract surgeons for the work of medical examination during the induction process and for the care of the health of the cadets. the large Barracks erected east of Robinson Laboratory for the School of Military Aeronautics were used partly for barracks and partly for quartermaster-department offices. Hayes Hall served for military headquarters and for barracks, and Page Hall, the Gymnasium, and the Shops Building were also used for barracks. Alterations were required in Page and Hayes Halls at a cost of $5,900. At first the men were messed at the Ohio Union in three shifts, but later the Aeronautical Laboratory was fitted up as a mess hall at a cost of $9,000 from the receipts of the Union and furnished meals at the rate of 2,000 an hour. Medical students in the Students' Army Training Corps were provided for in the Railway Y. M. C. A. Building in the city and dental students in one of the medical buildings on Park Street.

The S. A. T. C. was constituted a separate school of the University, and its affairs were administered separately under a special committee of the Faculty made up of Deans J. V. Denney, Alfred Vivian, and Edwin F. Coddington. This committee acted as occasion required under instructions from the regional director, President Raymond M. Hughes of Miami University. All cadets were assigned to their own classes and sections, which were limited to 30 members, except in the cases where it was permitted to increase the size of the sections to 40. The Faculty allowed regular students above freshman rank to enter the S.A.T.C., and a few of those who were under 20 years of age were assigned to the regular classes. By action of the Trustees, October 1, the incidental fee of $15 was refunded to all cadets. The administration of the corps as a separate organization enabled its classes to be conducted and any adjustments ordered by the Committee on Education and Special Training to be made without serious interference with the academic work of the regular students, except that the latter were deprived of small advanced courses in certain departments, which had an excessive number of cadet sections to instruct. It also happened that the S.A.T.C. caused a sudden demand for extra teachers in English, French, Spanish, mathematics, chemistry, and war issues. This demand was met by transferring instructors from departments where they were not needed and by employing new instructors as fast as they could be obtained.

The curricula prescribed by the Committee on Education and Special Training were five in number for men 20 years of age, these curricula being identified as programs A, B, C, D and E, and being intended for Infantry and Artillery, Air Service, Ordnance and Quartermaster Corps, Engineer, Signal, and Chemical Warfare, and Transport and Tank Service, respectively. Each of these programs required 12 weeks to complete it, the hours of work per week totaling 53. Three subjects formed the central feature of all five programs, namely, military instruction (11 hours), war issues (nine hours), and military law and practice (nine hours), counting more than half of the program. The differentiation of the programs was effected by coupling other subjects with these three. Thus, in program A for Infantry, Field Artillery and Heavy (Coast) Artillery, sanitation and hygiene (nine hours); surveying and map-making (12 hours), and an elective subject (three hours) were added. In program B for the Air Service the added courses were map-reading and navigation (12 hours) and elementary physics (12 hours). In program C for the Ordnance Corps and Quartermaster Corps 24 hours were distributed among accounting, business management, statistics, transportation, commerce, and allied subjects for the Quartermaster Corps, while an equal number of hours was assigned for physics, modern ordnance, business management, and an elective for the Ordnance Corps. In program D an approved schedule in any branch of engineering was required for the Engineer Corps, an approved schedule in chemical engineering or chemical technology for Chemical Warfare Service; and in program E for Transport or Tank Service 24 hours spent upon "subjects chosen from the list of allied subjects."

The program for 19- and 18-year-old men included some of the studies named above and left "about eight hours to studies already assigned" to the 19-year-old men and 11 hours to those assigned the 18-year-old men.

The men who were enroled in one of the enlisted reserve corps, such as the Medical Reserve, the Engineers' Reserve, or the Signal Reserve, were given an intensive training in the essential subjects of their branch according to special programs provided in medicine, dentistry, veterinary medicine, pharmacy, engineering, radio, etc. All of the above programs included two hours per day of military drill and two hours of supervised study, the latter requirement being generally neglected.

A Naval Unit of 91 men was also maintained, although it had a very uncertain status. Lieutenant Commander Evers of the Great Lakes Naval Training Station was on duty at the University at odd times, but the unit was looked upon as falling within the jurisdiction of the regular commandant. Special studies in seamanship, nautical astronomy, navigation, naval regulations, gunnery, and ordnance were included in the curriculum.

After a certain period of observation and testing of the cadets in the Students' Army Training Corps they were to be transferred to either an officers' training camp, a non-commissioned officers' training school, a vocational section for technical training, or a cantonment for duty as a private. The cadets were thus to be sorted according to the requirements of the service. The S. A. T. C. did not survive long enough, however, for this sorting process to affect many of the men. Only 109 men were transferred from the University to the camps.

On October 13, while the medical staff of nine men was conducting examinations of the cadets, the influenza epidemic, which was widespread throughout this country and Europe, made its appearance on the campus. The acting President, after consulting with the director of the student-health service, the City and State Boards of Health, and the medical staff, dismissed all students, except those in military service, and sent them home. As the others could not be dismissed without orders from the War Department, their classes went on as usual. The Military Hospital, with its 18 beds, proved to be much too small for the care of the large number of cases that developed, and it became necessary to utilize the east and northeast wings of the Barracks as hospital annexes for mild and convalescent cases. Sheets, blankets, and other supplies for the sick were, on request, immediately supplied in quantity by the Columbus Chapter of the Red Cross and City Federation of Women's Clubs. The corps of cadets was placed under limited quarantine, and a periodical inspection of housing quarters on the campus was carried on. Meals were sent to the patients from the Ohio Union, until the Department of Home Economics could send its kitchen equipment and its available staff to the Barracks. Faculty women and other willing volunteers also rendered valuable assistance to the nurses on duty in the hospital annexes. At one time or another the epidemic affected 440 men, and only eight deaths occurred in the Military Hospital.

Owing to this distressing episode, the University was closed to the regular students during a period of three weeks. A few days after their return, and before the effects of the epidemic had passed, the Armistice was signed, November 11, 1918. Then followed some days of uncertainty as to the continuance of the Students' Army Training Corps. According to the War Department's contract, that organization was to have lasted more than seven months longer; but the Federal Government changed its plan, and demobilization took place during December 10 to 12, 1918. If the signing of the Armistice brought general rejoicing, the disbandment of the S. A. T. C. diffused a less demonstrative but no less real sense of relief on the campus, although the unit had been in existence less than three months. Of its 2,018 members 109 had been sent to training camps, and 969 left the University at the time of the demobilization. These departing men were in need of money to meet their expenses in returning to their homes, but many of them had nothing but their warrants for their back pay, which the banks would not cash, and the financial officers of the Government were conspicuous by their absence. While the University had no authority to honor these warrants, it at least supplied the men with meals and beds until they could make arrangements to leave Columbus. Many of the cadets withdrew, especially those of 20 years of age who had been assigned purely military programs and therefore found it impossible to enter regular courses before the opening of the second semester. Not a few of these men returned to the University at that time. One thousand and thirty-one members of the S. A. T. C. remained and were at once transferred to a regular academic basis. Five hundred and thirty new students entered the University after the demobilization of the S. A.-T. C. The total number of instructors required to teach all sections and classes of the corps was 280.

In order to accommodate the former members of the Students' Army Training Corps who continued in the University, the announcement was made that for the remainder of the semester fees would not be collected from those who should complete the semester's work. The several colleges were empowered to allow partial or excess credit in S. A. T. C. courses for the current semester only; and it was promised that existing or equivalent courses would be given until the end of the half year, so that full credit might be gained by those taking these courses. It was under this arrangement that the courses in war issues, surveying, and map-making were continued to the end of the first semester. The Faculty voted that special classes should be formed to assist students in meeting the requirements for degrees or in preparing for second-semester courses, that courses usually announced for the first semester should be repeated for the second, and these should be followed in the summer session by such courses as might seem to be in demand. Finally, in view of the loss of time and the unavoidable distractions during the closing semester, the Faculty authorized instructors to report provisional or deferred credits at the mid-year, complete credit to be awarded where deserved at the end of the second semester or of the summer session. At the same time and for the same reasons the Christmas recess was reduced to nine days, December 21 to 29, inclusive, with the express understanding that New Year's Day should be devoted to classes. The Christmas holidays afforded the needed opportunity for the inspection and restoration of the University buildings that had been allotted to the uses of the Students' Army Training Corps.

At the time of the establishment of the S. A. T. C. it had been announced by the War Department that the amount of purely military instruction prescribed for the cadets would not preclude effective academic work. It is true that the academic work was in charge of a committee of the Faculty, but it is equally true that a staff of army officers controlled the time of the cadets under the sanction of military discipline, and that, the war being at its height, the chief interest of the student-soldiers was in the military side of their program. The younger officers of the military staff attached little or no value to the academic studies of the cadets and failed to coöperate with the members of the Faculty. A member of the Faculty committee reported that, "although supervised study at specific hours was early recommended by the War Department, it was not in effective operation here until nearly the end of the course when the assistance of the educational authorities in conducting it was permitted. Numerous students were kept from their classes for military duties and suffered loss of credit for no fault of their own. The result was a very inferior grade of educational work as even the liberal final marks given by the instructors show." It is revealing no secret to say that friction existed between different parts of the military establishment at the University in supporting the Government's plan of combined academic and military training for the cadets.

These conditions serve to explain the neglect of study and the absence from the classrooms that was so discouraging a feature of the S. A. T. C. Numbers of cadets were in the University without adequate preparation and obviously would not have been on the campus under ordinary circumstances. Even after the large rooms for "supervised study" had been provided in Orton and Page Halls, they remained deserted for the most part, while the lounge in Ohio Union was filled at odd hours by a genial throng of young fellows in khaki. At the time of demobilization Professor Edwin A. Cottrell, the liaison officer, reported to the Faculty that there had been 8,000 absences from classes, of which only 19 per cent had been excused, and that the majority of the absences had been "cuts." Nevertheless there were many serious students enrolled in the S. A. T. C. who made a creditable showing in their classwork, and there were many more with good intentions who were the victims of circumstances.

Taking off from the University Landing Field in wartime

Trustee Charles F. Kettering arriving after a flight from Dayton, Ohio

Professor W. A. Knight and a class in airplanes, after examining Trustee C. F. Kettering's flying machine

Barracks for the Army School of Military Aeronautics, built near Woodruff Avenue in wartime

CHAPTER III

WAR DRIVES AT THE UNIVERSITY

The University took an active part in all of the drives conducted in Columbus and Franklin County in connection with the war, as also in all of the state-wide campaigns. The latter included a campaign to get new members for the Red Cross; the tremendous drive during the spring and summer of 1917 for increased war-food production; a state-wide census of seed-corn in the early weeks of 1918; a conference followed by a campaign to promote the use of tractors in farming, the conference being held in February, 1918; a second drive for greater food production; campaigns to supply farm help during both years of the war; three "food pledge campaigns," one in the fall of 1917, the second in the following spring, and the third in December, 1918, besides bread-making and canning demonstrations in most of the counties. Most of the drives just mentioned were carried on under the joint auspices of the United States Food Administration in Ohio and the Ohio Branch of the Council of National Defense. The Executive Committee of the latter organization was the central agency through which the successive Liberty Loan drives were promoted in the State, operated locally through county committees. However, the Franklin County Committee treated the University as a separate unit, which in all drives for loans, except the first, maintained its own organization for securing subscriptions on the campus. The campaign for new members for the Red Cross was undertaken by the University Y.M.C.A. and Y.W.C.A. and by the Student Council and the Woman's Council, the University being regarded as a distinct unit in this drive. The same thing was true of later campaigns participated in by these organizations. For example, the Y.M.

C.A. solicited sums for the relief of college men in the prison camps of Europe early in April, 1917, and on the 18th of the following month it conducted a one-day subscription tour to help carry on the Army Y.M.C.A. work in the training camps. Seven months later still it again cooperated with the University Y.W.C.A. in a campaign to raise Ohio State's new quota for war work. Meantime, opportunities had not been withheld from the campus colony to buy thrift and war savings stamps, a fresh drive for the sale of the stamps being announced in convocation before the summer-session students on June 28, 1918.

Inasmuch as the campaigns relating to the production and conservation of food during the war and that to secure new members for the Red Cross have been described elsewhere in this volume, only the others will be dealt with here.

During the first week of April, 1917, a general appeal was addressed by the Young Men's Christian Association to the colleges, universities, and preparatory schools of the land for contributions with which to supply various forms of relief to the many college men who were already languishing in the prison camps of Europe. The total sum donated was reported on April 5, 1917, to be $120,000. Of this amount Ohio State University gave $5,500, being second in the list of contributors.

On April 24, 1917, or 18 days after the United States entered the war, Congress by a practically unanimous vote passed the Liberty Loan Bill, under the terms of which the first Liberty Loan was announced by the Government on May 2. On May 14 the Treasury Department made public the details of the loan, and on the following day a nation-wide campaign for the sale of bonds to the amount of $2,000,000,000 bearing three and one-half per cent interest was started. The University had at the time no committee to collect subscriptions from the officers, Faculty, and other persons on the payroll of the institution. Subscriptions on the campus were therefore taken by canvassers of the Franklin County Committee or through the Columbus banks. The campaign continued until June 15, but no separate record of bond sales to University subscribers was kept. For this reason neither the amount subscribed nor the number of persons subscribing is known.

Simultaneously with the launching of the first Liberty Loan drive, Columbus was asked through the city Y.M.C.A. to contribute $40,000 for the maintenance of "Y" huts in the training camps in the United States, for the support of Y. M. C. A. activities in the training camps across the water, and for the relief work in the prisoner-of-war camps for the remainder of the year. Under Faculty action in April and an executive order of Governor James M. Cox in May some 1,600 students had already withdrawn from the University to enter military, agricultural, and other forms of war service; and the University Y. M. C. A., like other student organizations, was badly disorganized. Nevertheless, a committee of 10 members of the "Y" undertook to raise money on the campus in a campaign limited to one day. These circumstances serve to explain why a comparatively small sum was secured.

The second Liberty Loan drive opened on October 1, 1917, and closed on the 28th. In the first Liberty Loan drive the University was not solicited as a separate unit and had no campaign committee of its own. This was undoubtedly due to the greatly disturbed condition of affairs on the campus at that time, which has been referred to in the preceding paragraphs. However, a campaign committee was organized to handle the new sale of Government bonds, Professor John A. Bownocker of the Department of Geology serving as chairman. During the opening week of the drive interest was aroused in the University and the city by the arrival of a fleet of nine airplanes from the aviation field at Dayton, an event which had been widely advertised. The planes began to arrive as early as 7 o'clock in the morning and circled about over Columbus in squadron formation until 10:30 o'clock, when they alighted on the new landing site on the campus west of Townshend Hall. The maneuvers were viewed by thousands of people from the city who came to the University to inspect the aircraft and be present when the mayor, officials of the Chamber of Commerce, and the Liberty Loan "boosting" committee welcomed the aviators. Columbus people made a gala occasion of the day. At the end of the campaign Professor Bownocker was able to report that 249 persons had subscribed $39,650 through the University committee and that a number of other Ohio State employees had subscribed more than $45,000 through their banks, bringing the total up to about $85,000. The Athletic Association bought a $3,000 bond and the Ohio State University Association, one of $1,000.

The showing made in the joint Y.M.C.A.—Y.W.C.A. drive to raise funds for war work in November, 1917, was also very gratifying. At that time the quota of the University was fixed at $17,000, but the committees of the two organizations had their campaign well planned, the spirit prevalent among the students and Faculty was very different from what it had been seven months before, and the giving was generous. The fraternities and sororities promptly decided to get along without formal parties for the year in order to devote the money that would be thus spent to the work of war relief. All kinds of sacrifices were reported, and individuals and groups showed surprising resourcefulness in meeting the liberal pledges they had made. The amount subscribed was $21,000, exceeding the quota by $4,000.

At the end of January, 1918, a committee of ten leading business and professional men of Columbus, of which Mr. S. P. Bush was president, Mr. Frederick A. Miller (Ohio State, class of 1901), vice-president, and Mr. A. T. Seymour (Ohio State, class of 1895), a member, undertook the task of establishing a Community War Chest to which every resident in the city able to do so was expected to contribute. The campaign to fill the chest was to occupy the first week of February, the advantages of the plan having been set forth in the city papers for weeks previously. The University went into this campaign better organized than for any of the earlier drives. An executive committee, consisting of Mr. Carl E. Steeb, chairman, William C. McCracken, superintendent of buildings and grounds, and Professors John A. Bownocker, George W. Knight, L. W. St. John, and Joseph S. Myers, appointed 11 teams each having a captain, a lieutenant, and eight other members. The *Ohio State Lantern* issued a special sheet on January 31 containing an urgent appeal to University employees to respond generously to the solicitors, whose names were printed in team lists, as well as the names of those to be solicited by each team. By this plan no person connected with the University was overlooked, and no subscription was accepted except by the team to which the assignment had been made. The object of the war chest was to provide an ample fund from which the subsequent quotas of the local community for various approved activities and relief work due to the war could be drawn on occasion, thus relieving the people of Columbus from later demands for money to meet the legitimate needs of the great organizations that were engaged in war work. The enterprise commended itself to the public, and, as subscriptions were payable in several installments, they were generally larger than they would have been otherwise. The number of University contributors, including officials, Faculty members, and employees, was 843, and the sum raised was $40,987.28. It was reported that this amount was nearly double what was expected from Ohio State by the committee of ten.

The captains and solicitors of the 11 University teams were again chosen to act in the third Liberty Loan campaign, which occupied the interval from April 5 to May 4, 1918. The date of the beginning of this campaign was also the first anniversary of the entrance of the United States into the war, the two events being celebrated jointly by the students in a big "Win-the-War-Day" demonstration, which included a parade, a regimental review, and a patriotic meeting in the University Chapel. By April 16, or nearly three weeks before the end of the drive, the executive committee of the University's campaign organization learned from the reports of the team captains that Ohio State had already exceeded its quota of the loan and invited the members of all the teams to a complimentary war supper, which was held in Ohio Union on the evening of the 18th. The total reported at the supper was $82,110, this amount being given in by Chairman Carl E. Steeb at a general meeting of the city teams on the following evening at Memorial Hall. When the drive closed, however, it was found that the total reached on the campus was $92,100, this amount being subscribed by 486 persons.

On Wednesday, June 26, 1918, the students and Faculty members of the summer session held a patriotic rally in the Chapel, the exercises consisting of singing, repeating the national pledge, prayer, and an address in the interest of the week's campaign to increase the sale of war stamps. The speaker stated that Franklin County had already raised $1,000,000, but wanted to secure $3,000,000 more through the sale of war stamps and pledges to buy them. He regarded this, he said, not only as a financial investment, but also as a patriotic and religious investment in the cause of liberty. On the second day of the campaign an airplane from the Fairfield Aviation School visited the city and University, showering them with small cards advertising the war-stamp sale. At noon the plane descended on the Ohio State landing-field. A stamp headquarters was opened in the city, and war stamps were placed on sale at booths on the street corners and in various stores. Persons connected with the University bought stamps or subscribed for them at these places, no separate record being kept for the institution.

Less than five months after the end of the third Liberty Loan campaign the fourth one began, the period in this instance being limited to three weeks, that is, from September 29 to October 19, 1918. The old campaigning organization with its 11 teams of 10 members each was again utilized under the chairmanship of Mr. R. M. Royer, the purchasing agent of the University, who filled the vacancy caused by the absence of Mr. Steeb, who had entered the service of the Government and was on duty in Washington, D. C. The actual work of soliciting subscriptions was not begun until the morning of September 30, the canvassers being instructed to employ the campaign slogan, "Buy twice as many!" in their appeal to purchasers of bonds, and the team captains were requested to report results to the executive committee every day at 4 o'clock P. M. in the bursar's office. A Liberty Bond sing was the novel feature of this drive, being held in the Chapel on the evening of October 4, under the direction of Professor Alfred R. Barrington, director of the various student musical organizations and chairman of music for the Franklin County Liberty Loan Committee. At the same time the young women of the University organized under class chairmen and class committees for the purpose of promoting the drive among the women on the campus. It was proposed that those who could not afford to buy bonds individually might be willing to join with others in purchasing one or more class bonds, which should be given to a fund with which to buy furnishings for the prospective Woman's Building. This movement had barely been started when the active solicitation closed on October 7, or 12 days before the date set for its termination, $93,650 being then reported. The teams making the largest sales were: Team No. 10, Coach Frank R. Castleman, captain, $16,800; Team No. 3, Professor Clarence D. Laylin, captain, $11,300, and Team No. 1, Miss Katherine A. Vogel, executive clerk, $10,350. Supplemental reports continued to come in for several days until the total reached $110,000, the number of subscribers being 600.

On Friday, September 27, 1918, Dr. John R. Mott, general secretary of the International Y. M. C. A., addressed a body of student delegates from 18 Ohio colleges, including 50 representatives of the Ohio State University, at the Virginia Hotel, in regard to a drive to be conducted during the week beginning November 11, in order to raise funds for seven national organizations engaged in war work, namely, the Y.M.C.A., the Y.W.C.A., the Knights of Columbus, the Jewish Welfare Board, the War Camp Community Service, and the American Library Association. Dr. Mott explained that heretofore these organizations had carried on separate campaigns for funds, but that at the request of President Wilson they had agreed to combine their efforts this year in raising the amount needed, $2,000,000. Ohio State was asked to subscribe $22,000, or one-fourth of the $88,000, which the 18 colleges represented at the meeting pledged themselves to raise. In view of the undenominational character of the drive, Jewish, Catholic, and Protestant students participated in it and, notwithstanding the fact that the Armistice was signed on the day it began, succeeded in gathering pledges to the amount of $16,500.

The last in the whole series of war drives on the campus was that to assist in floating the Victory Loan. The central committee in charge of the sale of the Victory bonds throughout the State met in Cleveland early in April and was attended by Professor Victor A. Ketcham of the Department of English as the representative of the Franklin County district. The drive was begun on April 21, 1919, more than five months after the signing of the Armistice, and lasted until May 10. The University campaign organization was called into service for the last time, Mr. Steeb being again at the head of the executive committee. The result fell short of that achieved in either the third or the fourth Liberty Loan campaigns, as was to have been expected. In this final drive 421 persons subscribed $82,200.

The various drives on the campus are tabulated herewith:

Drive	*Object*	*Dates*	Number of Subscribers	Amount Subscribed
Red Cross	New members	March 29, 1917	286	
Y. M. C. A.	Relief work	April, 1917	Not known	$ 5,500.00
First Liberty Loan	Sale of bonds	May 15 to June 15, 1917	Not known	Not known
Y. M. C. A.	For training and prison camps	May 15, 1917	Not known	Not known
Second Liberty Loan	Sale of bonds	October 1 to 28, 1917	249	$ 85,000.00
Y. M.-Y. W. C. A.	War work	Nov., 1917	Not known	$ 21,000.00
War Chest	War work	January, 1918	843	$ 40,987.28
Third Liberty Loan	Sale of bonds	April 5 to May 4, 1918	486	$ 92,100.00

War Drives

War Stamps	Sale of stamps	June 28, 1918	Not known	Not known
Fourth Liberty Loan	Sale of bonds	Sept. 28 to Oct. 7, 1918	600	$110,000.00
Menorah Society, Y. M. C. A., etc.	War work	Nov. 11, 1918, and after	Not known	$ 16,500.00
Victory Loan	Sale of bonds	Apr. 21 to May 10, 1919	421	$ 82,200.00

CHAPTER IV

RED CROSS ACTIVITIES[1]

In the spring of 1916, a full year before the United States became involved in the World War, the Columbus Chapter of the American Red Cross was formed, and Mrs. Snively, the wife of Major Harry H. Snively of the class of '95, and a member of the chapter, organized and conducted classes in first aid at that time. Late in March, 1917, the Columbus chapter, having but 350 members, started a movement to increase its membership to 10,000, in view of the crisis then existing in the relations between Germany and the United States. This movement included all of Franklin County and resulted in the organization of 113 units, among these being the North Side branch of the Columbus chapter, which met part of the time in the large basement room of the State Archeological and Historical Museum on the campus and included a number of University women among its workers. Another unit that was largely made up of University women was the surgical dressings or University branch, which was organized in the Home Economics Building and, during the first week of March, 1918, was transferred to the old Homeopathic Hospital on the corner of Tenth and Neil Avenues.

The enrollment of members for the Red Cross among students of the University was begun at the end of March, 1917, by four of the student organizations, namely, the Y.M.C.A., the Y.W.C.A., the Student Council, and the Women's Council. A committee of five representing these organizations was appointed, with Major George L. Converse, commandant of the

---

[1]For a part of the material in this chapter I am indebted to Professor Osman C. Hooper.

University Battalion, as chairman. At the end of a fortnight this committee was able to report the enrollment of 286 members.

Meantime, it was announced that all students were eligible to membership, but that women desiring to enlist in Red Cross service must have taken courses in elementary hygiene, home care of the sick, home dietetics, and preparation of surgical dressings. Men able to drive motor cars, or ready to serve as aids in base hospitals, would also be acceptable for enlistment. The University girls were told that they "ought to be the first to volunteer to give their services" by Professor Edna N. White of the Department of Home Economics, who was a member of the executive committee of the Columbus chapter and the chairman of its committee on dietetics.

On Friday, March 30, 1917, Mrs. Snively spent several hours in Orton Hall enrolling such young women as wished to enter classes in first aid. The schedule of classes in the other required subjects was announced on April 2. The course in dietetics was to comprise 15 lessons, that in surgical dressings 8 lessons, that in first aid 10 lessons, and that in elementary hygiene and home care of the sick 15 lessons. There was a registration fee of $2 for each of the first two courses and of $2.50 for each of the others. As these fees included the Red Cross membership fee of $1, anyone taking more than one course was not expected to pay the membership fee more than once. As instruction in the several courses was to begin immediately after the Easter recess, the young women were encouraged to enroll as soon as possible, but they were still registering at the rate of from six to eight a day in the second week of May. The instructors of these classes were Mrs. Snively, Mrs. Martin J. Caples, and Mrs. Edgar B. Kinkead, all of whom were downtown women. Beginning also in April, an elementary course in surgical dressings was offered to freshman girls in the Department of Home Economics, and a class was taught by Mrs. Grace G. Walker.

As the nation's preparations for war progressed and the need for the services of the Red Cross became more manifest, a Red Cross division of the University Women's Club was organized during the presidency of Mrs. Bruce, the wife of Professor Charles A. Bruce of the Department of Romance Languages. Members of this branch sewed each week day from 9 o'clock A.M. to 5 o'clock P.M. in the Home Economics Building, with an average attendance of a dozen. With the renewal of University activity in September, another group of members of the University Women's Club, together with some students and neighborhood women, was organized to make surgical dressings under the instruction of Miss Florence E. Heyde. The other group continued its sewing, Mrs. Grace G. Walker acting as the chairman and Miss Maude C. Hathaway as the secretary and treasurer of it. During the first week of March, 1918, the former group was transferred to the old Homeopathic Hospital. Later this group was moved to Oxley Hall, where its work was prosecuted to the end with Miss Heyde, Mrs. Raymond C. Osburn, Miss Eugenia C. Pavey, Miss Ruby Thomas, Mrs. Charlotte Dunn, and Miss Helen Dunn as instructors of the different classes, numbering in all six each week. Usually about 40 members were present at each class, although as many as 75 were present at one or two of the meetings.

The total registration in these classes was 307 women, of whom 31 were Faculty members and 150 University students and employees, the others being women of the neighborhood. The number of working hours was 7,970, the average number of hours for the Faculty women 60, the average for the students 22. The product in eight months was approximately 44,000 small gauze dressings and army pads. These, together with the surgical dressings made by the other branches of the Columbus chapter, were sent through the Red Cross headquarters at Cleveland to the hospitals in France. Owing, however, to an overproduction of the small dressings and a lack of the heavier pads, which were also needed by the front lines, the Government asked the Columbus chapter to stop making the former during the last three weeks of July, 1918. On August 6 all the Columbus branches engaged in making surgical dressings were compelled to cease their activities until September 1, on account of the great scarcity of gauze and absorbent cotton. The Red Cross workers of Franklin County, as also those in other parts of the country, had to wait until a new supply of these materials could be manufactured.

Connected with the Homeopathic Hospital there was a sewing group, the Homeopathic Hospital Auxiliary, with Mrs. A. E. Hinsdale as chairman, which operated from January to May, 1918.

Meantime, the sewing division of the University Women's Club continued for a time at the Home Economics Building and then was transferred to Westminster Hall on Fifteenth Avenue, where about 66 University and neighborhood women were engaged until the following February, under the chairmanship of Mrs. D. G. Sanor. Surgical-dressing work was also conducted there under the chairmanship of Mrs. T. A. Morton. In February, 1918, the groups of workers under the supervision of these two ladies were transferred to the large basement room of the State Archeological and Historical Society Museum on the University grounds at the High Street entrance. They constituted what was known as the North Side Auxiliary. During the greater part of the summer of 1918 the classes of this auxiliary met every Tuesday, Wednesday, Thursday, and Friday, Thursday afternoons being reserved for the making of surgical dressings. Fifty-one Faculty women were engaged in the work here for different periods ranging from six to 184 hours. The average daily attendance of this auxiliary during the summer season was not less than 75 persons. In the closing days of July the women were not only filling orders for surgical dressings, but were also doing a great deal of sewing for the French and Belgian refugees, including French orphans. Besides other garments, they were turning out 100 shirts a day. A survey of their workroom showed heaps of new garments of various kinds, large piles of knitted goods for soldiers, made at home, and numerous boxes of dressings and bandages. The auxiliary produced a total of about 50,000 large absorbent dressings and numbers of pneumonia jackets, in addition to the other articles. The work here was greatly facilitated by the use of an electrical machine for rolling bandages, which was devised by Professor F. C. Caldwell and Mr. W. R. Alexander of the Electrical Engineering Department. By means of this invention an expert operator could roll five yards in 40 seconds, a task which when performed by hand could not be done in less than 25 or 30 minutes. With the introduction of this machine at the Museum workroom, it was possible for Mrs. Wilbur H. Siebert to do practically all of the bandage-rolling not only for the North Side branch, but also for the Columbus chapter. All the other local branches were thereby released from the necessity of making bandages by the tedious hand method. Plans had been made for producing the machines for use throughout the country when the war ended.

For this branch, too, Professor Eldon L. Usry of the Manual Training Department provided portable screens, shelving, markers, and other equipment. Professor Frank E. Sanborn of the Industrial Arts Department perfected and offered to Red Cross headquarters a device for handling heavy bolts of cloth that were to be cut into shape for garments. Both in the University and outside of it there was a fine spirit of helpfulness, whatever the need of the workers might be.

A knitting group was organized by the women employees of the University as a division of the State employees' branch. Money was contributed by the men employees for the purchase of yarn, and many articles were made and distributed through the secretary of the State branch.

The greatest interest and activity of the brief period of America's participation in the war was displayed by the Red Cross workers of the University during the spring of 1918. This fact is explained in part by the signing and ratification of the peace between the Bolsheviki and Germany in March, and the announcement in the same month that American troops were occupying trenches at four different points on French soil. These items of news were quickly followed by the reports of the German drives that were made between

March 21 and April 18. But the interest of the University girls in war activities was also stimulated by the forming of a new war organization during the period of these events. Minnette Y. Fritts was the head chairman of this organization and Joy N. Rogers, Harriet A. Day, Lucille Whan, Helen D. Dustman, Harriett E. Daily, Vivian S. Townsend, Margaret E. Fisher, and Florence L. Whitacre were in charge of its sections. The chairmen of the class committees were as follows: senior, Jessie F. Masteller; junior, M. Dorothy Kramer; sophomore, Margaret Welch; freshman, Florence Wolf. Through the efforts of these students and their committees hundreds of University girls were registered for war work, only a portion of which could be regarded as strictly Red Cross.

Some of the young women who attended the summer sessions during the war period were readily persuaded to enter the Red Cross classes. A class in first aid of over 34 members was conducted during the summer of 1917, Dean E. F. McCampbell of the College of Medicine, then a captain in the Medical Reserve Corps, being one of the lecturers before this group. Captain McCampbell explained the fact that the majority of wounds were received by the soldiers as injuries to the head and face, due to the modern method of trench fighting, although the dropping of bombs into the trenches, he added, often resulted in injuries to the arms and legs. This explanation was preliminary to the discussion of the methods of treatment for such wounds. On July 1, 1918, classes in surgical dressings were organized at Oxley Hall.

When the University opened in the fall of 1918, first-aid classes for sophomore girls were formed and began to meet in the week of September 30. The large size of the Tuesday morning class made necessary its division into two sections. Other classes met on Tuesday afternoons and on Wednesday mornings and afternoons.

During the latter part of November, 1918, after the Students' Army Training Corps had been established at the University, the girls belonging to the Ohio State branch of the Red Cross undertook to mend and sew for the cadets and for the soldiers at Camp Sherman. The clothing from the camp at Chillicothe that needed repair was sent to the campus by the Columbus Chapter of the Red Cross. The workrooms in the Home Economics Building were open every afternoon, and a competent adviser was in attendance to care for the articles received and instruct the girls who went there to do this form of reclamation work. Ten committees of from 15 to 19 members each, the total membership being 173, were assigned to this patriotic service.

Soon after the declaration of war Mrs. George W. Knight went to Chicago and later to Detroit to fit herself to be an instructor in surgical dressings and first aid. Returning, she was appointed an instructor and supervisor by the Columbus chapter. She immediately began giving two courses of instruction, one (eight lessons of three hours each) which produced about 200 supervisors and assistant supervisors, and the other (14 lessons of three hours each) which produced seven instructors, some of whom were drafted for work elsewhere. In June, 1917, she was able to surrender the supervision to those she had taught and in July was designated as chairman in surgical dressing, a position which she occupied until the work ceased with the signing of the Armistice in November, 1918. She organized and directed the work, securing material and designating supervisors, in 15 surgical-dressing branches in Franklin County and had general supervision of the surgical-dressing work in 12 counties in central Ohio. What with teaching, speaking, visiting units, ordering supplies, and appointing supervisors, Mrs. Knight's service was a notable one. In the various units and branches there were approximately 3,000 workers, and the quantity and quality of the output were such as materially to assist in giving to the Columbus Chapter of the Red Cross the high reputation it achieved. As a reward for her volunteer service, Mrs. Knight was awarded the Red Cross badge with the two stripes, representing 2,700 hours.

Faculty women who became supervisors, most of them in the classes of Mrs. Knight, were: Mrs. Raymond C. Osburn, Mrs. Wilbur H. Siebert, Mrs. George B. Kauffman, Mrs. Edgar

S. Ingraham, and Miss Mary Henderson. Mrs. Kauffman organized a large and active branch of workers in Clinton Township, supplied a workroom for it in her home on North High Street, and directed it with such success that a Red Cross banner was awarded to her group. In November, 1917, Mrs. Alfred D. Cole, the wife of Professor Cole of the Department of Physics, organized a sewing and knitting group at the Tenth Avenue Baptist Church, in which from 20 to 40 women, some of the University, worked faithfully to the last.

An unusual record of service is that of Mrs. Franklin A. Ray, the wife of Professor Ray of the Department of Mine Engineering. Mrs. Ray had the advantage of being a graduate nurse of St. Luke's Training School of Chicago, Ill. On June 8, 1917, she was registered as a Red Cross nurse for home service. By reason of her special training she felt obligated to devote as much of her time as necessary to giving instruction in elementary hygiene and home care of the sick and conducted classes in Columbus, Newark, Granville, and Alexandria. Living near Granville, O., her qualifications were promptly recognized there, and she was made a member of the executive committee of the Licking County Chapter of the Red Cross, chairman of its committee on nursing activities, and chairman of the Granville branch of the Red Cross. Those who are acquainted with Mrs. Ray do not need to be told that her services were gratuitous.

Faculty women engaged in the Red Cross canteen work in Columbus were: Mrs. Raymond C. Osburn, Mrs. William T. Magruder, Mrs. E. A. Cottrell, Mrs. Alfred Vivian, and Miss Grace Chandler. From January to June, 1919, that is, during the period of the return of the troops from overseas, these ladies served at the clubroom on High Street, opposite to the Union Station, meeting soldiers who called, providing for their comfort in various ways, and giving them needed information and counsel. Mrs. W. O. Thompson supervised the making of the University's great service flag and did canteen work both in Columbus and New York City.

The service flag contained 2,640 gold stars at the time of

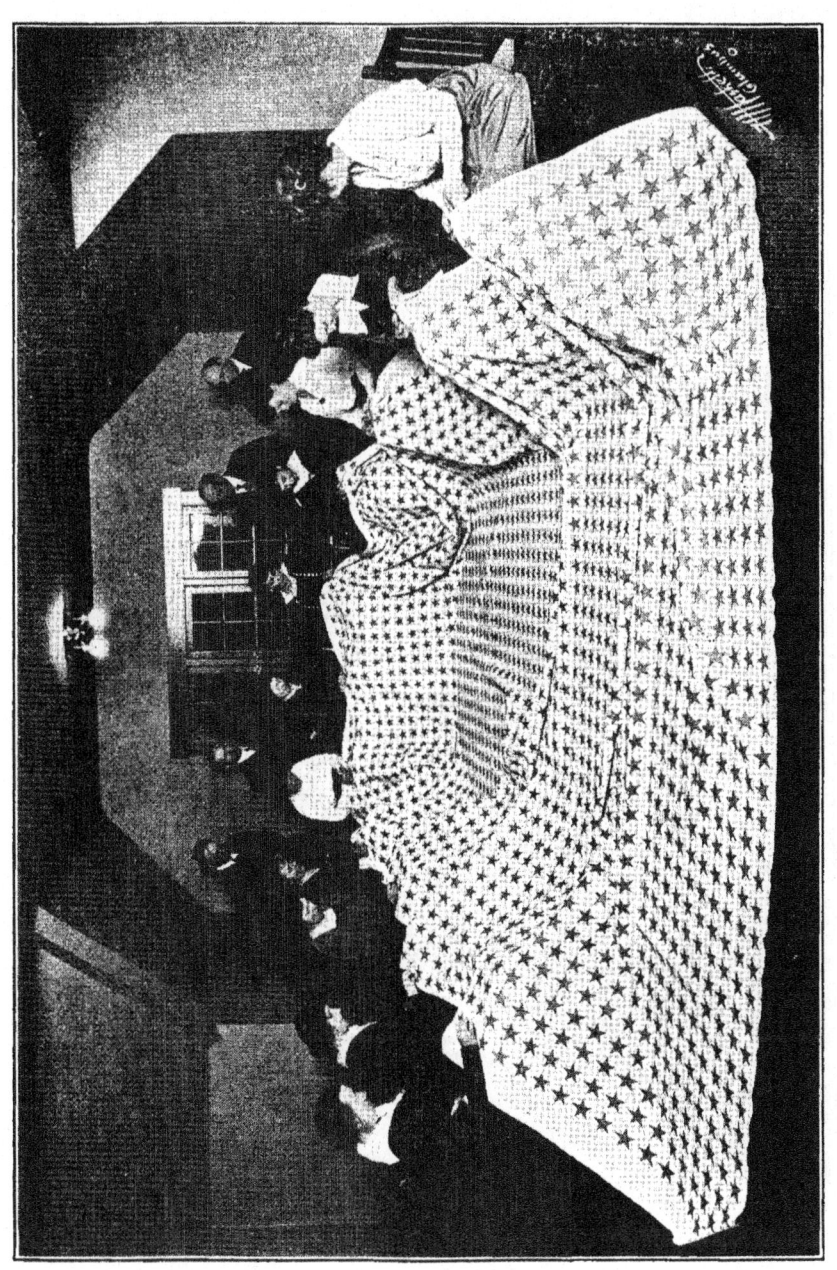

Mrs. W. O. Thompson and ten other ladies finishing the service flag.

The service flag displayed on the front of the Library.

its dedication on Saturday afternoon, May 25, 1918. At that time the only service flag known in the country to have more stars was that of the Bell Telephone Company in New York City. At the dedicatory exercises, which were held in front of the University Library in the presence of a throng of people, the president of the Alumni Association, Burton D. Stephenson presided, and Lowry F. Sater gave the address, at the close of which he presented the flag, which hung suspended against the front of the Library, to the University. President Thompson accepted it in a stirring speech and was followed by former Governor James E. Campbell. Messages of regret at their inability to be present from President Wilson, Governor Cox, Secretary of War Baker, Secretary of the Navy Daniels, and United States Senators Harding and Pomerene were read. The occasion was most impressive. Later the several addresses were published.

Several of the younger men in the University Faculty took part in the activities of the Red Cross overseas. Nearly two years before the United States became involved in the war, Assistant Professor Walter T. Peirce of the Department of Romance Languages became a Red Cross worker in France, spending the summers of 1915 and 1916 as an orderly in the American Ambulance Hospital at Neuilly, near Paris.

Professor Peirce was the first of our University teachers to go into war work. On his return in the autumn of 1916 he was soon in demand as a speaker on the relief work of the American Red Cross, under whose auspices he had gained his experience. During the next 10 months he gave more than 60 addresses before societies, clubs, and larger audiences. As he had brought back a large number of photographs which he had taken in France, he illustrated many of his talks with pictures thrown on the screen. Besides speaking a number of times in Columbus, he gave addresses in Chillicothe, Portsmouth, Circleville, Springfield, London, Urbana, Marysville, Newark, and Delaware, finding opportunities to establish local chapters of the Red Cross and to encourage sewing for the hospitals overseas. Audiences, clubs, and individuals contributed money for the purchase of materials for bandage making, and various women's organizations about the University, including the Woman's Council, the French Club, and six sororities, prepared hospital supplies in sufficient quantity to fill 10 cases, which were shipped to France in May, 1917.

The supplies consisted of sheets, towels, wash cloths, shirts, pajamas, knitted articles, tray cloths, napkins, surgical dressings, and gauze. Furthermore, a relief unit was formed by Mrs. Joseph V. Denney among the University women for the purpose of providing the necessary money, materials, and work to continue furnishing such supplies. The ladies who were associated with Mrs. Denney in the relief unit were: Mrs. John A. Bownocker, Mrs. Charles St. John Chubb, Mrs. George L. Converse, Mrs. Clair A. Dye, Mrs. Wallace S. Elden, Mrs. George W. Knight, Mrs. Henry C. Lord, Mrs. William T. Magruder, Mrs. Wilbur H. Siebert, and Mrs. Alfred Vivian.

Late in June, 1917, Professor Peirce sailed for Bordeaux in company with Dr. Albert R. Chandler of the Department of Philosophy and Thomas M. Magruder, a son of Professor W. T. Magruder. Early in July Drs. Chandler and Peirce took up the work of orderlies in the hospital at Neuilly, while young Magruder became driver of an ambulance at the front for the same establishment. The hospital at Neuilly had been opened by American residents in Paris in August, 1914, immediately after the outbreak of hostilities, to help care for the French wounded. Its supporters also maintained a considerable number of motor ambulances at the front. After continuing as orderlies until early in October, Messrs. Peirce and Chandler enrolled as field delegates of the Bureau of Refugees of the American Red Cross in Paris, Mr. Peirce being sent to northern France to distribute supplies to the war sufferers in that region. With the establishment of General Pershing's headquarters in France, in the winter of 1918, Mr. Peirce was appointed an interpreter in the Intelligence Division of the headquarters of the American Expeditionary Forces. At this time he was commissioned a second lieutenant. He was soon made responsible for the translating and publishing through the proper channels of all military correspondence carried on between the American and Entente officers. In December, 1918, he was appointed translator for the United States delegates to the Peace Conference, and about the same time he was promoted to the rank of first lieutenant. The importance of Lieutenant Peirce's new position may be estimated from the fact that he was the exclusive translator of all that was said in French on the floor of the conference, of which the notes were taken by the French stenographers who were under his charge.

As a field delegate Mr. Chandler was a guest of the British Quakers at Troyes for a few days in October, 1917, where he became acquainted with the measures they were taking to relieve the wretched condition of the refugees under their care. After the Italian retreat to the Tagliamento, at the end of October, 1917, and to the Piave, in the early days of November, before the advance of the combined German and Austrian forces into Italy, Mr. Chandler was sent by the Red Cross down to Rome, being among the first workers dispatched into that territory. Thence he proceeded to Milan, where thousands of refugee families were collecting. There he helped the American consul and a committee of resident Americans to establish a home and kitchen for refugees, besides engaging in other Red Cross activities. Large numbers of fugitives were housed in extensive dormitories provided by two local Italian organizations and hitherto used for the accommodation of emigrants passing through the city. Thousands of families had also to be sheltered in tents. Mr. Chandler was a witness of the thrilling demonstration in the Scala Theater in honor of the first contingents of French and English troops that passed through Milan on their way to the Italian front.

After spending two months in Milan, Dr. Chandler was transferred in January, 1918, to Chioggia, a fishing town in the lagoon, about 20 miles south of Venice, where he was the only foreigner in a district of 70,000 inhabitants. Here the Red Cross delegate kept a canteen in readiness in anticipation of another retrograde movement of new troops and a new flight of refugees. The population of the district was now chiefly women and children, most of the men being away at war. As there was plenty of relief work to be done, Dr. Chandler and his staff of a few soldiers and Venetian girls opened a free soup kitchen which filled the pails of hungry people with hot and nourishing food. This supplemented one maintained by the Italian authorities. A workroom was also found where some of the Chioggia women were kept busy making clothing for ragged war orphans and the needy children of soldiers at the front. Shoes, stockings, and other articles of apparel were also distributed.

During January and February, 1918, Venice was harried by air raids, which caused many refugees to leave during the weeks immediately following, but they did not go to Chioggia. It was therefore necessary for Mr. Chandler to divide his time between his headquarters and Venice during March and April so as to assist the Red Cross delegate there in distributing food to the departing refugees from the little Red Cross room in the railroad station. Closing the canteen at Chioggia late in November, 1918, Mr. Chandler continued his work in Venice until March 1, 1919. In February he had been given the rank of captain, and in that and the following month he made two trips to Fiume to distribute clothing to certain Crotians, who were naturalized American citizens and eager to return to the land of their adoption.

On April 1, 1919, Captain Chandler was transferred to the Red Cross Commission for Europe, whose headquarters were in Paris. From there he was sent with other workers to Berlin in the third week of April to assist the Red Cross delegation there in caring for Russian prisoners, only to learn that the need for new workers had ceased. Thence he returned to Paris, was soon released from further service, and arrived in New York on June 22, 1919.

Another member of the University staff who entered the service of the American Red Cross in Italy was Dr. Robert G. Paterson, assistant professor of Public Health and Sanitation in the College of Medicine. Dr. Paterson arrived in Rome on October 6, 1918, with a tuberculosis unit, which became the Tuberculosis Department of the American Red Cross Commission for Italy. He helped to organize the medical and public-health service in the peninsula and the adjacent islands, his unit discontinuing its labors on May 14, 1919. Major Paterson was then transferred to the headquarters of the American Red Cross Commission for Europe at Paris and remained there until his discharge in June, 1919.

Besides the three members of the Faculty who were engaged in Red Cross work abroad, Professor Osman C. Hooper and Professor Joseph S. Myers of the Department of Journalism, Professor Arthur M. Schlesinger of the Department of American History, and Dean James E. Hagerty of the College of Commerce and Journalism rendered various services in connection with the Columbus Chapter of the Red Cross.

In the spring of 1917 Dean Hagerty was appointed chairman of the Civilian Relief Committee, and as such became chairman of the Home Service subcommittee. He directed the work of material and advisory aid of the families of soldiers and sailors, giving to the men needed information before going to camp and after discharge and to their families information and aid of various kinds until the readjustment to industrial and community life was complete. He organized a corps of investigators, which was aided by a consultation committee that met at stated intervals to consider the more difficult problems. Two members of the University Faculty served on this committee, namely, Professor Hooper and Professor Schlesinger. Mr. Stockton Raymond, an alumnus, was also a member of the committee, while four alumnae served in various capacities—Miss Florence Covert and Miss Elizabeth Long as executive secretaries, and Miss Julia Griggs and Mrs. Eleanor Ryan Hixenbaugh as visitors.

At the invitation of the American Red Cross, Dean Hagerty organized at the University a Home Service Institute for the training of investigators and office managers in civilian relief work, and this institute was conducted under the joint auspices of the American Red Cross, its chapter in Columbus, and the University Department of Economics and Sociology. Three classes were instructed, one in 1917 and two in 1918, each doing six weeks of classroom and field work, the latter in connection with local philanthropic organizations. Some of the students became volunteer workers in the civilian relief department of the Columbus Chapter of the Red Cross, while others returned to the counties from which they came to render similar service. A number of permanent social workers were prepared by these classes.

In the summer of 1918, when there was pressing need for nurses, a campaign was conducted in Columbus for the enrollment of graduate nurses and of young women willing to take the training necessary to become nurses. Professor Joseph S. Myers was chairman of the committee that opened headquarters at the Deshler Hotel and within a fortnight enrolled 203 nurses and 126 young women willing to take the training.

At the outbreak of the influenza epidemic among the cadets of the Students' Army Training Corps on the campus, in October, 1918, nothing like an adequate supply of bedding, towels, and other articles required for the care of the scores of the sick were at hand. Through the prompt action of Mrs. Lowry F. Sater, Mrs. Frank A. Ray, and Professor and Mrs. W. H. Siebert, the Columbus Chapter of the Red Cross, and the City Federation of Women's Clubs generously and fully met these needs without delay, the Red Cross purchasing what it did not already have in stock and supplying in addition a number of trained nurses.

It is, of course, impossible to give an exhaustive account of the Red Cross activities of the women graduates of the University. A few examples must suffice to illustrate the fact that not a few of the alumnae rendered a devoted service at home or abroad, as the case might be. Miss Ola Mae Arick of the class of 1918 engaged in civilian relief work in Cleveland. Miss Esther Eaton (M.A., 1912) went to France in April, 1918, to do child-welfare work in the devastated districts that were then being rebuilt. Miss Mary Agnes Kelly (class of 1906) of Los

Angeles was sent to Italy in October, 1918, as an interpreter for the Red Cross. Miss Margaret Teachnor (class of 1917) became connected in the latter part of October, 1918, with the personnel division of the American Red Cross Commission in Paris and was later stationed in the village of Brest, Brittany, with the canteen, where on December 13 she had the honor, with six other American Red Cross girls, of greeting President and Mrs. Wilson, Miss Margaret Wilson, and General Pershing at the landing pier. Miss Teachnor remained at Brest until in April, 1919, when she accompanied the Army of Occupation as a Red Cross worker to Coblenz, Germany. Miss Florence E. Welling (class of 1910) sailed for France late in November, 1918, to serve as an entertainer in the aviation camps. Miss Charme M. Seeds (class of 1915) arrived in France early in April, 1919, to become a casualty searcher in the personnel department of the American Red Cross. Miss Helen Hayward, '14, accompanied a party of sixty young women overseas in January, 1919, for canteen work in France. She first served in London for three weeks, then in Liverpool for a brief time, after which she went to France.

CHAPTER V

WAR WORK OF THE RELIGIOUS ORGANIZATIONS

There are four or five religious organizations in the University, besides the Y. M. C. A. and the Y. W. C. A. Among these is a Catholic organization and a Jewish organization; the others are Protestant. In general, then, the war activities of the Y. M. C. A. and the Y. W. C. A. were inclusive of the great majority of the students, and it may be asserted without fear of contradiction that sectarian lines were not drawn among the students in the promotion of patriotic enterprises.

The Y.M.C.A. had never been in as excellent a condition at Ohio State University as when the war started. This was due to the determined effort the association put forth during the academic year 1916-17 under the able leadership of its secretary, Huntley Dupre, to gain the support of the student body. The result was that the association enrolled the largest membership of any student Y. M. C. A. in the world. The leading religious organization among the young women was the Y. W. C. A., and the two other leading student organizations of a general nature were the Student Council and the Woman's Council. When, therefore, the Columbus Chapter of the American Red Cross began its movement at the end of March, 1917, for a greatly increased membership, it wisely secured the appointment of a committee representing these four organizations to enroll members among the students. However, it may be said frankly that the outcome of the two weeks' campaign for new members did not fulfill the expectations of its sponsors in the city. Only 286 persons joined the Red Cross, whereas it had been hoped that 10 times that many would join. Doubtless, the figure set was beyond reason in view of the harrowing uncertainty existing in the minds of the students, especially of the male students, during this period, and also in view of other war activities that were being started simultaneously on the campus and that were nearer to the hearts of the students.

The general appeal addressed to the colleges and preparatory schools of the country by the Young Men's Christian Association early in April, 1917, for a fund with which to carry relief to college men in European prison camps stirred the sympathies of the young people to whom it came, all the more that it was emphasized by the declaration of war by the Government. Within a few days $5,500 was subscribed by the students and Faculty, this being the most successful campaign to raise money that had ever been conducted by any student organization of the University up to that time.

In the last week of April, after hundreds of young men had left the University to go into agricultural and military service, the Y. M. C. A. was called on by the Young Men's Christian Association of Columbus to raise part of the $40,000 required during the rest of the year to support wartime activities in the military training camps on both sides of the Atlantic, as well as in the prison camps overseas. The student association had lost many of its most active members, and the Faculty were aware that they would soon be given the opportunity to subscribe to the first Liberty Loan. These circumstances interfered materially with the success of the Y. M. C. A. solicitation, which secured a disappointing sum.

By virtue of the trying experiences of the spring semester of 1917, the University Y. M. C. A. gave itself with a new ardor to the work of disseminating the spirit of service among the students when Ohio State opened in the fall. As soon as the training camps were occupied by enlisted men, members of recent cabinets of the University Y. M. C. A. were to be seen in charge of the "Y" huts at various camps.

Those members who still remained at the University found the time in which to organize 33 Bible-study classes in fraternity houses and boarding clubs, and in November, 1917, the Y. M. C. A. and Y. W. C. A., acting jointly, surprised the community by raising nearly four times the amount for war work that had been secured for the Y. M. C. A. alone in its boasted campaign of the early days of April of the same year, that is, the two associations raised the sum of $21,000, exceeding the quota apportioned to the University by $4,000.

The fall and winter of 1917 was a busy season for the two associations at the University in more ways than one. They assisted freshmen in entering the institution, finding rooms, boarding places, and church homes; they held receptions for the new students as well as the old; the Y. M. C. A. arranged a series of weekly religious meetings which were addressed by prominent men of the Faculty, city, and State; it sent out six gospel teams, and maintained an employment bureau for students who were earning their way through college in whole or in part.

Already in August, 1917, J. Ruskin Dyer of the class of '16, who had been a member of the Y. M. C. A. cabinet, had gone to France to work with the American Army Y. M. C. A. and had been stationed at the artillery Campe de Mailly. In the following December he had been transferred to the French Y. M. C. A. and sent to the front. It was at this time that William E. Wright of the class of '12 joined the Sixth French Army as a worker in the French Y. M. C. A. at Soissons and vicinity. Mr. Wright was decorated with the Croix de Guerre for bravery during the German advance on the Aisne in the second battle of the Marne, July 18–August 4, 1918. Early in December, 1917, Professor Henry R. Spencer arrived in Paris on his way to Italy as a Y. M. C. A. volunteer. He became regional director, being stationed at the headquarters of the Third Italian Army, being ten miles north of Venice until Trieste and Trent were occupied by the Italians, November 3, 1918, and after that at Trieste. By January, 1917, Huntley Dupree of the class of '14 (Law School, 1916) and Don L. Demorest of the class of '16 were in France. For the next three months they were engaged there in the prison relief work of the International Committee of the Y. M. C. A. During the months of April, May, and the opening days of June, 1917,

Mr. Dupre was with the American Army Y. M. C. A. in Paris. From June 5 until July 9 he was engaged in organizing the Y. M. C. A. at St. Nazaire for the First Division of the American Expeditionary Force, the first American troops to disembark in France, their landing being effected on June 26, 1917. In July he organized the association work at Nevers, in August at Alvord for the Lafayette Esquadrille aviators with the French Army, in September he assisted in organizing the Y. M. C. A. in the Neufchateau and Bourmont areas for the Twenty-Sixth and Third Divisions, A.E.F. Mr. Dupre was the first American to be sent with the French Y. M. C. A. to the front. This was in October, 1917, and the following months into January, 1918, he spent with the Sixth French Army on the Aisne, his headquarters being at Soissons. In January he was transferred to the French Y. M. C. A. at Villers-la-Fosse and Crecy-au-Mont, where he devoted his activities to the Eleventh Army Corps of the Sixth Army. In February he enlisted as a private in the 26th Regiment of Infantry, First Division, A. E. F.

From this point on Mr. Dupre's record corresponds very closely with that of his friend, Mr. Demorest, and the two records, will, therefore, be given together, after the first part of the latter's record has been recounted. After doing prison-relief work in France, Mr. Demorest spent six months or more in organization work. In April, 1917, he organized the Y. M. C. A. headquarters in Paris and then in succession he formed the branch associations for the Artillery of the Twenty-sixth Division, A. E. F., at Chateauroux; for the Fifteenth Regiment of Engineers, A. E. F. (the first American Engineers in France) at Vierzon; for the American Aviation Camp at Issoudun; and for the Heavy Artillery Camp at Mailly. From October, 1917, to February, 1918, he was with the French Army Y.M.C.A. at Ville en Tardenois and in the vicinity of Rheims and at Fort de la Pompelle and, like Mr. Dupre, he enlisted as a private in the 26th Regiment of Infantry, First Division, A.E.F. From March 8 to April 1, 1918, the two friends saw service in the trenches; from the last-named date until July 9 they were together in the Army Candidates' School (Infantry) at Langres, being then commissioned as second lieutenants; for the next fortnight they were enrolled in the Student Army Gas School, A. E. F., serving as instructors in this school from July 23 to September 1; during the next 10 days they were on special duty, Demorest with the Seventy-seventh Division and Dupre with the Twenty-sixth, on the Vesle front at the time of the German retreat in the second battle of the Marne; then both took up their work as instructors in the Army Gas School at Rolampont and continued in it until in early December, 1918, both being promoted to first lieutenancies on November 13. In February, 1919, both returned to the United States, but three months later Demorest returned to France to take up work with the French Y. M. C. A.

J. Ruskin Dyer, like Demorest and Dupre, enlisted as a private in February, 1918, but in the Artillery and was sent to the First Division, A. E. F. He was in the Artillery Training School at Saumur from April to July, when he was commissioned a second lieutenant. In the fall of 1918 he saw service with a coast-artillery battery, and in the spring of 1919 he was promoted to a first lieutenancy. After his service in France Huntley Dupre returned to the University and the secretaryship of the student Y. M. C. A., but in January, 1920, resigned his position in order to become educational secretary of the University of Prague in Bohemia. His work there consisted not only of Y. M. C.A. activities among the 7,000 students of the institution, but also of educational work among the people of the historic old city, in which he took up his duties on March 1, 1920.

Aside from the five members of the University Y. M. C. A. whose war records have been given above, a list of 57 was printed in the *Makio* of 1919, out of an estimated total of 75 men who had served in the association cabinets during the previous four years, who went into military service.

The Rev. Dr. Gaius Glenn Atkins of the class of '88 also did Y.M.C.A. work in France. He was first regional secretary of the *Americaine Foyer de Soldat* (Y.M.C.A.) with the French Army in the summer of 1918 on the Montdidier Sector, being in charge of the cantonments half-way between Beauvais and Amiens, with his headquarters at Maisoncelle-Tuilleries. In September he was transferred to the American Army and given direction of the Y.M.C.A. Department of Religious Work in the first region, with his headquarters at Brest. He served in the Pontánazen Hospital during the influenza epidemic and for a brief time later with the 26th Division in the Verdun combat area.

Several of the University women participated in Y. M. C. A. activities abroad. The first of these to leave for France was Mrs. Guy W. Mallon of Cincinnati, O., who was formerly a student in the College of Arts, and whose husband was a trustee of the University. Mrs. Mallon served as Y.M.C.A. hostess at Saumur, France.

Miss Winifred A. Tunell, former secretary of the Y. W. C. A. at Ohio State, was one of those in charge of the hostess house and an aide in the hospital at Tours, where she entered upon her duties early in July, 1918. Miss Nan Cannon of the class of '01, secretary of the Ohio State University Alumni Association in 1917-1918, spent two weeks in December of the latter year attending a conference of Y. M. C. A. workers from all over the country, at the end of which she sailed for France to work at the "Y" headquarters in Paris. Miss Isabel McNeal, formerly an assistant in the registrar's office, became the chief statistician of the Bureau of Claims and Adjustments, Red Cross, at Bordeaux and Paris.

Miss Ednah H. Pugh, former secretary in the office of the Entrance Board of the University, who was active in Y. W. C. A. work after the beginning of the war, went to Barnard College, New York City, in the fall of 1917 to take a course of intensive training. In February, 1919, she was sent to do overseas work with the Y. M. C. A. At the same time Miss Florence Gilliam of the class of '09 sailed for France to act as interpreter for the association.

The enlistment of numbers of students in military service

during the months following the declaration of war by the United States Government was first commemorated in bronze on the University grounds by the local Y. M. C. A. At Christmas time, 1917, the association had an enduring tablet set in the large granite boulder near the main walk at the southeast corner of University Hall. The inscription on the tablet, which was written by Professor Joseph Russell Taylor of the Department of English is as follows: "In honor of those sons of the Ohio State University who have answered the call to the colors in the year 1917." The dedicatory ceremony at the unveiling of the bronze plaque was conducted by President W. O. Thompson. The plaque is so placed that it is frequently seen by the throngs of students who pass on their way to and from University Hall, being thereby reminded of the self-sacrifice of the men who offered themselves to uphold the cause of humanity.

In speaking of this memorial plaque, the *Makio* of 1918, which was issued about fourteen months after the United States entered the war, stated that according to estimate approximately 4,000 graduates and former students of the University had answered the call to the colors and that 300 Ohio State men were then fighting under the Stars and Stripes in France. The total number of enlistments in all branches of the service during the war period was 6,593.

With the establishment of the School of Military Aeronautics on the campus in May, 1917, and the subsequent opening in rapid succession of three other military schools under the jurisdiction of the War Department, the hundreds of men who were ordered here from all parts of the United States to receive their ground training were confined within stated boundaries during the period of their stay. For them the University was a military post, with its rules of strict discipline. To meet the needs of these cadets the University Y. M. C. A. obtained from the War Work Council of the general association games of various sorts, a victrola and set of records, writing materials, and other supplies for the use of the successive squadrons, whose members were confined to the campus for three months, except when granted a very brief leave, which happened but rarely.

The presence of the Students' Army Training Corps at the University in the fall of 1918 caused a radical change in the work of the local Y. M. C. A., which was at once transformed into Army Y. M. C. A. work. All college associations were taken over by the National War Work Council. The student secretaries were made Army secretaries and became responsible to the War Work Council. This was done in order to preserve the identity of the student associations and to enable them to resume their regular activities when peace should return. At Ohio State the association tried to fill the needs of the S. A. T. C. cadets in particular, needs that were emphasized by their confinement to the campus, as in the case of the students in the earlier military schools. It sought to further the religious life of the men by holding weekly devotional meetings, by personal efforts, and by distributing quantities of Scripture leaflets and pamphlets. For the diversion of the cadets it held entertainments in the Chapel every Saturday night. It welcomed the cadets to the Y. M. C. A. offices, which were visited by an average of 500 men daily. During the months of October and November, 1918, nearly 25,000 letters were written on paper furnished by the Y. M. C. A. The only branches of the regular work that were maintained as in former years were the employment bureau and the foreign-student department.

The following members of the Y. M. C. A. cabinets of the years 1915 to 1918, inclusive, were in war service:

Arden O. Basinger	Alexander Glenn	Carl Marquand
Leo Bayles	Lloyd Hanson	Robert Nevin
Earl F. Baum	Charles Harley	Ellis Noble
Clifford C. Boyd	Frank Hartford	Virgil Overholt
John W. Bricker	Bryan Heise	W. R. Palmer
Kenyon S. Campbell	John Hendrix	Joseph Park
Bert Chambers	Donald Hoskins	Jack Pierce
S. L. Cheny	George Hoskins	Allen Rankin
Dana Coe	William H. Houston	Ralph Roehm
George Coe	Ray Hoyt	Melvin Ryder
Luke Cooperider	Ralph Howard	George Schuster
Fred Croxton	Carl L. Kennedy	Dudley Sears

Religious Organizations

Edmond Deibel
Don L. Demorest
Maynard Donaldson
William A. Dougherty
Charles B. Dunham
Huntley Dupre
J. Ruskin Dyer
Luther Evans
Roy Ferguson
Mark Fuller

Herbert Kimmel
Chauncey Lang
Ralph W. Laughlin
  (killed in action)
Gladden Lincoln
Samuel Linzell
  (with Canadian Army)
John Luttrell
Martin Mansperger

Frank Shaw
Gordon Smith
Paul E. Sprague
Luther C. Swain
Dann O. Taber
Gerald Tenney
Galen Weaver
William Willing
Harold Yost

At the end of a year of hostilities the Jewish organization, known as the Menorah Society, had 32 members who were graduates of the University in service as follows:

Theodore Beekman
Bernard Benjamin
B. A. Bergman
J. E. Blum
Marvin Blum
Dervey Brumberg
Samuel Cohn
E. A. Deutsch
J. B. Duga
A. Eidelman
Maurice Epstein
H. H. Felsman

M. Friedman
Leon Friedman
H. Greenberger
Nedward Gross
Ralph Gross
William V. Gross
Irving Klein
Jesse Kleinmeyer
Stanley Koch
Leon B. Komisaruk
Walter Krohngold

Jack Kuertz
R. Levison
Louis Posovick
Phillip Sanders
A. S. Shapiro
Edwin A. Weil
Harvey Weiss
J. Wilkoff
Bert Wolman
Leo Yassenoff
Solomon Yassenoff

T. M. Magruder and his ambulance on the road at Maison Rouge, near the Chemin des Dames, September, 1917.

T. M. Magruder (in center) and his ambulance just south of Beauvais, France, April, 1918.

Columbus, Ohio, Red Cross Hospital Unit No. 5 at the Naval Operating Base, Hampton Roads, Virginia, April 17, 1919.

CHAPTER VI

THE OHIO UNION IN WARTIME

It is safe to say that the men's club house, the Ohio Union, was put to uses for more than a year and seven months during the war which were never dreamed of by the enthusiastic body of students who succeeded in obtaining from the General Assembly of the State in 1907 the appropriation of $75,000, which made possible the realization of their cherished plan for a building adapted to the needs of the University boys. Continuously from May 21, 1917, until December 20, 1918, the Ohio Union served as an important adjunct to the five military schools which the War Department at Washington maintained for longer or shorter periods at Ohio State University.

On the first-mentioned date there arrived at the University 16 cadets to receive intensive training in the first of the schools that was established on the campus, namely, the United States School of Military Aeronautics. From that time until the end of August, 1918, when the Aeronautical School was discontinued after the Engineer Officers', the Aero-Squadron Adjutants', and the Balloon Adjutants' Schools had closed, the dining-room of the Union was the mess hall for the cadets. With the opening of the University in the fall of 1918, the Union became at once the lounge and mess room of the much larger number of cadets who were being rapidly inducted into the Students' Army Training Corps, which was demobilized a few days before Christmas of the same year.

The original number of 16 aeronautical cadets was steadily added to, until in August there were more than 200. By the middle of January, 1918, the average daily number had increased to nearly 350. In February it leaped to 725, rose to over 830 with the starting of the Balloon Adjutants' School in March, and thereafter declined until there were less than 350 aviation pilots when the Aeronautical School was closed, August 31, 1918.

During the summer of 1917 Mr. Edward S. Drake, the manager of the Union, and his civilian employees were confronted with the problem of taking care of both the cadets of the Aeronautical School and the students of the summer session. The former were seated on one side of the dining-room and the latter on the other, but it was necessary to have the cadets come in two relays. The Union still continued to function as the social center for the students of the University.

Before the opening of the institution in the autumn word was received that the Government would increase the number of cadets to about 400. Accordingly, an addition, which increased the seating capacity of the dining-room one-third, was rushed to completion; a storeroom of two floors was erected on the west side of the building, and a complete refrigerating system was installed. The dining-room was closed to all but cadets, and the Union literally went on a war basis. The only privilege accorded the University students in the building was that of using the meeting and committee rooms on the second and third floors. Although the Engineer Officers' School was added to the Aeronautical School on October 19, 1917, but few officers were sent to the campus, and the combined average daily number did not run above 265.

At the beginning of January, 1918, the Union officials were instructed to prepare for a total of 900 men, as the Government had decided to establish two additional military schools, one for aero-squadron adjutants and the other for balloon adjutants. In two weeks of the coldest weather known for years a frame annex, 60x30 feet in dimensions, was added to the kitchen, and equipment was installed. Before this addition was completed, the former of the new schools was opened, January 12, and the average daily number of cadets rose to about 350. By the end of February it ran over 800, remaining stationary during the month of March, in which the School for Balloon Adjutants was started. During the next five months the number of cadets gradually declined to less than 350, when the last of the military schools was discontinued. A total of 3,232 men were stationed at the University during the duration of these schools and were fed at the Ohio Union.

In addition to furnishing a mess hall, the Union was practically the only place for recreation and social enjoyment open to the cadets. From Sunday evening until Saturday evening they were not allowed to have "liberty," that is, to leave the campus. From Monday to Friday nights, inclusive, their study hours began at 7:30 o'clock P. M., and all were required to be in barracks at that time. Most of the men spent the interval between the evening meal and the study period in the Union, and the building was crowded to capacity. They occupied it to the exclusion of all others and made free use of the billiard, reading, and writing rooms, while there was scarcely space for standing in the lounge.

Even on Saturday nights the cadets were not permitted to leave the campus until after they had been in training three weeks. Accordingly, on that evening the third floor was given over to some form of entertainment for those who could not or did not care to visit the city. Dramatic and musical organizations of Columbus kindly offered their services to the manager of the Union, and these, with talent drawn from among the cadets, furnished the entertainment. These affairs were discontinued after warm weather came.

When the University opened in September, 1918, 1,800 young men promptly signified their intention of being inducted into the Students' Army Training Corps, the fifth and last of the military schools which the Government maintained at the University during the time of belligerency. The Union was asked to feed these men. As fast as they were sworn into the service they began coming to the Union for their meals, and the building remained closed to all but cadets. Within a short time 1,350 men had completed enlistment. These were fed in three shifts of 450 each, the dining-room having been equipped with regulation barracks tables so that the maximum seating capacity could be obtained. There were still over 650 men to be enlisted, but no more could be taken care of at the Union, and three shifts were already overtaxing the employees and equipment, besides being very inconvenient to the military staff. Therefore, the University authorities decided to allow the Union to utilize as a mess hall the large building that had been recently erected as an Aeronautical Laboratory. This was arranged to seat 900 at one time. It was well past the middle of November before equipment could be obtained and the mess hall opened. The Union then reverted to the use of the non-military students. Meantime, the Armistice had been signed, a number of cadets had dropped out, some others had been transferred to training camps, and the number fed at the new mess hall averaged about 1,650. Preparations were soon made to discontinue the Students' Army Training Corps, the last cadet was discharged, and the mess hall was closed, December 20, 1918.

One feature of the work that ought not to be overlooked was the part the Ohio Union took in helping to maintain the Military Hospital, which was erected near Woodruff Avenue not far from the Barracks. This hospital had 18 beds. Among so many men as there were in the Students' Army Training Corps it was inevitable that there should constantly be some in need of medical attention. The hospital was opened soon after the S. A. T. C. was established, but kitchen equipment was not installed until several weeks later. During this interval all food for the patients was cooked at the Ohio Union and sent over to the hospital. When the influenza epidemic assumed large proportions, late in October, 1918, and it became necessary to appropriate for hospital use two rooms in the Barracks building for the accommodation of the sick, then numbering more than 100, it was no longer possible to cook in the Ohio Union kitchen, with its limited space and equipment, regular meals and the special diet required by the patients confined in the hospital. Although the hospital kitchen was put in operation under the management of the Department of Home Economics, all supplies were still drawn from the storeroom of the Union. While the epidemic was at its height it was impossible to obtain enough helpers to operate the hospital properly, and Manager Drake and several employees of the Union gave their services to the extent of six hours daily for about a fortnight as hospital assistants. All this work was done by a force of employees that was made up almost entirely of women. Every male employee, except four or five who were not within the age limits for the service or were physically unfit, had gone into the Army. One officer from the inspector general's office remarked that he had learned at the Ohio Union that in such times more men could be released for the actual fighting forces by substituting women to do the cooking in the home camps. The work of the Ohio Union during the war was not spectacular, but it was no sinecure; and all who remained on duty throughout this period felt that they had had a small part in the great task.

CHAPTER VII

CAMPUS PUBLICATIONS DURING THE WAR
By Professor Carl Wittke

Campus journalism is the mirror in which are reflected most of the important events and interests of University life, and student and alumni publications have always constituted one of the most valuable source materials for the study of University activities. The record of the University's part in the World War is written large on practically every page of the campus publications issued during the critical years, 1917 to 1919, and other chapters of this University war history which chronicle the achievements of University men and women in the war, could not have been written without constant reference to the files of University publications. It is the purpose of this chapter to discuss the effect of the war on campus journalism itself—the problems and difficulties of campus publications in wartime; the effect of the war upon the character, appearance, and subject matter of these journals, and their share and influence in the mobilization of student opinion for the material and moral support of the Government's war policies.

There was not a campus journal which did not feel the effects of the war and which did not, at some time during the war years, find it extremely difficult to maintain publication. When one learns that the school year 1918-1919 opened with but two members of the Student Council in college,[1] and that of the 75 men who had served as members of University Y. M. C. A. Cabinets 60 were in the service[2], it is not difficult to appreciate the inroads the war made upon the staff and organi-

---
[1] *The Ohio State Lantern*, Sept. 25, 1918.
[2] *The Makio*, 1919, p. 217.

zation of campus publications. As a result, the way was opened for woman's entry upon her rightful place in college journalism. Within a month after the declaration of war the University daily, *The Ohio State Lantern*, reported the loss of over half of its men reporters and two issue editors. It became necessary to abolish the *Lantern's* weekly woman's page in order to release the women responsible for that feature for regular reportorial work, and the woman's editor was made issue editor.[3] More and more frequently "Today's News Editor" was a woman, and in the summers of 1917 and 1918 the editors-in-chief were women students. The September, 1917, draft claimed the business manager of the *Lantern* and the business manager-elect of *The Makio*.[4] The photograph of the *Lantern* staff reproduced in the 1919 *Makio* shows to what an extent women students had come into control of the University daily. On the staff were 20 women and but three men, and for probably the first time in the history of the *Lantern* its business manager was a woman, Miss Jean K. Fitzgerald.[5] In spite of the extraordinary difficulties which were encountered on every hand, and the constant necessity of rearranging the editorial and business staffs, it is to the credit of those in charge during the war years that there were only two interruptions in publication. On January 14, 1918, the *Lantern* failed to appear because the shortage of coal made it impossible to heat the Shops Building where the *Lantern* was printed, and from October 11 to November 12, 1918, the *Lantern* was forced to suspend publication due to the closing of the University during the influenza epidemic.

The Sun Dial in 1918 had its first woman editor,[6] and the first issue of that year was sold on the campus by a staff of 20 women students. The majority of the editorial and business

---

[3] *The Ohio State Lantern*, May 10, 1917.
[4] *Ibid.*, Sept. 28, 1917.
[5] The fact that all but one of the news-desk positions, formerly held by men, had been assigned to women prompted the editorial admission that to women must be conceded "the right to equal consideration with the men in the awarding of important positions on University publications in the future." *The Ohio State Lantern*, Nov. 15, 1918.
[6] See *The Ohio State Lantern*, Nov. 22, 1918.

staffs for 1918 were women.[7] The 1919 *Makio*, by tradition the junior class annual publication, was prepared by a staff selected from all classes.[8] The business manager of the 1918 staff left for military service in April; the editor-in-chief for 1919 was also called into service, and Miss Helen D. Dustman was appointed to succeed him, and thus received the distinction of being the first and only woman editor *The Makio* has ever had.[9] The staff for the 1919 yearbook was composed of 13 men and 18 women.[10] Two former editors-in-chief, Lawrence Yerges of the 1914 *Makio* and Ralph Laughlin of the 1916 *Makio* were killed in the service.

The Agricultural Student, a long-established, monthly, student publication of the College of Agriculture, experienced even greater difficulties. Its editorial staff suffered from numerous changes, due to the war. In the fall of 1918 the editor enlisted in the Students' Army Training Corps, the business manager was summoned to Camp Hancock, Ga., and the circulation manager also found it impossible to return to the University. The staff became so disarranged that it became necessary for the Faculty of the College of Agriculture to take over the publication of the magazine in order to avoid complete suspension. Consequently, the issues of *The Agricultural Student* from November, 1918, to March, 1919, were the work of a Faculty committee, headed by Professor Alfred C. Hottes. *The Veterinary Alumni Quarterly*, in an editorial of March, 1918, complained of similar difficulties as a result of the war. The treasury was becoming exhausted, the committees in charge of the publication were disintegrating, and articles for publication were becoming scarce, due primarily to the diversion of the interests of veterinarians to actual war problems. *The Ohio State Engineer* began its existence as a campus publication in January, 1918. Its editorial staff soon felt the effects of the war. The first volume of this quarterly contained only two numbers, and the second only one. *The*

---

[7] See photographs in the 1919 *Makio*, pp. 204, 205.
[8] *The Ohio State Lantern*, Nov. 18, 1918.
[9] *Ibid.*, Nov. 15, 1918.
[10] *The Makio*, 1919, p. 201.

Ohio State University Monthly, the organ of the Ohio State University Association, in October, 1918, found it necessary to make certain changes in publication which materially altered the size and appearance of the magazine. Due in part to the decrease in receipts on account of the absence of alumni in war service, and in part to the increased cost of paper and cuts, and the requests of the Government to economize, the *Monthly* was issued in smaller type and on cheaper paper, and was substantially reduced in size. The editor, at the close of the war, left for France to engage in Y. M. C. A. canteen work.[11]

The Ohio State Lantern during the war assumed an appearance and character which sharply distinguished it from the *Lantern* files of normal times. The old familiar news items and editorials about new buildings, Faculty changes, student activities and social life, the honor system, overconfidence in athletics, plans for a new Stadium, Farmers' Week, the nurture of college traditions, etc., gradually disappeared from the front page during the war years, and were supplanted by feature articles, news items, and war headlines which rapidly converted the appearance of the first page of the college daily to something closely resembling the front page of a city paper. Most of the war activities of the campus, from the mission of President Thompson to serve as chairman of the Commission of Agriculture for the reclamation work in devastated France, to the daily routine of S. A. T. C. barrack life, or the sending of candy by the University girls to Camp Sherman, were reported at length in the columns of the daily *Lantern*. The reports of what remained of the social activities of the University in wartime were relegated to the inside pages. A mere glance at the headlines of any issue during the war strikingly proves to what a great extent the life of the University campus from 1917 to 1919 was really a vital and inseparable part of the life of the nation. The following headlines, selected at random from front pages of *Lantern* issues, are typical of the

---

[11] *The Ohio State University Monthly,* Jan., 1919.

war period. The issue of April 10, 1917, carried on its first page these headlines:

    University Will Train 2000 City Men on Campus.
    Western Schools Take Active Part in War Movement.
    Professor H. R. Spencer Gives Motives of United States in World War.
    Ohio State Will Not Discontinue Spring Athletics.

In the issue of July 4, 1917, we find:

    Preparing Flying Field for Student Aviators.
    Study Broken Jaws in Dental War Clinic.
    Speaks on Necessity for Bullets of Bread—Dean Vivian.

The first page of the issue of July 11, 1917, contained little else but war news, with these headlines:

    History Teachers Unite to Spread Knowledge of War.
    Strength and Health Needed in War Work.
    Appeal to Engineers.
    To Discuss Income Draft.
    Members of Faculty Doing Share in Work.
    First-aid Class Learns Kinds of War Injuries.
    Extra Buildings Authorized for Aviation School.
    Klingberg Lecture. (On the Mistakes and Menace of German Foreign Policy.)

The *Lantern*, during the war period, also frequently reported mass meetings and the war work of organizations off the campus, in the city.[12] Several new features and departments were added as a result of the war. As early as February, 1917, the *Lantern* began publishing letters from Huntley Dupre and Don Demorest, two University "Y" men who wrote interestingly and informingly of their observations and experiences in Y. M. C. A. work in France.[13] On October 2, 1917, a new department, known as "Ohio State's War Diary," was begun with a letter from Margaret A. Knight, M.A. '15, then in war service in France with the Northwestern University Base Hospital Unit.[14] Throughout the war this department reprinted letters home from University men and women in the service, some of which constitute a valuable and interesting

---

[12] See *The Ohio State Lantern*, April 2, April 3, 1917; Nov. 12, 1918.
[13] *The Ohio State Lantern*, Feb. 13 and 20; March 7, 12, 26, 1917.
[14] *Ibid.*, Oct. 2, 1917.

part of the University's war records. October 22, 1917, an editorial announced the weekly appearance of a short story in French, no doubt prompted by the great increase in enrollment in the Department of Romance Languages, due to the war, and a week later the first *"Article Francais,"* [15] a short story entitled *"Autre pays, autre moeurs,"* made its appearance. A column of Current Events was added for the enlightenment of the student body in wartime; bits of war poetry occasionally appeared on the editorial page, as did also reprints from the editorial columns of other college newspapers dealing with various phases of university war activities. In November, 1918, another new column was added, containing news notes from the various companies of the S. A. T. C. quartered on the campus. Each company had its own news reporter, and an effort was made by this means to have the *Lantern* supply the want of a camp paper and to help develop an *esprit de corps* in the student army.[16] The "Social Life" section of the *Lantern* was greatly affected by the war, and soon was full of accounts of military weddings in which Ohio State men and women were the principals. Only "The Idler's Chronicle and Comment" very rarely betrayed the influence of war conditions, and with its gentle musings and leisurely style remained a pleasing contrast to the other departments of the paper, all of which were engulfed in the hustle and whirl of campus war activities. As the war progressed, the *Lantern* printed long reports of the winning of decorations and citations by University men; war photographs frequently appeared on the front page, and with the coming in of the casualty lists the records of those fallen in battle were printed, together with an occasional editorial tribute to the more prominent of the University men who died in the service. For a number of months after the close of the war, stories of the experiences of soldiers returning to the campus after demobilization, continued to be featured. The effect of the war upon the American language can also be discovered in the files of the *Lantern*. The reporters were quick to add to their journal-

---

[15] *The Ohio State Lantern*, Oct. 22, 29, 1917.
[16] *Ibid.*, Nov. 13, 1918.

istic vocabularies such phrases as "carry on," "over the top," "do your bit," "drive," "camouflage," and other expressions coined during the war.

The general appearance of *The Sun Dial* was also quick to respond and yield to war influences. Many of the jokes and cartoons were concerned with war matters; the term "camouflage" was pressed into service and perhaps overworked; several numbers contained gruesome war stories, strikingly contrasting with the rest of the magazine, designed in a lighter, humorous vein. The October, 1917, number, dedicated to Ohio State men in the service, contained serious editorials, appealing to students not only to support the war in a general way, but to engage actively in some special kind of war work. The November, 1917, issue was enlivened by two drawings by the art editor of the Cornell *Widow*, the artist at that time being quartered on the campus as a member of the Aviation School. In February, 1918, the *Sun Dial* issued a special "Aviation Number." In contrast with earlier practice, it contained serious editorial paragraphs dealing with the war, by such eminent Americans as Roland G. Usher and Meredith Nicholson, and a poem, "Democracy at War," by Hamlin Garland. The issue of November, 1918, was the "S. A. T. C. Number," and the last issue of the year the "Homecoming Number." [17]

The same evidences of the influence of the war are discernible in *The Makio*. The 1917 *Makio* was dedicated to Huntley Dupre, former University Y. M. C. A. secretary, engaged in war work abroad. But the number had been compiled before the United States actually entered the war as an active participant, and therefore it showed much less of the war influences than succeeding numbers. That the University community had not yet completely surrendered its earlier prejudices against drill to the new spirit which tended to glorify all things military, is evidenced by the "Satire Section" of the 1917 *Makio*. Enclosed in heavy black lines of mourning, the section is dedicated to the Military Department, "for whom everyone has a sore spot on his shoulder, chilblains on his feet,

---

[17] *Sun Dial*, Dec., 1918.

90   HISTORY OF THE OHIO STATE UNIVERSITY

and a brick in his hand." The 1918 *Makio*, especially its alumni section, was full of war items. There were many individual and group photographs of University men in the service; pictures of the Officers' Training Camp at Fort Benjamin Harrison were included in the "Military Section," as were also photographs taken at the Texas flying fields and at other camps. Many names in the lists of fraternity members were starred, to indicate enlistment, and near the end of the book appeared the first tribute to "Ohio's Honored Dead." [18] But it was the 1919 *Makio* which was really the War Number. It was dedicated to the Ohio State boys in the war, and devoted its space largely to the military features of the war, with the purpose of telling "the story of the war as seen on the campus." It contained the names of 4,662 University men in the service, of whom 60 had lost their lives in the war.[19] There was also included a signed statement from each of the deans and the University librarian, showing the war work done by each college, and the effects of the war upon the colleges as such.[20] There was a section devoted to "Co-ed War Activities" and preceding the membership lists of each sorority was a paragraph or two dealing with the war activities of the organization. The foreword to the section devoted to fraternity life recorded the hardships that had resulted from the war for the Greek-letter organizations. The Athletic Section was noticeably smaller than in other years, and perhaps as further evidence of the war's effect upon campus interests and standards, the famous "Rosebud" Section was supplanted by the photographs of the University's 18 "most representative women students."

The alumni news in *The Agricultural Student* as early as March, 1918, contained numerous reports of enlistments and other activities connected with the development of the war program. The September, 1918, issue was dedicated "To Our Farmers' Sons in the War, who willingly and gladly laid aside their labors in the field to perform a noble and glorious

[18] 1918 *Makio*, pp. 458-459.
[19] 1919 *Makio*, p. 60.
[20] *Ibid.*, pp. 52-53.

duty for their country." Many of the editorials urged greater production of food and the conservation of our resources. A notable and valuable section was the one headed "Letters from Over There." Professor Wendell Paddock was especially active during the war in communicating with former students in the camps and at the front, and most of the letters received and printed were addressed to him or to Professor Scherer. They sometimes constitute an interesting running comment on the experiences and progress of the war.[21]

The Veterinary Alumni Quarterly very early in the war called upon veterinarians to enlist in the Veterinary Officers' Reserve Corps, provided by the National Defense Act of June 3, 1917. Each member of the profession was urged to enter the service "with the spirit of undying loyalty and red-blooded patriotism," in spite of the fact that the profession had "not yet received from our Government the recognition it deserves." ".... To quibble about our 'rights'," the article continued, "indulge in seditious criticism perhaps, and refuse to 'get into the game' are not only poor ways to exhibit patriotism, but miserable methods of promoting the best interests of our profession at this critical time in our country's history....."[22] When the June, 1917, issue published a translation of an article by Professor R. Eberlein of Berlin, dealing with his experiences with horses on the European battlefields, the editor found it necessary to prefix this explanation: "While Professor Eberlein may be our enemy in a military sense, nevertheless we should remember that he is one of the most eminent veterinarians in the world..... For the acts of brutality practiced by the German Army, to which Professor Eberlein was temporarily attached, he cannot be individually responsible. Science is international, world wide....."[23] Such an explanation seemed necessary in 1917 to ward off hostile criticism of a magazine which ventured to reprint articles by enemy subjects, even though those articles were of a purely scien-

---
[21] See *The Agricultural Student*, Nov., 1918, pp. 178, 179; Dec., 1918, pp. 244, 245; Jan. 1919, p. 300; Feb., 1919, pp. 367, 368.
[22] June, 1917.
[23] *The Veterinary Alumni Quarterly*, June, 1917.

tific nature. The *Quarterly* printed many valuable articles on the organization and work of the Veterinary Corps during the war. Its alumni notes contained reports of the activities of the graduates of the College of Veterinary Medicine during the war, and in September, 1918, a new feature, "Letters from Alumni" (in the service), was added. An editorial in the January, 1918, issue vigorously opposed the movement then under way to lower the standards for admission to veterinary colleges due to the decrease in enrollment as a result of the war.

The Ohio State Engineer, in each of the issues which appeared so irregularly during the war, contained some material which was the direct result of the new interests aroused by the war. The first issue was dedicated to Charles Franklin Kettering; the second contained a long article on the construction of an army cantonment, and suggested that all the facilities of the University should be placed at the disposal of the engineering and military departments, even though this might mean the suspension of many of the normal activities of the University. Needless to add, the suggestion elicited vigorous opposition from some members of the Faculty.[24] *The Sansculotte,* a magazine which expired after the appearance of the third number, in April, 1917, contained no reference to the war except in a review of Bertrand Russell's "Why Men Fight." The reviewer's attitude toward the war can be discovered in a sentence which contained a caustic comment to the effect that a nation sometimes goes to war "for a trade route blubbering over human rights." [25] The School of Military Aeronautics, located on the University campus, was re-

---

[24] *The Ohio State Engineer*, April, 1918, p. 55.

[25] April, 1917, p. 8. The review continues with a criticism of the American professor class, who "have been the good and faithful servants of a State which conserves the interest of a capitalistic class; they have given themselves to the manufacture of an uninquiring, listless, Philistine student body, 'moulded' to react to that series of stimuli termed 'good citizenship.'" . . . The magazine was generally regarded as the work of ultra radicals. See *The Ohio State Lantern,* Oct. 3, 1917. But for another view, see Ludwig Lewisohn's comment—"The magazine was crude enough. But it was alive. There was verse in it, unrythmed and gawky, but hopeful, and prose with some close thinking in it and a social outlook and a breath of the future." *Up Stream,* p. 164.

sponsible for the publication of *The Pilot* and the Adjutant's School for the *Esprit de Corps*. Both magazines appeared but once. *The Pilot* (August, 1918,) a magazine of 32 pages, was really designed to serve as a souvenir of the School of Military Aeronautics. On its staff were former newspaper men from the *Chicago Daily News*, the *Tribune*, and *Herald-Examiner*, as well as young business men connected before the war with some of the country's largest industrial and business concerns. With the exception of the humorous section and a short story, the magazine was given over almost entirely to pictures of the campus, the Aviation School, and a roster and directory of its officers and men. The *Esprit de Corps* appeared March 26, 1918, as the publication of Squadron 8, Adjutants. It was smaller than *The Pilot*, and of similar contents. On its editorial staff were the former city editor of the Hagerstown (Md.) *Morning Herald*, the proprietor of the California *Blythe Herald*, and college journalists from the University of Wisconsin *Sphinx*, the University of Pittsburgh *Owl* and *Pitt Weekly*, the Harvard *Lampoon*, and the University of Pennsylvania *Punch Bowl*.

The Ohio State University Monthly, as the official publication of the alumni, very naturally devoted most of its space in the period from 1917 to 1919 to a chronicle of the services and sacrifices of Ohio State graduates and ex-students in the war. Even before the United States formally entered the war there were occasional articles dealing with war-relief work done by Ohio State men in Europe.[26] The April, 1917, number, published just after the official declaration of war, printed an appeal from the president of the University Association calling upon all graduates and ex-students to answer the summons of their country. In the next issue the section devoted to "War News of the Campus" made its first appearance.[27] Although the June issue was devoted primarily to commencement news, it contained a great mass of war items dealing with the services of University men on and off the campus. By the

---
[26] See *The Ohio State University Monthly*, Jan., 1917, pp. 20, 21.
[27] *The Ohio State University Monthly*, May, 1917, p. 5.

fall of 1917 war news made up the greater part of the magazine. There was a section devoted to "Letters from the Front," and beginning with December, 1917, a constantly growing list of University men serving in the ranks or commissioned as officers. The first 16 pages of the first issue in 1918 were devoted exclusively to war news. The *Monthly* also printed several articles designed to inform its readers of some of the problems and results of the war. As examples may be mentioned articles by Professor Denney on "War and Poetry," [28] Mr. Knipfing's "The Case Against the Peace Discussers," [29] Mr. Reeder's "Library Service at Camp Sherman," [30] an article on the coal problem,[31] and one by Professor Siebert on "Independence for Armenia."[32] Every issue was profusely illustrated with war photographs. The May, 1918, number was the "Service Number." It appeared with a front cover-page of stars in a blue field, and a back cover representing a service flag, and was dedicated "To Our Wartime President." The first 38 pages were devoted to photographs of Ohio State's army and navy officers, and the following 100 pages to a roster of University men in the service. Supplemental lists and the "Roll of Honor" were printed in many of the later issues. "Letters from the War" continued to be published for months after the close of the war. Much of the alumni news printed in the *Monthly* of 1919 reflected the spirit of patriotism and the new interests aroused by the war.

An article published in the *Monthly* before the United States was actually at war, but after diplomatic relations with Germany had been severed, threatened for a time to give rise to an unfortunate controversy, which was, however, averted by the editor's prompt decision to close the columns of the *Monthly* to all further discussion of the incident. The article involved was a summary by Charles F. O'Brien, '03, of his observations in Germany in the fall of 1916. It appeared under

---

[28] April, 1918.
[29] Jan., 1919.
[30] Feb., 1918.
[31] April, 1918.
[32] Feb., 1918.

the title, "Behind the Scenes in Warring Germany."[33] The writer contended that Germany was neither starving nor hungry, commented on the marvelous achievements of the German Government and German scientific men during the war period, and represented the war as a clash between a highly socialized state and states which represented the principles of *laissez-faire* and individualism. The writer refused to predict which would win, but suggested, perhaps, "a happy mean." The article represented Germany as the victor in the field at that time and commented on the disastrous results of the submarine campaign in England. "England cannot afford to lose much more. She is plainly worried. .... Time will tell and shortly. ...." The article was written in a "breezy," not to say flippant, style, but contained hardly anything which would not now be admitted to have been a fair estimate of the state of affairs which existed late in 1916 and early in 1917. The article brought a vigorous resolution from the New York Ohio State University Association, denouncing it for its "pro-German undertone and its inaccuracies," and by implication mildly criticizing the policy of the editor in publishing an article whch might, at that critical time, seem to reflect the views of the association. The resolution of protest was published in the *Monthly*, together with a letter from Edward Orton, Jr., in which he admitted the possible value of the article, but contended that no American had the right to think or express such "frank sympathy with the German cause" two weeks after the severance of diplomatic relations between the United States and Germany.[34]

In addition to mirroring and reporting the war activities of the University and its student organizations, campus papers were also influential factors in molding student opinion in support of the war measures of the Government and in maintaining the morale of the student body during the disturbances and interruptions of war times. In the performance of these im-

---
[33] *The Ohio State University Monthly*, March, 1917, pp. 17-19.
[34] *Ibid.*, June, 1917, p. 53.

portant tasks, the *Lantern,* as a daily paper which reached most of the student body, was naturally most active.

The editorial columns of the *Lantern* during the war period are full of good advice, intended to hold the student body strictly to its war tasks. Cutting classes was denounced as unpatriotic,[35] and students were urged to "carry on" and finish their college work in spite of all the discouraging interruptions that resulted from the war. The winter of 1918 was especially bad in this respect. Due to the war, the weather, the coal shortage, the influenza epidemic, and other causes, the work of the students was constantly interrupted by rumors of the closing of school, and the worst of these disturbances occurred just before the final examinations at the end of the first semester. Probably not often before in the history of the *Lantern* had an editorial reminded the student body that in spite of all apparent excuses, "personal and school honor must be reflected in the grades of the final examinations. The order is 'carry on'."[36] There were frequent appeals to a patriotism that would "go deeper than sentimental tears or talk of the 'red, white, and blue'."[37] The women were urged to attend all the Chapel addresses on the preparation, production, and conservation of food;[38] mass meetings were advocated to get every University woman into war work;[39] and when vacation time approached, several editorials demanded the use of the vacation period for profitable war service, and denied the right of anyone to consider it a time for rest and leisure.[40] There were articles on the virtue of optimism and the dangers of exaggerated optimism, and the necessity of "banishing the grumbler" from the campus. The editor rejoiced because "horse play" had been eliminated from student life,[41] and welcomed the S. A. T. C. as an organization which would spread

---

[35] *The Ohio State Lantern,* May 7, 1917.
[36] *Ibid.,* Jan. 9, 1918.
[37] *Ibid.,* Aug. 15, 1917.
[38] *Ibid.,* Feb. 14, 1918.
[39] *Ibid.,* Oct. 8, 1918.
[40] *Ibid.,* May 20, June 25, 1918.
[41] *Ibid.,* Nov. 22, 1917.

"the *esprit de corps* of the army" on the campus.[42] All forms of war work and patriotic interests received constant editorial endorsement and praise. At the same time an effort was made to combat the many unfounded and malicious rumors that were afloat in wartime and often threatened to undermine the influence and support of such organizations as the Red Cross and the Y. M. C. A.[43] One editorial deplored the new fad of excessive smoking;[44] another demanded respect and recognition for the college professor, who had at last, by his war work, demonstrated the fallacy of current opinion that all professors were mere theorists.[45] The student body was urged to attend debates and lectures on important war questions, and was especially advised to enroll for the "War Issues" course, devised by the Faculty to set forth the historical background and the aims of the war. When statistics were collected by the Department of American History which showed that of all the students enrolled in the fundamental course in the History of the United States, only about one in 15 was actually reading President Wilson's war messages, a *Lantern* editorial commented on the deplorable lack of interest and urged the development of a more intelligent patriotism.[46] As a new feature, there appeared occasional articles especially addressed to students, by such men as P. P. Claxton, head of the United States Department of Education, and Secretary of War Newton D. Baker, provided by the Patriotic News Service of the National Committee of Patriotic Societies.[47] Another new feature was a column headed "Some War Doings of the Past Week at Other Colleges."[48]

In spite of the splendid response of University men and women to the call to war service, some of the campus publications frequently found it necessary to criticize the war work being done on the campus, and to spur the student body to

[42] *The Ohio State Lantern*, Oct. 2, 1918.
[43] *Ibid.*, Feb. 11, 1918.
[44] *Ibid.*, March 25, 1918.
[45] *Ibid.*, March 15, 1918.
[46] *Ibid.*, Dec. 7, 10, 1917.
[47] *Ibid.*, Oct. 24, Nov. 8, 1917.
[48] *Ibid.*, April 24, 1917.

greater efforts. *The Sun Dial* was the first to sound this critical note. In an editorial which appeared during the first month of America's participation in the war, the spirit of Eastern institutions was contrasted with that of Ohio State. "The student body lacks something. And sadly," the editorial began. "Whether it's 'school spirit' or whether it's patriotism or whether it's the desire to think, we don't know. . . . . A large percentage of them (students) have settled into the attitude of smug indifference over the war question. . . . . It's the superior air of 'let the Yokel do the fighting' that we are aiming at; it's the lethargic air which pervades the campus that we're talking about. . . . ."[49] Several weeks later the *Lantern* was forced to report that the new volunteer system, designed to interest the student body in Saturday drill, was a failure. But one upperclassman had reported.[50] In an editorial on "Patriotic Knitting," written in the fall of 1917, the *Lantern* criticized the work of the women students: ". . . . The *Lantern* hopes that in the near future gray and olive-drab yarns will take the place of the pink, green, and blue now so much in evidence among campus knitters."[51] Some fraternities were criticized for their neglect with reference to the regulations of the Food Administration and their failure to observe a meatless and wheatless day each week.[52] A public criticism of University women, in an address by Mrs. George Wells Knight, in the Home Economics Auditorium, in which the speaker asserted that the University women "stand lowest in patriotic work," resulted in a vigorous recruiting campaign the week following to enroll each girl for at least one hour of Red Cross work per week.[53] The *Lantern* a week later reported that less than half of the women of the University had enrolled to date for Red Cross work.[54] In April, 1918, the University arranged a great "Win-the-War Day" celebration in the Uni-

---

[49] *Sun Dial*, April, 1917.
[50] *The Ohio State Lantern*, May 1, 1917.
[51] *Ibid.*, Sept. 28, 1917. See another editorial on "Pig Knitters," in the issue of Oct. 12, 1917.
[52] Editorial—"Not a Subject for Jesting,"—Jan. 23, 1918.
[53] *The Ohio State Lantern*, March 28, April 4, 1918.
[54] *Ibid.*, April 12, 1918.

versity Chapel, and succeeded in filling just half of the Chapel. Faculty and student body were promptly and severely censured in the editorial columns of the *Lantern*,[55] and a summary of Ohio State's war activities for the first year brought the admission that ". . . . the things of which we are most proud have been done by those who have 'gone out' from the University."[56] There were some difficulties in collecting the funds pledged for war purposes on the campus, and the Y. M. C. A. was forced to make a special "drive" to collect overdue subscriptions which amounted to approximately one-fourth of the total pledged.[57] The conclusion of the Armistice, on the campus as elsewhere, brought a decline in interest in war work, and in February, 1919, the *Lantern* once more felt it necessary to criticize the women students for their failure to report in the University sewing-rooms to finish their assigned tasks.[58] In all of these criticisms there may have been elements of exaggeration. In any case, there were probably no more "slackers" in war work among the University community than could be found in any other community of similar size and composition. That the constant vigilance and criticism of the University daily had much influence in holding war activities to a standard of greater efficiency seems certain.

The urging of students to greater activity in support of the war did not blind the University publications to the fact that in accordance with the theory underlying the selective-service act, it would be best for many of the student body to remain at their books. The *Lantern* ventured the suggestion that it was the moral duty of all youths under 21 to make the most of their opportunities, for they had been "drafted for education."[59] An editorial pointed out the "inefficiency of sending into the trenches men of high scientific attainments . . . . which would be invaluable to the country if applied in other ways. . . . ."[60] In the second year of the war the stu-

---

[55] *The Ohio State Lantern*, April 8, 1918.
[56] *Ibid.*, April 9, 1918.
[57] *Ibid.*, April 11, 1918.
[58] *Ibid.*, Feb. 13, 1919.
[59] *Ibid.*, Oct. 10, 1917.
[60] *Ibid.*, Feb. 13, 1917.

dents were advised to become teachers, as "a war necessity" and a patriotic duty, in order to help meet the crisis due to the sudden shortage of teachers.[61] Medical and engineering students were especially urged to finish their courses.[62] *The Ohio State Engineer* pointed out the great need for trained engineers "to lead the world in reconstruction," and concluded that "it was probably the wisest and most patriotic thing to remain in college and obtain as much knowledge and technical training as possible. . . . ."[63] *The Agricultural Student* also was concerned with the dangers that might come from the promiscuous enlistment of agricultural students, and protested, furthermore, against the plan to mobilize the idle class of the cities for farm labor. "The farmers need help, but they do not want parasites." [64]

In the numerous "drives" conducted during the war for the raising of funds for war purposes, the support given by the University publications, and especially by the *Lantern*, left nothing to be desired. "Buy Big Bonds and Beat the Beast of Berlin" was the glaring streamer which appeared on the first page of the *Lantern* on "Win-the-War Day," [65] and every Liberty Loan campaign received unstinted editorial support, news space, and advertising space in the University daily. Practically the entire issue of January 31, 1918, was devoted to publicity for the Columbus War Chest. The Red Cross, Y. M. C. A., thrift-stamp sales, and the special campaign to raise Ohio State's quota for the maintenance of the American University Union in Paris were all prominently featured and supported. *The Sun Dial* [66] and other campus publications likewise devoted considerable space to these campaigns.[67] The

---

[61] *The Ohio State Lantern*, May 21, 1918.
[62] *Ibid.*, May 4, 1917; *The Ohio State Engineer*, Jan., 1918.
[63] January, 1918, p. 23.
[64] June, 1917.
[65] April 6, 1918.
[66] Oct., 1917.
[67] An interesting collection of the posters, programs, and other notices used to carry on these campaigns on the campus is preserved in the Library *Memorabilia Collection*, Vols. 24, 25, 26, and in the collections of the Historical Commission of Ohio, at the Ohio Archaeological and Historical Society Museum.

CAMPUS PUBLICATIONS 101

Lantern and the *Sun Dial* were sent to many army camps in this country and abroad, along with other reading matter collected on the campus in a special campaign to provide "A Book for Every Soldier." [68]

In the campaign for the conservation of the nation's resources and for greater food production, *The Agricultural Student* very naturally played a leading role. *The Agricultural Student* maintained that upon the farmers "will rest the final responsibility in winning the war." [69] Its pages abound in appeals for greater production of food products, recipes for making "war bread" and other wartime substitutes, methods of conserving fuel, appeals to increase poultry and egg production because "the humble hen can play a prominent part in preventing the progress of the Prussian peril . . . .," etc.[70] Special attention was given in the "Home Economics Department" of the magazine to the question of conservation by college girls, not only in the matter of food, but in wearing apparel as well.[71] *The Sun Dial* emphasized the development of "war gardens,"[72] and the Lantern appealed to college students to become farm laborers.[73] During the influenza epidemic, the *Lantern* made a special effort to arouse the student body to an appreciation of the necessity of maintaining a sound mind and body in wartime.[74] As a special form of conservation, peculiarly emphasized in college circles, the elimination of many formal and other social functions is worthy of mention. In May, 1917, when the first detachment of University students left for the Reserve Officers' Training Camps, an editorial in the *Lantern* urged the elimination of most social affairs, formals, flowers, taxis, etc., as forms of unjustifiable waste in time of war,[75] and this opposition to all kinds of "ex-

---

[68] *The Ohio State Lantern*, March 21, 1918.
[69] May, 1917.
[70] *The Agricultural Student*, Jan., 1918.
[71] *Ibid.*, Nov., 1917, Oct., 1918.
[72] Feb., 1918.
[73] *The Ohio State Lantern*, May 15, 1917.
[74] *Ibid.*, March 18, Oct. 1, and 7, 1918.
[75] *Ibid.*, May 11, 1917.

travagant and frivolous living" was continued to the end of the war.

In addition to articles and editorials supporting and reporting University war activities, there was some little discussion of war aims and the problems of reconstruction in campus publications, and an effort was made to develop an intelligent patriotism among the student body by editorials designed to throw light upon the fundamental issues at stake in the war. Frequently articles from other sources appeared on the *Lantern* editorial page. Those selected from other college papers were frequently very serious and courageous discussions of war questions.

During the first year of America's participation in the war, the *Lantern* editorials displayed a sanity of judgment on some war questions which could not be found in a large portion of the public press which had already yielded to a blind, and sometimes cruelly vindictive, war hysteria. Again and again the *Lantern* made its appeal to reason and to the spirit of charity. ". . . . The war is not going to be won by any outburst of hysterics or by venting our wrath upon a few persons who may or may not be guilty. . . ." [76] And again: "Apathy need no longer be feared, with the American people roused to their present pitch, but just as great a danger lies in hysteria." [77] The student body was reminded that college men were educated for leadership, in a time of national crisis, but not for privilege.[78] When Dr. Harry W. Laidler, secretary of the Intercollegiate Socialist Society, who before the outbreak of the war had taken a prominent part in the anti-war demonstrations in Belgium and England, was permitted to speak in Townshend Hall on "The Socialist Challenge to the College-bred," the *Lantern* editor made it the occasion for an editorial, "No Intolerance Here," in which he pointed with pride to the liberal spirit prevailing at Ohio State.[79] There were no indications in the *Lantern* editorial columns at the beginning of

[76] *The Ohio State Lantern*, April 19, 1917.
[77] *Ibid.*, May 4, 1917.
[78] *Ibid.*, April 2, 1917.
[79] March 8, 1917.

the war of that form of war hysteria which found in German art, books, music, and the study of the German language in American schools something which must be exterminated in the interests of a thoroughgoing Americanism. An editorial written two months before the actual declaration of war by the United States commented upon the cosmopolitan character of the University community. "Our experience has shown us that the line of nationality is a vague demarcation, as far as single individuals are concerned. .... What the Civil War meant to communities in the Border States, war with a great foreign power would mean, on a smaller scale, to a university community in either country. .... There are Germans who have built up warm friendships in the University. ...."[80] *Der Deutsche Verein* was able to present Sudermann's "Heimat" in the University Chapel at a time when our relations with Germany were most critical, and when a large part of the public press was already bitterly attacking everything of German origin. The *Lantern* advertised the play and gave a most favorable review of the production.[81] The movement for the abolition of the teaching of German and against the performance of the music of German masters was consistently denounced as an absurd form of war hysteria and perverted patriotism. "It is a ground for self-congratulation," an editorial commented, "that the illogical wave has not struck Ohio State. One evidence that we are still in possession of reason is the coming production of the annual German play, without the slightest unfavorable comment. ...."[82] When the discussion over the inclusion of Bach and Beethoven on concert programs and the playing of the national anthem at symphony concerts became acute in the public press, the *Lantern* deplored such "inane discussion" and hoped that it would not progress to such a stage "as to deprive the people of good music—the thing of beauty so much needed in these chaotic times—a con-

---

[80] *The Ohio State Lantern*, Feb. 7, 1917.
[81] *Ibid.*, March 26, 1917.
[82] *Ibid.*, March 22, 1917.

dition which might easily come about if the public attempts to entirely dictate the program to be played at concerts." [83]

To develop an intelligent patriotism and a thorough and sane understanding of the issues of the war, the *Lantern* frequently featured interviews with Faculty members dealing with the problems and developments of the war.[84] The series of lectures arranged and given by the History Departments and dealing with the background of the war, American ideals, traditions, aims, etc., were reported at great length in the *Lantern* columns, and students were repeatedly advised to enroll for the new "War Issues" course and to study the war by means of the latest books acquired by the University Library.[85] In September, 1917, two new features were added to the *Lantern*. The first was a column of "Current Comment" by Professor Henry R. Spencer, which continued to appear until the time of Professor Spencer's departure for Italy to engage in Y. M. C. A. work. In this column many angles of the war situation were discussed for the information of the student readers. Perhaps the best in this series was the first article, an admirable exposition of the question of the proper bounds between free speech and treasonable utterances.[86] The other new feature was one which has been mentioned before—a column of Current Events, designed to give a brief and convenient summary of important items which might otherwise be overlooked in the excitement of campus war activities. As another method for the enlightenment of the student body, frequent attendance at Convocation and the reading of history was strongly recommended.[87] As the war progressed into the spring and summer of 1918 and long casualty lists began to appear, the *Lantern*

---

[83] An editorial of March 2, 1917, in the *Lantern*, quoted at some length from a leaflet issued by the Collegiate Anti-Militarism League, entitled "Collegians, Protect Your Ideals." An editorial of April 16, 1917, denounced the work of the League—"Persons behind the move are unwilling to bear their share of the work of American citizens, and are clothing their tendency to shirk under a fabric of theories . . . ."
[84] Professors G. W. Knight, H. R. Spencer, and Joseph A. Leighton seem to have been the most popular sources for these interviews.
[85] *The Ohio State Lantern*, Feb. 13; Nov. 27, 1918.
[86] *Ibid.*, Oct. 1, 1917.
[87] *Ibid.*, March 5, 1917; Nov. 25, 1918.

editorials, like those of most of the public press, changed their tone and were more often the result of passion and a bitterness of heart than of sound and calm reasoning. Perhaps the worst example of this style is an editorial which appeared April 10, 1918, under the heading, "Hell and Who Made It." The article reveals a flippancy of expression and an immaturity hardly to be expected of a college man.[88]

The months immediately following the cessation of hostilities brought forth some discussion of the problems of reconstruction and some bits of advice to the demobilized college man, but very naturally the campus press was soon more interested in a return to the "normalcy" of college life than in the technical and difficult problems of the peace conference and the reconstruction of the world. The demobilized members of the S. A. T. C. were advised to remain in school and to keep their army insurance, and owners of Liberty Bonds were urged to hold their investments. *The Agricultural Student* gave some space to the question of settling the returning soldiers upon farm lands,[89] and suggested the use of army motor trucks to transport pupils to and from the centralized schools in rural communities.[90] The *Lantern* gave its editorial support to a series of lectures arranged by the Y. M. C. A. on "World Problems," [91] and heartily endorsed the work of the Historical Commission of Ohio, which was housed on the campus and engaged in the preservation of Ohio's war records.[92] In spite of the fact that an earlier editorial had pronounced military training "the great democratizer" and had concluded, quite seriously, that "there are no snobs in the army," [93] other new reasons for opposing universal military training were soon discovered, and by the close of 1918 the *Lantern* was opposed to the plan.[94]

But the student body was, after all, most interested in the return of the "good old times" of college life. In 1918 the Jun-

---

[88] See also an editorial of March 27, 1918.
[89] Dec. 1918, pp. 211-214.
[90] May, 1919, p. 535.
[91] *The Ohio State Lantern*, Feb. 25, 1919.
[92] *Ibid.*, Feb. 5, 1919.
[93] *Ibid.*, March 6, 1918.
[94] *Ibid.*, Dec. 6, 1918.

ior Prom had been sacrificed to the war,[95] and other social functions had either been abandoned or seriously curtailed. Soon after the Armistice, a *Lantern* editorial urged the restoration of "the traditions" and called for the return of Panhellenic banquets, the Junior Prom, the Co-ed Prom, the May Fete, the Sphinx, and Bucket and Dipper ceremonies, and all the other social functions of campus life.[96] At the close of 1918 the first Women's Council supper for two years was reported.[97] A headline of December 19, 1918, announced the "Gaiety of Other Years Comes With Christmas—Sororities and Fraternities Make Merry With Dances and Parties, as in Pre-war Days." The following February the Men's Glee Club was reorganized,[98] and when it was decided to re-establish the Junior Prom, the *Lantern* urged that it be made a formal event, as before the war.[99] For several months reports of demobilization and an occasional story which was the result of the war appeared in the *Lantern*, and the University *Monthly* continued to publish the news of demobilized Ohio State men in a section headed "Swords Into Plowshares." But these were mere survivals of other days. More and more rapidly the campus publications assumed their pre-war appearance. It was the *Sun Dial* of February, 1919, which officially heralded the return to "normalcy" in its "Old Times Number." It was dedicated to "the good old times and to the good old-timers," and in it the editor summoned all loyal sons of Ohio State to put away the uniform for the "dress suit." And then: "Let's all dance our first dance for the sake of 'Auld Lang Syne'."

---

[95] *The Ohio State Lantern*, Feb. 20 and 21, 1918.
[96] *Ibid.*, Nov. 29, 1918.
[97] *Ibid.*, Nov. 26, Dec. 13, 1918.
[98] *Ibid.*, Feb. 5, 1919.
[99] March 10, 1919.

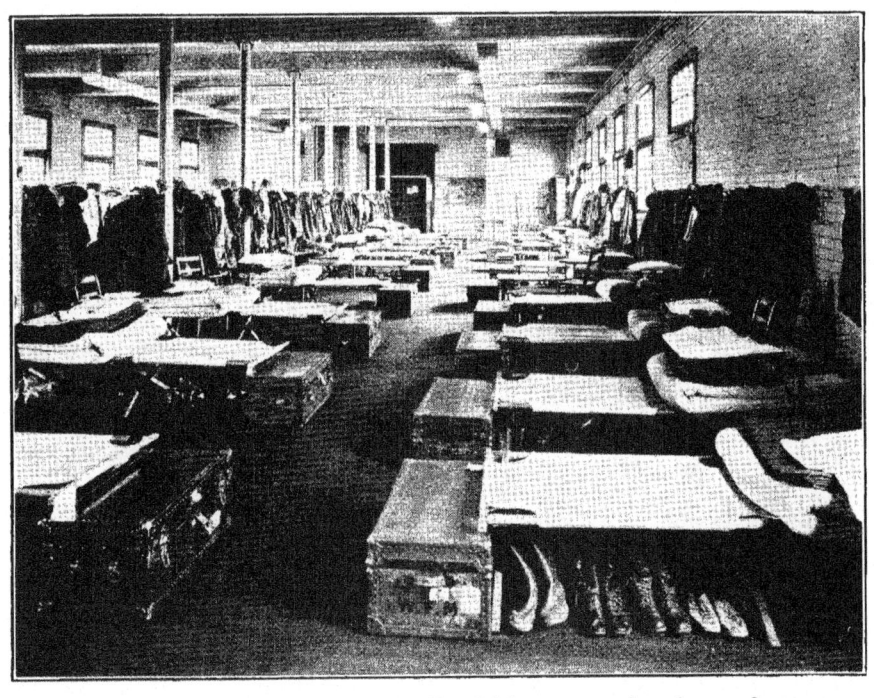

Interior of part of Hayes Hall, which was used as barracks

Cadets engaging in one form of recreation

The Military Hospital where two hundred influenza patients of the S.A.T.C. were treated in the autumn of 1918

A class in surveying, Army School of Military Aeronautics

CHAPTER VIII

ATHLETICS DURING THE WAR

Recognizing the fact that athletic training is valuable in fitting young men for military service, the University did not neglect its sports during the war. As in other similar institutions, the frequent departure of athletes to go into service was keenly felt and necessarily lowered the quality of the teams. But with others stepping in to fill the vacancies, a continued interest was maintained, and the primary purpose of training the men was fulfilled.

The entrance of America into the war, in April, 1917, was quickly followed by the exodus of a large number of University men, who responded to the call to military service or farm work. The effect of this on spring athletics, however, was not so marked as might have been expected. The baseball team played 15 games during the season, winning 14 and the Western Conference title. The track team engaged in four dual meets and was victorious in the Big Six, although by a narrow margin only. Nevertheless, indications of what was to follow were not lacking. The baseball season was little more than half over when Ohio State's star catcher, Howell I. Jones, went to Fort Benjamin Harrison. The track squad lost the services of its captain, Robert B. Nevin, and five other point-winners during the spring. The tennis team was able to play through most of its schedule, although Northwestern, Wisconsin, and Kenyon canceled their meets on account of the departure of players from those institutions.

On June 6, 1917, representatives of the various universities in the Western Conference met at Chicago and decided to continue intercollegiate athletics as usual during the following year. The war drains on the colleges were not felt to any great extent even in the fall of 1917. With one or two exceptions, the members of the 1916 championship team who were eligible for another season returned. The result was another title-winning "aggregation," which was not scored upon during the season. In addition to the regular football schedule, two games were played for the benefit of soldiers in the training camps. One of these was a contest with the Auburn Polytechnical School eleven at Montgomery, Ala., November 24, 1917, before the soldiers of Camp Sheridan. Not yet recovered from the Illinois game of a few days before, and lacking the services of their quarterback, who had left for the navy, State's eleven gave a rather listless exhibition, the game resulting in a scoreless tie. On Thanksgiving Day the Camp Sherman team, comprising five former all-American players and other lesser stars, was defeated on Ohio Field by a score of 28 to 0. Immediately after the close of the season nine members of the team entered some form of military service.

Basketball began auspiciously with two veterans of the 1917 squad on hand. Early in the year, however, the Gymnasium was transformed into a dormitory for the School of Military Aeronautics, leaving the Varsity team without a place to practice until the Indianola floor could be secured a little later. When, soon after, the two principal players were called into service, Ohio State was represented on the floor by five men with no previous Varsity experience. In basketball, as in football, the Camp Sherman team from Chillicothe was defeated, the game running overtime and the score being 36 to 31. No showing was made in the Western Conference, although a momentary flash of form made possible the defeat of the Northwestern five, who had been expected before the encounter to win the Conference title.

The inroads of the war were more obvious when the spring sports opened in 1918. At this time the Varsity "O" Association had but four men left of all those who had gained their letters during the preceding year. This number was greatly increased by the initiation of 40 new men in the spring.

In track athletics the losses of the preceding year had been heavy. Sixteen men had been decorated with letters in 1917, and some freshmen had been considered promising; yet when the candidates were called out, it was found that but one sure high point-winner remained. Only two dual meets were scheduled, one with Indiana and the other with Ohio Wesleyan. In both of these State's athletes captured the majority of points. The Big Six meet, which was advanced a week on account of the early commencement, resulted also in the customary victory.

Hammond and Nevin, who were members of this track team, were later to give up their lives in the service, both succumbing to the ravages of the influenza epidemic of the ensuing fall.

The baseball season of 1918 opened with two of the four eligible letter men present. Both had been rejected for military service. Coach L. W. St. John had been appointed director of recreation in the School of Military Aeronautics and was unable to give much time to the development of a team. Since the other universities and colleges were suffering from similar handicaps, the conditions of rivalry were fair. The Ohio nine won eight of the 10 games, losing the championship honors to Michigan in a close contest. A game arranged with Camp Sherman was never played, probably on account of overseas departures from the camp, which were taking place at that time in large numbers.

No men with previous Varsity experience in tennis returned for the 1918 season. Many candidates of ability made possible a good record against Ohio colleges, but little showing was made against the racket-wielders of the Western Conference.

Although the effect of the war was distinctly noticeable in the record of the year 1917-1918, it was not until the fall of the final year of the great conflict that the University's sport program was completely upset. With Americans actively engaged in the closing battles of the war on the fields of France, with the transformation of the universities all over the country into military training camps, it could not be expected that the events of college life would take their regular course.

Upon the organization of the Students' Army Training Corps early in October, 1918, the direction of athletic activities was taken over by the military authorities. The ruling of the United States War Department was to the effect that all members of the training corps were to be permitted to compete for teams, regardless of university eligibility requirements. This decree enabled freshmen to play. The time allotted for practice was to be determined by those in command at the various institutions. The Ohio State team was allowed only one hour a day, which usually came after dark. Other colleges with which games were played were more fortunate in this respect.

Eleven men of the 1917 football squad, who normally would have been back for another year, were at this time in service. No letter men returned. Only four squad members remained, two of these being transferred to training camps after the first few games. The development of a team was further interfered with by the fact that Coach J. W. Wilce, owing to his duties as a member of the Medical Corps, had little time to devote to his football work. The team was strengthened, however, by the arrival of a member of the 1916 team and another player from Ohio University at Athens. These men had been sent to join the Naval Reserve Unit on the campus. The remaining positions were filled largely by sophomores, who had gained some experience on the freshman squad of the preceding year. Freshmen were also available, but only one played regularly on the team. The influenza epidemic during the latter half of October and after was another factor contributing to the unsettled conditions in 1918. Two regular players were absent from the lineup at the time of the Denison game on account of it. The Northwestern game had to be canceled because of the epidemic and the difficulties of travel. Of the six games played, three were with Ohio colleges and resulted in victories. The only trip of the year was to Urbana, where Illinois defeated the Varsity by a score of 13 to 0. Games with Wisconsin and Michigan were also lost.

The signing of the Armistice on November 11, 1918, gave bright prospects for the future. No captain was elected for the eleven at the close of the season in anticipation of the return during the year of a large number of former players.

Two prominent football men were claimed by death during the war. Fred Norton, a member of the 1916 championship team and an all-around athlete, died of wounds received in action while fighting German airplanes. Harold J. Courtney, captain of the 1917 team, died of pneumonia while at sea.

Intramural athletics scarcely existed during wartime. Shortly after the declaration of hostilities the usual spring carnival was held, but this was the last of such events until after the signing of the Armistice. A little activity among class and fraternity teams was attempted the following year, but was soon given up. The taking over of the Gymnasium by the military authorities early in 1918 left no place for intramural sports, while the chapter houses and classes were losing numbers of their men by withdrawal from the University.

CHAPTER IX

THE SORORITIES AND FRATERNITIES DURING 1917 AND 1918

THE SORORITIES

The greater part of the years 1917 and 1918 was a period spent by most of the organizations of the University in war work, of which the sororities and fraternities did their full share. The sororities were not, of course, so seriously affected by the war as were the fraternity chapters, for the upper class members of the latter, with but rare exceptions, enlisted in the Army and Navy or, if prevented by physical disability from so doing, left the campus to enter other forms of patriotic service. This withdrawal of the older and more experienced men reduced most of the fraternity chapters that rented houses to such a financial condition that they were forced to give these up until the cessation of hostilities enabled them to recover. The few sororities, however, that were occupying rented houses were able to retain them. The others were holding their chapter meetings in rented rooms near the University.

The extent and variety of the war activities of the sororities appear in the following summary of their more important efforts, chapter by chapter, which also shows how their social life was colored by the time. A year or more before the United States was dragged into the war, Mrs. Dorothy Canfield Fisher of the class of 1899, who is a member of Kappa Kappa Gamma, went to France and established a relief station at Meudon-val-Fleury, a suburb of Paris on the electric railway to Versailles. There in the "Kappa" rooms, just behind the *Mairie* or town holl, she made weekly distributions of the garments sent to her by American friends, especially by the University and alumnae chapters of Kappa Kappa Gamma. Every Sunday morning a medical dispensary was held in the rooms, which were given, rent free, by the mayor of the village, the dispensary being under the supervision of a Red Cross physician. It was while engaged in this benevolent work that Mrs. Fisher wrote and published a book of notable short stories, entitled *Home Fires in France,* which she dedicated to her friend and former professor in the University of Kansas, General Pershing. Besides contributing generously to Mrs. Fisher's relief enterprise, the Kappas participated in the Y. M. C. A., Red Cross, and Patriotic League activities, and in December, 1918, were one of the first organizations to volunteer to fill a number of Christmas boxes for the soldiers at Camp Sherman. In the previous summer Miss Minnette Y. Fritts of the active chapter enlisted as a student nurse in the expectation of being sent to a military hospital in France.

The members of Kappa Alpha Theta participated extensively in war relief activities. The chapter adopted a French orphan to whom it sent several boxes of clothing. It pledged and paid the sum of $300 towards the amount raised by the Y.M.C.A. during the early part of April, 1917, besides the contributions made by individual members. Each Theta tried to do her share of Red Cross work in making surgical dressings and in answering such other calls as came from Red Cross headquarters and from the Military Hospital on the campus. Later the active chapter and the alumnae united in establishing a dispensary in France, which was under the direction of the American Committee for Devastated France and bore the name of the sorority.

In June, 1918, Mary Rowlen, ex-'20, began her training as a Red Cross nurse. Soon after Mrs. McManigal (Elizabeth Hoffman, ex-'19) enlisted as a naval yeowoman and was stationed at Baltimore, while Juliann E. Whitehill was awaiting her call as a Red Cross nurse. Early in December, 1918, Monabelle Lentz of the class of 1917 entered the Walter Reed Hospital at Washington, D. C., to become an instructor in occupational therapy, after preparing for this position at the Albright Art School in Buffalo during the previous summer. Miss Lentz's patients were soldiers who had suffered from shell shock.

Every member of the chapter of Pi Beta Phi joined the Red Cross and the Patriotic League, while the chapter itself took a life membership in the Red Cross. It also raised over $1,000 as its contribution to the relief fund of the University Y. M. C. A. and Y. W. C. A., partly in the form of individual pledges, but chiefly through the cooperative work of the whole chapter. For example, it held several subscription dances, gave a musicale, and sold special issues of the *Ohio State Lantern* and the *Sun Dial* in raising the money it had subscribed. On Christmas eve the chapter presented a play for the benefit of the soldiers at Camp Sherman. One of the former members of Pi Beta Phi, Miss Ednah H. Pugh, enlisted for canteen work.

Alpha Phi assumed an unusual number of war obligations. It undertook to maintain a *foyer* or home at Roanne in France, where the munition toilers might come for rest and recreation in their leisure time. This home was under the supervision of the Y. M. C. A., but was in charge of a member of the sorority and was known as the Alphi Phi *Foyer*. The chapter helped to raise the sum of $750, which the members subscribed in the University Y. M. C. A.–Y. W. C. A. drive of November 1917. It also filled 30 one-pound boxes with candy and nuts and distributed them in December, 1918, among the needy families it was caring for. Many of the members served on committees for the Liberty Loan campaign, and many of them sewed for the soldiers. Alpha Phi also ascertained the winter needs of a little fatherless French girl and sent her a complete outfit of comfortable clothing. The alumnae of Columbus held fortnightly meetings, which were largely devoted to whatever war activities seemed to be most urgent, such as Red Cross sewing or mending. On one occasion 40 shirts were made. Several graduates of the chapter rendered special service. Evangeline Wolfel of the class of 1914 engaged in the civilian relief work of the Columbus Red Cross; Caroline Herman of the class of 1917 was secretary of the free labor exchange which was the sole employment bureau for all labor employed in the construction of Camp Sherman; and Vernette Boylan, a former member of the class of 1917, sailed for France in the spring of 1919 to engage in canteen work under the auspices of the Y. M. C. A.

Every member of Delta Delta Delta was a member of, and a worker in, the Red Cross and the Patriotic League. As a chapter they contributed $350 to the Y. M. C. A.-Y. W. C. A. relief fund. The pledges of the sorority bought a $50 Liberty Bond, which they presented to the chapter. All of the girls knitted articles for the soldiers and sailors and contributed during two years to the support of a French orphan.

By personal pledges, selling *Sun Dials,* and giving a subscription dance, the chapter of Delta Gamma exceeded its pledge to the Y. M. C. A. and contributed to the Belgian relief fund of the national order. It gave support and sent a Christmas box to a French orphan. Its Patriotic League work consisted of the making of garments for Belgian children. Several of the former members of the chapter found special duties to perform. Bertha Holtcamp served as a bacteriologist at Camp Jackson, South Carolina; Margaret McNaghten was yeomanette in naval service at Newport News; Margaret Johnson and Enid King were occupied with Government work in Washington, D. C.

All of the members of Phi Mu did sewing or bandage making for the Red Cross and contributed to a fund which the national order used to establish a nurses' hut in France. The chapter also bought a Liberty Bond and gave a subscription dance, the proceeds of which went to the Y. M. C. A. war relief fund. Five members served on committees for University war work. Rose Waring Russel of the class of 1918 entered Government service in Washington, D. C., and Mabel Ensign of the class of 1914 accepted a call to go to France.

Alpha Gamma Theta devoted much time to Red Cross work, making surgical dressings and convalescent robes, besides knitting numerous socks and sweaters. As a Patriotic League unit it met regularly during the summer of 1918 to sew for the Belgians. This work was continued with enthusiasm during the remainder of the war. When the Patriotic Glee Club was organized in June, 1918, under the magnetic leadership of Miss Lillian Stocklin of the class of 1910, four members of Alpha Gamma Theta were included in the organization. One member of the chapter did volunteer motor driving for the Red Cross, another served in the office of the United States Food Administration in Ohio, and still another aided in food demonstrations in Columbus. Two members of the sorority were employed by the Government as laboratory technicians: Helen Eisele was connected with General Hospital No. 19 at Azalea, N. C., and Ruth Williams with General Hospital No. 17 at Markleton, Penn.

Besides the personal pledges of the members to the Y. M. C. A. relief fund and for thrift stamps and Liberty Bonds, the members of Delta Zeta as a chapter subscribed $250 to the Y. M. C. A. and Y. W. C. A. relief fund in November, 1917. The money usually spent for "spreads" was devoted to war work, and at the few parties held the girls made bandages. The active and alumnae chapters together adopted two French war orphans. While the active chapter gave many hours to Red Cross work, the alumnae chapter was organized into a Patriotic League unit. Helen Murray of the class of 1913 was in the Ordnance Department at Washington, D. C. Ruth Murray of the class of 1915 went into training as a war nurse. Mildred Foureman became information clerk in the hostess house at Wright Flying Field, Dayton, O.

Alpha Xi Delta supported a French orphan girl, sending her clothing and money and exchanging numerous letters with her. Every member of the chapter did her share in making surgical dressings and in sewing for Belgian children and American soldiers. All belonged to the Patriotic League. Helen McKinley and Florence Watson were in the home-service department of the Columbus Chapter of the Red Cross. By means of individual pledges, the selling of flowers at the games and sandwiches to the University girls, and the managing of a moving picture theater the chapter was able to contribute to the Y. M. C. A. relief fund. Among the alumnae Mrs. Kelly Enzor gave her entire time to war work, dividing it between the motor corps, canteen service, and surgical-dressing work. Several of the graduates fitted themselves for reconstruction and social-service work in France. Rhoda Shick of the class of 1917 gave concerts and lectures, and Grace Cicle, a former member of the class of 1918, lectured in various cities of the State on food conservation.

Established in the fall of 1918, Chi Omega was the latest addition to the University's roll of Greek-letter societies within the period of the war. Nevertheless, the chapter promptly assumed responsibility for two French children who had been orphaned by the strife. Corinne Waters spent the summer of 1918 in lecturing throughout Ohio in behalf of food conservation, and later during the influenza epidemic among the cadets of the Students' Army Training Corps she volunteered her services as nurse's aid in the University Hospital. Catherine Allison took employment on a farm near Mechanicsburg, O., during the summer of 1918, and Esther G. Shreider found occupation in an airplane factory at Dayton. Margaret E. Fisher acted as publicity agent for the University unit of the Patriotic League.

THE FRATERNITIES

The fraternity element among the students of Ohio State University is distributed among 40 chapters of as many national orders, and at the outbreak of the war comprised a total of about 1,000 members. The common interests of these two score chapters are vested in a representative committee known as the Men's Panhellenic Council, which deals with policies affecting the inter-relations of the component groups under the supervision of the Faculty committee on fraternities, which makes its recommendations to the University Faculty. A similar system exists in connection with the sororities; but since the latter constitute only a little more than one-fifth of the entire number of the Greek-letter societies—men's and women's together—in the University, and since the sororities were far less affected by the war than the fraternities, the Women's Panhellenic Council and the Faculty committee on sororities were not confronted by the problems which the state of belligerency brought before the corresponding committees in connection with the fraternities.

Indeed, no permanent organizations in the University were so shaken by the war as the fraternity chapters. Within a month after hostilities were declared by the United States, they received a staggering blow through the withdrawal of more than 1,000 students to go into farm work, military service, or some other form of war work. Needless to say, many of these departing students were fraternity men. As numbers of other students, including many more of the Greeks, were preparing to follow them, some of the fraternity houses closed at once. Phi Kappa Psi rented its house to families and did not occupy it again until early in 1919. Beta Theta Pi opened its domicile during the first two weeks in the fall of 1917 with a small number of members, initiated several new ones on October 12, but these joined the Students' Army Training Corps and went into barracks, while half of the old members withdrew to training camps, leaving the Beta house all but empty. It was opened again in the second semester of 1918-1919.

The dental fraternity, Xi Psi Phi, gave up its clubhouse, because all but four of its active members went into the S. A. T. C. Thereafter it held its weekly meetings in a large room rented for the purpose and did not re-open its house until in September, 1919. Only seven members of Alpha Gamma Rho returned to college in the fall of 1917, and these, with the exception of one man, went into barracks with the S. A. T. C. The chapter rented its house to the military staff of the S. A. T. C. for an officers' club, the active and alumni members of the chapter being admitted to the house when they wished to use it. Full possession of the property was regained after the demobilization of the Students' Army Training Corps in

December, 1918. Three-fourths of the active members of Sigma Pi were in the service during the year 1917, and in the fall of 1918 the S. A. T. C. took the rest. The chapter, therefore, gave up its house and for the next 15 months held its meetings in an apartment of five rooms, which it rented. Alpha Chi Sigma, the chemical fraternity, had only six members in college in the fall of 1918, and five of them were quartered in barracks as S. A. T. C. cadets. For the next seven months the chapter got along without a house, moving into its new home late in the spring of 1919. At the beginning of the war 14 of the 17 members of the legal fraternity, Delta Theta Pi, went into military training or engaged in agricultural pursuits. When only four members of the society returned to the University in the fall of 1917, several of whom were awaiting the call to service, the chapter gave up its house and occupied an apartment during the next two years. It moved into its present house in September, 1919.

About half of Lambda Phi Omega's men enlisted or withdrew to officers' training camps by June, 1917. The others went into the Signal Reserve Corps and the Engineers' Reserve Corps. These organizations were incorporated with the Students' Army Training Corps in the fall of 1918 and the chapter gave up its house and sold its furniture at auction, in anticipation of another year or more of the war. A month after the signing of the Armistice the members of the chapter were discharged from the S. A. T. C., December 10, 1918, and became scattered in residence but continued to hold their weekly meetings. The fraternity, which had been an Electrical Engineering organization, was now changed so as to include men from all the engineering departments. This gave the chapter a wider range of membership, and in the fall of 1919 it furnished and moved into another house.

Numerous other chapters passed through the trying experience of closing their houses for a longer or shorter period in consequence of the war, and several that were ready to build homes of their own in the spring of 1917 were forced to postpone indefinitely the execution of their projects. This was true of Phi Delta Theta, Delta Tau Delta, and Kappa Sigma. Zeta Beta Tau managed to complete the foundation for its new house, when the beginning of hostilities prevented further operations. Among the chapters that found it expedient to surrender their domiciles temporarily were several of the oldest ones in the University.

According to definite reports received from chapter officers, seven fraternities were able to keep their houses open during wartime, and there were doubtless others. Phi Delta Theta was so fortunate as to have 21 members remaining in its chapter at the end of the college year, 1917-1918, but during the first semester of the following year its house contained only six occupants, namely, one junior, one sophomore, and four freshmen, until the demobilization of the Students' Army Training Corps in December, 1918. Seven men maintained the house of Sigma Alpha Epsilon during the fall and winter of 1918, while 14 of its members were living in the S. A. T. C. Barracks. Delta Chi had only six men occupying its new house and two additional ones boarding there at one period during the war. The clubhouse of Acacia was kept open through the fortunate circumstance that the chapter had some members in the Aviation School, several of these being regarded as "transfers" from other chapters, and it had others who were instructors in the University. Sigma Phi Epsilon started in the fall of 1917 with 18 men out of 32 active members and pledges of the previous year. Those who had failed to return were in active service or were awaiting the call. The chapter soon added 24 by initiation or by pledge, a larger number than usual being taken on account of the uncertainty of the times. Of the total membership of 42 thus secured, 33 joined the S. A. T. C. in the fall of 1918, leaving nine men to run the chapter and maintain the house until the Armistice was signed. Three of these occupants of the house were pledged men. Phi Sigma Epsilon kept its house open, notwithstanding the fact that only three or four members of the fraternity lived in it during a part of the period of belligerency. Another chapter that retained its house throughout the war was Alpha Tau Omega.

While some of the chapter houses closed promptly after the withdrawal of hundreds of students in April and May, 1917, others weathered the storm until their younger classmen were ordered into barracks as S. A. T. C. cadets in the autumn of 1918. Already in November of 1917 the many fraternity houses still remaining open were displaying service flags bearing from one to 22 stars in honor of brothers called to the colors. The first and second officers' training camps at Fort Benjamin Harrison, Ind., contained dozens of Ohio State fraternity men, and they were soon to be found in more or less numerous groups in other camps throughout the country.

During the summer and fall of 1918 the departure of University men for military and naval service reduced fraternity ranks to such an extent that when college opened in mid-September conditions were worse, instead of better, for the chapters. It was even feared that Greek-letter life might become a thing of the past. Upper classmen were very scarce around the fraternity houses. The prospect was that most of these domiciles would be closed by October 1. Several of the chapters were keeping their houses open only by renting a part of them to other societies. For example, Acacia, the Masonic fraternity, was sharing its house with Phi Alpha Gamma.

Not only were the chapters so depleted that they were either abandoning their domiciles or admitting other organizations as co-occupants, but the Men's Panhellenic Council was also badly shattered. Nevertheless, a meeting of that body was called for the night of Wednesday, September 25, 1918, in Ohio Union to consider both the critical condition of the chapters and the continuance of the Panhellenic Council itself as a functioning organization during the college year. So many members of the council were in service, including its president, that it looked as though an entirely new committee would have to be chosen. A great number of freshmen had poured into the University to join the Students' Army Training Corps, and many of them were experiencing serious difficulties in securing rooms for the two weeks during which they would have to maintain themselves prior to their induction as cadets, when they would receive from the Government the pay of enlisted men. Several chapters rented the vacant rooms in their houses to some of these freshmen. This plan commended itself to the Panhellenic Council, which was eager to find a way of improving the chapter-house situation. There was, however, a University rule against freshmen being initiated and living in chapter houses, but it was suspended for a time. The few remaining brothers, on whose shoulders rested the financial support of their partly occupied chapter houses, now proceeded to initiate a sufficient number of new men to fill their vacant rooms, and the fraternities were thus transformed into groups composed chiefly of "yearling members."

Within a few days, however, the cadets of the Students' Army Training Corps were ordered into barracks on the University grounds, and the fraternity houses were again left partly vacant and financially unproductive. The chapters occupying rented houses now leased them and disbanded for the present or moved into apartments. Liberty from barracks for the initiated cadets came at uncertain intervals and rendered regular assembly nights impossible for most chapters. Military restrictions also interfered with the proper organization of the Panhellenic Council, and very few meetings were held.

The ordinary social life and activities of the students were suspended for the most part and, insofar as they survived, were conducted on a much reduced scale. As already noted in the earlier part of this chapter the sororities occasionally gave subscription dances for the purpose of raising part of the sums pledged by them towards the Y. M. C. A. and Y. W. C. A. relief fund. In the spring of 1918 Phi Kappa Psi secured most of the $500 it had subscribed to this fund by means of a dance and Captain Burr's lecture at the Hartman Theater. The social life of Xi Psi Phi, the dental fraternity, was not materially hampered by war conditions. The society usually held a dance once a month and a dinner dance at the end of the year, besides an occasional smoker. Acacia did very little in the way of social activities. Its efforts were chiefly devoted to correspondence with those of its members who were in active service, with a view to enabling them to meet with other brothers who might be on duty in their neighborhood. Such meetings not infrequently took place, to the great delight of all concerned. Sigma Phi Epsilon enlivened the approach of Army life by some kind of entertainment every week in the form of smokers, parties, and an occasional house dance. Refreshments were never served at these affairs. Although the house of Phi Sigma Epsilon remained open during the war, the chapter held no social events of any kind. These few instances suffice to show that several of the fraternities pursued widely different policies in regard to social activities. In general, however, the closing of so many of the chapter houses, the substitution of war interests for the ordinary social interests, and the constant withdrawal of men to enlist in different branches of the service deprived most of the students of either the opportunity or the inclination to indulge in social affairs.

After the Armistice was signed, a communication bearing the date of October 16, 1918, reached the University from the War Department to the effect that fraternity activities and military discipline were incompatible in the very nature of things, and that it was to the best interests of the service that the operations of fraternities in institutions where units of the Students' Army Training Corps had been established be suspended for the period of the present emergency. In particular, the War Department objected to cadets living together in fraternity houses and to their participating in functions or meetings of a social or ceremonial nature, but not of a business character; yet, as was made plain in the communication, the Government was not seeking to prevent the resumption of fraternity activities when the existing emergency should have passed.

Professor A. H. Tuttle, chairman of the Faculty committee on fraternities, in publishing this order stated that, on inquiry among such chapters as he could reach, he was convinced that the fraternities at Ohio State were living up to the letter and the spirit of the order, but he called attention to the fact that the order was still in full force (November 18, 1918), and that, until it should be modified or rescinded, he was sure the chapters would continue to observe it in every detail.

Within the month following the receipt of the above order the Students' Army Training Corps was demobilized, and with the return of many of the older brethren from service, the fraternities began to recover their normal status. However, six of them had not sufficiently recovered by the time the *Makio* of 1919 went to press, either on account of temporary disbandment or the continued absence of their leading members, to be represented with their service lists in the fraternity section of that publication. When the University resumed its activities in February, 1919, the chapters in general were larger than ever before in their history. In the previous fall the chapters had initiated more men than usual before the termination of hostilities, because of the prospect of many withdrawals and the Faculty's action permitting the initiation of freshmen. Hence, the return of the older men from military service swelled the numbers to the point where 35, 40, and even more members were common. One effect of this rebound was seen in the immediate organization of 26 fraternity basketball teams, which were grouped into four leagues and were playing nearly every night in the week in the Armory.

The part taken in the war by the fraternity men reflects nothing but credit upon the University. The service lists of the chapters show that more than 2,700 Greeks of Ohio State, including undergraduates and alumni, responded to the call of the Government. This total takes into account about 450 cadets of the Students' Army Training Corps, 46 members of the Naval Reserve, 34 of the Medical Reserve, 30 enlisted men who were awaiting their call, eight members of the Engineering Reserve, and four of the Signal Reserve, all of whom were in the University when the Armistice was signed. Many of the Ohio State Greeks who got into the war in the

126 HISTORY OF THE OHIO STATE UNIVERSITY

opening days served as commissioned officers in all grades from that of second lieutenant up to that of brigadier-general, and some of them won decorations for meritorious service or gallant conduct on the field of action. The two chapters that appear to have supplied the largest contingents were Phi Kappa Psi and Beta Theta Pi, each having a record of about 125 men. Sigma Alpha Epsilon had a list of 110 members in the service, among whom were 26 officers. Eighteen other chapters were represented by groups of from 52 to 97 men. The younger chapters, having smaller numbers of alumni, naturally did not furnish as many men as the older ones. Their records range from 46 down to 25 members in the service.

Of the 136 University men whose devotion to their patriotic duty cost them their lives, 65 belonged to fraternities. The list of these honored dead is as follows:

FRATERNITY	NAME	CLASS	CASUALTY
Phi Gamma Delta	Carl R. Crites	1919	died of wounds, Oct. 10, 1918, received in the Meuse-Argonne.
	Alva K. Overturf	1919	died of disease at Camp Taylor, Ky., Feb. 5, 1920.
Phi Kappa Psi	Adelbert M. Agler	1912	killed in action in the Ardennes, France, Nov. 5, 1918.
	Drew S. Webster	1915	killed in an automobile accident in France, July 16, 1918.
	Edwin D. James	1918	killed in an airplane accident at Ellington Field, Tex., Jan. 31, 1918.
	Carey R. Evans	1918	killed in action at Passel, France, Apr. 5, 1918.
	Thurman G. Flanagan	1913	died of wounds received in action in the Meuse-Argonne, Oct. 5, 1918.
	Harold A. Husband	1919	drowned at sea in line of duty, Aug. 12, 1918.
Sigma Chi	Errett Skinner	1920	died on May 22, 1918, following an operation.
Phi Delta Theta	William P. Bancroft	1918	died at Cambridge, Mass., Oct. 22, 1919, of disease resulting from war injuries.

SORORITIES AND FRATERNITIES

FRATERNITY	NAME	CLASS	CASUALTY
	Charles A. Navin	1920	died of disease at Camp Taylor, Ky., Nov. 25, 1918.
Beta Theta Pi	Ralph T. Saunders	1917	died of disease at Camp Eustis, Va., Oct. 12, 1918.
	Edward Sigerfoos	1891	died of wounds received in action on the western front, Oct. 7, 1918.
	Wallace C. Sabine	1886	developed disease during war service in Europe; died after surgical operation in Boston, Jan. 10, 1919.
Sigma Nu	Donald H. Charlton	1918	killed in airplane accident at Taliaferro Field, Tex., July 22, 1918.
	Almar H. Dechon	1917	died of disease, Feb. 1, 1919.
	Jay Norton Dyer	1920	killed in airplane accident at Pensacola Bay, Fla., May 17, 1919.
Sigma Alpha Epsilon	John C. Dugan	1911	died of disease at Camp Taylor, Ky., Jan. 11, 1919.
	Joseph C. Monnier	1913	died of disease, Oct. 1, 1918.
Kappa Sigma	Melvin D. Gladman	1921	died of disease, Oct. 18, 1918.
	Burnham B. Matthews	1917	died of disease in France, Nov. 26, 1918.
Alpha Tau Omega	Harry J. Myers	1918	killed in airplane accident at Ft. Worth, Tex., May 10, 1918.
Alpha Kappa Kappa	John C. Bowman	1914	died of disease in Naval Hospital, Philadelphia, Oct. 2, 1918.
	Ira G. Allen	1918	died of disease in Roosevelt Hospital, New York City, Oct. 27, 1918.
	Halstead R. Wright	1895	died of disease, Oct. 17, 1918.
	John K. Lawson	1916	died of disease at Romage, France, May 28, 1919.
Delta Tau Delta	Alvin R. Roberts	1912	died of disease in France, Jan. 9, 1918.
Delta Upsilon	Lawrence C. Yerges	1915	died of wounds received in action in France, Oct. 24, 1918.
	Cyril F. Carder	1918	died of wounds received in action at Chauteau-Courcy, France, July 22, 1918.

128   HISTORY OF THE OHIO STATE UNIVERSITY

FRATERNITY	NAME	CLASS	CASUALTY
Delta Upsilon	Harold J. Courtney	1918	died of disease on board S. S. *Louisville* on way to France, Sept. 21, 1918.
Sigma Delta Chi	Lawrence C. Yerges		(see Delta Upsilon, p. 127).
Alpha Gamma Rho	Russell H. Arnold	1921	died of disease at Manitowac, Wis., Oct. 24, 1918.
	Raymond H. Baldwin	1920	killed in action near Landres, France, Nov. 2, 1918.
Phi Beta Kappa	Charles A. Bruce	1895	died of disease Apr. 3, 1918, developed at Camp Sherman, O.
	Latimer Johns	1912	killed in action near Gesnes, France, Sept. 30, 1918.
	Edward Sigerfoos		(see Beta Theta Pi, p. 127).
	Wallace C. Sabine		(see Beta Theta Pi, p. 127).
Sigma Xi	Wallace C. Sabine		(see Beta Theta Pi, p. 127).
Acacia	Harry A. Heifner	1916	died of disease, Oct. 4, 1918.
	Guthrie O. Burrell	1916	died at Blerecourt, France, of wounds received in action in the Argonne Forest.
	Oscar O. Johnson	1911	died of disease in Dec., 1918.
	Laird K. Roberts	1919	died of disease at Brest, France, Jan. 15, 1919.
	Carl R. Stebbins	1913	died of disease, Oct. 12, 1918.
Alpha Sigma Phi	Murton L. Campbell	1918	killed in action on the Somme front, near Baupum, Aug. 23, 1918.
	Ralph J. May	1921	died of disease, Nov. 24, 1918.
Sigma Pi	Thomas W. Barrett	1919	killed in an airplane accident at Tours, France, June 28, 1917; was first Ohio State University man to lose his life in the war.
	Samuel J. Covert	1916	killed by a sniper's bullet at the front, Sept. 28, 1918.
	James E. Graham	1922	died of disease at Ft. Worth, Tex., Oct. 24, 1918.
	Harold L. Hissem	1920	died of disease at Camp Sherman, O., June 8, 1919.
Pi Kappa Alpha	Vaughn R. McCormick	1918	killed in action at St. Mihiel, Defensive Sector, Sept. 12, 1918.
Phi Rho Sigma	Guthrie O. Burrell		(see Acacia above).

Sororities and Fraternities

Fraternity	Name	Class	Casualty
	Hadley H. Teter	1916	lost at sea, Sept. 26, 1918, when U. S. cutter *Tampa* was sunk in Bristol Harbor.
Phi Sigma Epsilon (later Theta Chi)	William A. Wirth	1917	died of disease, Oct. 8, 1918.
Delta Chi	Ralph W. Laughlin	1917	killed in action at Catelet, St. Quentin Sector, France. Sept. 30, 1918.
Alpha Zeta	Edgar M. Allen	1908	died of disease at Los Angeles, Calif., in 1918.
Delta Sigma Rho	Fred S. Haynie	1910	died of disease, July 2, 1919, resulting from Army service.
Phi Kappa (formerly the Newman Club)	Fred W. Norton	1917	died on July 23, 1918, of wounds received in action.
	August H. Bornhorst	1911	died at Civilian Hospital, Sedro Woolley, Wash., Dec. 7, 1918.
	Charles M. Elder	1915	died of disease, Oct. 7, 1918, at Camp Sherman, O.
	Charles A. Navin	1920	died of disease at Camp Taylor, Ky., Nov. 25, 1918.
Phi Delta Kappa	Carl K. Hammond	1919	died of disease, Oct. 31, 1918.
Alpha Pi Upsilon	Fred W. Norton		(see Phi Kappa above).
Psi Omega	Alexander H. Jones	1911	died of disease at Army Post Office 714, France, Oct. 1, 1918.
Phi Kappa Tau	Stanley C. Miller	1915	killed in airplane accident at Evanton, Wyo., Oct. 15, 1919.
	Frederick F. Searle	1915	died of disease in France, Oct. 12, 1918.
Alpha Mu Pi Omega	Ralph T. Saunders		(see Beta Theta Pi, p. 127).
	Thomas P. Johnston	1910	died of disease at Base Hospital 101, France, Oct. 8, 1918.
	Charles E. McClelland	1902	died of disease, March 27, 1926, contracted in the war.
	Carl C. Smith	1911	died of disease in France, Feb. 17, 1919.

Fraternity	Name	Class	Casualty
Eta Kappa Nu	Harland H. Cowle	1915	died of disease in Base Hospital, Tours, France.
	Wayland W. Cowle	1915	died of disease at Denver, Colo., Oct. 12, 1919.
Gamma Phi	Karl S. McComb	1916	killed in action, American Expeditionary Force, Defensive Sector, Aug. 12. 1918.

CHAPTER X

THE COLLEGE OF AGRICULTURE AND THE FOOD PROBLEM

The college first to engage as such in war activities was the College of Agriculture. This was due to the urgent and imperiling food situation in the United States and the associated countries. The available food supply was being rapidly diminished by the prosecution of hostilities on a scale never witnessed before, and the gigantic conflict had been waging for more than two and a half years. The law of diminishing returns was operating in a way that called loudly for the production of greater supplies of food to counteract it. This was generally realized, but especially by the agricultural colleges of the country.

Governor James M. Cox did a very wise thing when, on April 11, 1917, he conferred with President W. O. Thompson, chairman of the executive committee of the Association of Agricultural Colleges and Experiment Stations, Dean Alfred Vivian, Director Clark S. Wheeler of our Agricultural Extension Service, Chairman T. J. Duffy of the Ohio Industrial Commission, Secretary George Stauffer of the Ohio Board of Agriculture, and Mr. Fred C. Croxton of the Ohio Institute for Public Efficiency. This conference decided to promote agricultural production throughout the State: (1) by means of county food and crop commissioners and a vigorous campaign among the farmers for increased acreage and more intensive farming; (2) by supplying farm labor through about a dozen new Employment Exchanges; (3) by enlisting the granges in the campaign for food production; (4) by calling on the colleges and high schools to release their young men for farm and garden work; and (5) by requesting the Home Economics

Department of the State University to conduct a state-wide canning, or food conservation, campaign.

A Committee on Food Conservation and Supply was promply organized, which, under the able leadership of Mr. Croxton, vice-chairman and director of the Ohio Branch of the Council for National Defense, launched a great drive throughout the State for food production and conservation. The principal agencies in this drive were our College of Agriculture and its Agricutural Extension Service, and the State Department of Agriculture. In the spring of 1917 there was a pressing need to teach our country and city people how best to conserve, utilize, and increase the food supply. The slogan of the agricultural drive in Ohio, as in other states, was "Food will win the war." For the past twenty years our College of Agriculture had been teaching scientific agriculture to increasing numbers of students, and for twelve years its Extension Service had been doing the same thing in more popular form in the counties of the State. The war gave a new impetus and thrilling significance to this work. Most classes in the college were greatly reduced in size during this period by the withdrawal of students to go into agricultural and military service, the great exodus taking place early in May, 1917. However, already in April about four hundred students had departed from the College of Agriculture and about a hundred more from the other colleges. Some of the classes were entirely suspended, or combined with others. But the whole agricultural staff of the University suddenly became extension workers. All its members, from Dean Vivian through the list, traveled over the State, making numerous addresses on food production and conservation. From the University at large, including the College of Agriculture, more than a thousand students withdrew from May 4 to 10 to work on farms. Our Agricultural Extension Service during the years 1917-19 had the advantage of some increase of funds, partly due to the normal increase in the Smith-Lever fund, partly to a larger State appropriation, but especially to war emergency sums provided by the United States Department of Agriculture. In the fiscal year 1917-18 the amount available from these sources was $197,300 and in 1918-19 it was $220,700.

When the Federal Food Administration in Ohio was created in September, 1917, our College of Agriculture was not overlooked. It supplied four of the eight agricultural advisers to that body, namely, Dean Vivian, Clark S. Wheeler, Professor F. S. Jacoby, and Professor Thomas D. Phillips, the last named being given charge of the Division of Grain Threshing, while Professor Edna N. White became the home economics director. Dean Vivian had already served for several weeks as adviser to Mr. Herbert C. Hoover, the United States food administrator, in Washington, D. C. In addition to these officers, the University furnished nine other members of its Faculty as members of divisions or directors, besides five graduates, to the State Food Administration.

Fortunately, our College of Agriculture had completed a more effective organization by the beginning of the great war. Each of its eleven departments became responsible not only for resident teaching and research, but also for extension service in the counties. Departments were also created for the supervision of county agents, boys' and girls' clubs, farmers' institutes, and agricultural publications. This new organization enabled the college to do its war work surprisingly well, although during hostilities nineteen members of seven different departments entered military service. At the beginning of the academic year 1917-18 there were twenty-six county agents, at its close fifty, and during 1918-19 seventy. A number of these agents were emergency appointees. The formation of farm bureaus was also stimulated. They were organizations of the farmers within the counties which cooperated with the county agents. In 1914 there were only four thousand farm-bureau members in Ohio as compared with fifty thousand at the end of June, 1918.

In the fall of 1917 the college had ten home demonstration agents in counties and eight in cities. A year later the number had increased to eighteen in the counties. They supplied information and guidance in home economics, especially about canning and drying fruits and vegetables; they trained volunteer workers; assisted in Red Cross activities; and, with twelve county leaders in as many more counties, organized a large number of boys' and girls' clubs for gardening, corn raising, poultry tending, etc.

Professor Edna N. White had charge of the home demonstration agents. She was chairman of the Conservation Committee and director of home economics on the staff of the Federal Food Administration in Ohio, and likewise chairman of the Food Department of the Woman's Committee in the Ohio Branch of the Council of National Defense. She took a leading part in the conference of trained helpers at the University in May, 1918. These persons were promoters of food conservation. Following the conference, two-day institutes were conducted in a number of the counties for the training of volunteer workers. Under Miss White's supervision the trained and volunteer workers gave demonstrations in canning and drying vegetables and fruits and making "victory bread" before gatherings of housekeepers in 48 counties. During June, 1918, 395 demonstrations and talks were given; during July, 424; and during August, 67. This record does not include the home demonstration agents. They also made a fine record. During 1918 the urban agents gave more than 1,100 demonstrations and about 770 talks, besides holding 217 public meetings. The total attendance was more than 332,000 in the cities of Akron, Canton, Chillicothe, Cincinnati, Cleveland, Columbus, Dayton, Toledo, and Youngstown. The rural or county agents gave more than 525 demonstrations and nearly 200 talks before organizations, and more than 50 demonstrations and 25 talks before public meetings, with an attendance of more than 41,000. Miss White also directed the work of the home economics or girls' clubs, which had a membership of over 6,000 and received systematic guidance through the Extension Service. These clubs were visited twice each summer by home economics teachers.

Through the Food Department of the Ohio Branch of the Council of National Defense, Miss White and her committee of women carried out a comprehensive program for maintaining food committees in every county and township, for promoting war gardens, poultry raising, and milk production; for teaching uncomplaining compliance with the Government's food regulations; for the report of violations of these regulations on the part of merchants, hotels, restaurants, and individuals. During the summer and autumn of 1918 a series of food round tables was held under the auspices of the women's committee at Akron, Cambridge, Cincinnati, Columbus, Oberlin, and Toledo, which were attended by representatives of the adjacent counties. These meetings were for the purpose of spreading information and enthusiasm among the army of women workers. During this summer also a motor truck, equipped for canning and egg-candling demonstrations, visited more than 60 towns and villages off the main railroad lines in 14 counties. By this means the Food Administration, assisted by Professor Jacoby, its adviser in poultry husbandry, succeeded in reaching 9,300 persons. Under Miss White's supervision 14 leaflets and two bulletins dealing with food conservation were published and distributed throughout the State. The Agricultural Extension Service circulated similar publications on meat substitutes, victory breads, and food conservation. It has been officially stated that the saving of food by voluntary cooperation of households was "the greatest single achievement of the Federal Food Administration in Ohio." This achievement was due in no small part to the efforts of the College of Agriculture and its Extension Service.

The staff of the Department of Agricultural Chemistry and Soils instructed farmers on the best methods of increasing crop yields. The department cooperated with the Ohio Experiment Station in preparing and distributing circulars on soils and fertilizers, in supplying articles for the farm press, and in holding meetings at the experimental farms for the discussion of fertilizers and soils. Such activities greatly stimulated the use of fertilizing materials. The Department of Agricultural Chemistry and Soils agreed with the county agents to recommend phosphates to the farmers and thereby greatly increased their use.

All the agencies working together brought a larger acreage under cultivation and a larger crop yield; Ohio's wheat record before and during the war will illustrate this:

Year	Acres	Bushels	Bushels per Acre
1912-16	1,623,000	23,822,000	15
1917	1,870,000	41,140,000	22
1918	2,290,000	43,225,000	19

The acreage was, of course, very materially affected by the larger price prevailing during the war, but a considerable part of the increased yield can be safely credited to the efforts put forth to bring this about. The aim had been to bring the wheat crop up to 3,000,000 acres, with an average yield of 20 bushels per acre.

The Ohio Board of Agriculture gives the following figures for the other staple crops:

INDIAN CORN

Year	Acres	Bushels
1916	3,154,480	96,352,296
1917	3,387,459	122,204,661

OATS

Year	Acres
1916	801,639
1917	1,538,843

RYE

Year	Acres
1916	68,669
1917	101,372

BARLEY

Year	Acres
1916	27,683
1917	50,447

POTATOES

Year	Acres
1916	5,460,008
1917	11,802,020

In view of these results, largely attributable to the increased production program of April, 1917, another campaign for greater crops was launched early in 1918. In this drive, prosecuted under the joint auspices of the Federal Food Administration in Ohio and the Ohio Branch of the Council of National Defense, the general use of tractors was advocated, and a tractor school was conducted by our College of Agriculture for one week early in February at the University. The school was attended by about two thousand farmers. It was followed by smaller schools in the counties conducted by tractor manufacturers. The outcome of these and other efforts was the addition of at least two thousand machines to those already owned by Ohio farmers. A survey made in the autumn of 1917 showed about the same number then in use.

In January, 1918, the College of Agriculture made investigations into the supply and quality of seed corn in the State and found that it was very poor and wholly inadequate for existing needs. The wet season in corn harvest in 1917, followed by an early and extremely cold winter, had ruined much of the corn for planting. It was found that about 32 per cent of the former year's crop was soft and unfit to plant. This was the lowest germination test in the history of Ohio. Together with other agencies, the college issued a call to all superintendents of rural schools to attend a conference in Columbus for the purpose of enlisting the children in a seed-corn census of the State and locating the corn left over from previous seasons. The teachers were asked to test samples of seed corn in their schoolrooms. During February and March twelve testing stations were established to serve the people in all parts of Ohio. More than four hundred and six thousand ears of corn were tested at these stations. The methods for conducting the census were devised by the college, which soon discovered that neither the low germination seed nor the old seed would suffice. Hence, contrary to its established policy, the State University engaged in the purchase and sale of seed corn in order to handle quickly a large importation from outside the State. Plans for buying this seed in southeastern Pennsylvania were formed early in March, 1918, and Mr. W. E. Hanger, the specialist in farm crops, was authorized to obtain this "war emergency seed corn." Before the corn could be loaded into cars for shipment, it must be sampled from the cribs and the type approved, tested, and inspected.

Through the efforts of Director Clark S. Wheeler of our Agricultural Extension Service a contract was signed by the Stokes Seed Farm Company, the Seed Stocks Committee of the United States Department of Agriculture, and the University, whereby the Seed Stocks Committee agreed to finance the purchase of fifty thousand bushels of corn from the Stokes Company, to be selected by agents of the University. Late in March it was learned that not more than fourteen thousand bushels of seed corn could be procured from southeastern Pennsylvania, and after more investigation it was decided to get the rest from Delaware. All of this corn was shipped from the purchasing points between March 20 and April 25, 1918, and was distributed in forty-two counties in Ohio. In addition, thirteen thousand bushels were bought by the Seed Stocks Committee under the same plan and shipped to Toledo as a reserve for late orders. This supply was also sent out widely through the State. The prompt execution of this whole enterprise was highly creditable to all who shared in it, including our College of Agriculture, its county agents, and the farm bureaus. The great result achieved was that many thousands of acres were planted with good seed that would have been planted with poor seed, or not at all.

In the program adopted by Governor Cox's conference in April, 1917, the need of supplying farm labor was fully recognized. Hence fourteen employment offices were opened in as many cities by May 1 of that year, in addition to the seven already in operation. Both the old and the new offices were placed under the direction of Mr. Fred C. Croxton and his staff. Professor Matthew B. Hammond of our Department of Economics was one of the four men chosen to organize the new offices. As several thousand college and high-school students were released for farm work early in May, including more than one thousand from our University, Professor H. C. Ramsower of the College of Agriculture was appointed enrolling officer and secured the information about the fitness of the applicants for farm jobs. He was able to place several hundred of these on farms, or in war industries, before they left the University. This work was carried on through the Agricultural Extension Service. Professor Ramsower had to abandon his teaching in agricultural engineering during eighteen months. Professors Thomas G. Phillips and L. O.

Lantis were likewise released from their teaching of rural economics in order to engage in the employment service and food administration in Fayette, Greene, Logan, and Union Counties. Both continued in this work from about May 1 until September 1, 1917. Professor Phillips was then given charge of the Division of Grain Threshing of the Federal Food Administration in Ohio and the placing of farm labor.

Meantime, the employment offices were exercising great care in the choice of men sent to farmers and were placing many of the students who applied to them. The work of the Grain Threshing Division was to prevent waste of wheat and rye during the threshing season, since the estimated loss of these grains during threshing in 1917 amounted to nine hundred thousand bushels in Ohio alone. Accordingly, early in the spring of 1918 meetings of farmers and threshers were held in the important grain-producing counties, under the direction of Professor Phillips. At these meetings county threshing committees were formed to urge all possible care in the handling of grain from the field to the market. Posters were printed and distributed at the expense of the Ohio Department of Agriculture; pledge cards were circulated and signed by over two thousand owners of threshing-machines, and reports from fifty-six of the eighty-eight counties of Ohio indicated that not less than two hundred thousand bushels of wheat alone were saved that otherwise would have been lost.

Early in 1918 the question of supplying farm-hands became more serious than ever. At this time Professor Phillips was assigned to the employment service as farm-help specialist. He conducted a series of drives through the employment offices, assisted by about eighteen hundred volunteers, to secure orders from farmers for such labor as they might need. The first drive was organized in February, with the necessary publicity to persuade experienced men to take up farm work. Despite the great shortage of labor and the more attractive offers to workers in the cities, these drives were so successful that no appreciable fraction of the harvest was lost from lack of farm-hands. Under the leadership of Mr. L. J. Taber, master of the State Grange, the granges cooperated in reporting the labor needs of the farmers.

During the period from May 1 to December 31, 1917, nearly six thousand farm-hands were reported as placed, most of them being employed by the month. The results of the drives in the spring of 1918 were as follows: during March 906 farm-hands were reported placed; in April, 738; in May, 529, and in June, nearly 1,100. During the following months the record was equally good.

In February, 1918, a Federal Milk Commission for Ohio was appointed by United States food administrator, Herbert Hoover, to deal with questions of price and supply. This was done at the request of Mr. Croxton, since there had been sudden advances in price in several cities, notably in Columbus, in November and December, 1917. Although our College of Agriculture was not officially represented on the Milk Commission, two members of the Department of Rural Economics, Professors J. I. Falconer and H. E. Erdman, rendered valuable assistance, the latter giving much of his time during 1918 and all of it during the summer of that year to the commission.

The extensive work carried on by our College of Agriculture during the war through its Extension Service is shown by a few figures. In 1917-18 the number of workers in that service reached a total of 119 and in the following year, 162, as compared with 74 in 1916-17. Of the number in 1918-19 23 were specialists, giving their full time to their respective departments. That same year the Agricultural Publications Department sent out nearly three and a quarter millions of circulars, bulletins, and posters, as compared with nearly two million eight hundred and twenty thousand in 1916-17. The county agents engaged in many activities that cannot be expressed in figures, but a partial list of these included over 66,000 calls by farmers at agents' headquarters, over 19,300 visits to farms, more than 2,000 demonstrations, some 250 meetings to explain demonstration work, at which the attendance was 29,600; about 2,200 meetings at which plans were outlined and the attendance was nearly 67,700, and 2,340 miscellaneous assemblages, with an aggregate attendance of 153,400. By the end of the war there were over 1,150 boys' and girls' clubs, with a total enrollment of about 11,450 members. The value of the commodities produced by these clubs was a little more than $99,000. In 1918-19 the 26 home demonstration agents conducted 1,800 demonstrations in food conservation, canning, home nursing, etc. About 97,000 persons attended these demonstrations. In addition, more than 4,500 meetings were held, with an attendance of 101,300. Over 6,000 visits were made to homes. In a word, all of the eleven departments of the College of Agriculture rendered most unusual and valuable services to the State and the Nation during the war.

Effects of the War on the College of Agriculture

Let us now look at the effects of the war on these departments and the college as a whole. In 1917-18 there were 1,198 students registered in the college, while in the following year the number had dropped to 825 and in 1918-19 to 722. Four of the younger instructors in agricultural chemistry and soils soon went into the Army. The teachers of soils who were left gave much time to preparing articles and circulars on soils and fertilizers and to farmers' meetings for the purpose of explaining the best means of increasing crops. Some lectured in various parts of the State on food production and conservation. The numbers in the classes in agricultural chemistry and soils fell off until only the foreign students, or those physically disqualified for service, remained. The courses for advanced and graduate students were largely abandoned during the war years, and those maintained were but poorly attended. The depletion of the soils staff became more rapid than the decrease in the number of students, because the farmers needed the help of experts in improving the fertility of their land. It was the Agricultural Chemistry and Soils Department that arranged meetings at the experimental farms, where improved methods of soil treatment and cultivation were presented and explained to the farmers. The county agents were supplied with the best suggestions the department could offer concerning methods of increasing yields. Much time was spent in keeping informed about the latest developments in the fertilizer and limestone industries and in bringing pressure to bear, when necessary, for the prompt delivery of materials for soil improvement.

Two members of the Agricultural Engineering Extension Service were called out in the first draft, making it necessary for Professor H. C. Ramsower to assume their duties. Other members of the department took over his classes. A special course on motor transports was given for the benefit of a unit of the Students' Army Training Corps and drew a large enrollment. In all other courses the registration was very light until the second half-year of 1918-19, when there was a marked improvement.

In animal husbandry the enrollment in 1916-17 was 933. In the following year it dropped to 618, and in 1918-19 to 352. In the Department of Farm Crops there was a similar falling off. From 389 students in 1916-17 the number fell to 264 in 1917-18 and then to 173 in the year following. A gain of only 16 was made in the autumn of 1919. The Botany Department had a registration of 825 in 1916-17. This dropped to 555 in the year following, but the number rose to 642 in 1918-19. Six hundred and twenty-two students were enrolled in 1916-17, 285 in 1917-18, and only 148 in 1918-19. In Horticulture and Forestry the student enrollment was 750 in 1916-17. In the next year it declined to 382, the number of classes remaining the same. In 1918-19 it descended to 190. The Department of Landscape Architecture did not exist during the two war years on account of the absence of Professor Philip H. Elwood, who was in military service overseas. With the revival of the department in September, 1919, the enrollment returned to nearly normal. The opportunities of many of the men who had been in military service to see something of landscape gardening in Europe prepared them for the acceptance of foreign standards in landscape design and park making.

Early in the spring of 1917 the staff in Home Economics was "mobilized" for general service. The department had sent letters to a number of trained women asking them to register as volunteers in food conservation work. During May all colleges and universities in Ohio having home economics departments were visited, and the interest of the teachers and students was sought. About four hundred volunteer workers were thus enlisted. Then the larger cities of the State were visited, and the home economics teachers and other trained women were given the plan for conducting the initial work as well as demonstrations in the new canning methods. Fourteen leaflets on foods, a bulletin on canning and preserving, and a book of recipes were prepared for the Ohio Branch of the Council of National Defense and distributed. A bulletin on substitutes for meat and another on those for flour, with recipes for quick bread, were compiled, published, and sent out by the University's Agricultural Extension Service. The volunteer workers were supplied with an outline and bibliography for food conservation talks. The Federal Food Administration in Ohio was much aided by articles prepared by members of the Home Economics Department and printed in the press. Various activities were carried on through the extension service of the department, including hundreds of demonstrations before summer canning clubs, farm women's clubs, girls' clubs, and farmers' institutes; food exhibits at the State Fair and National Dairy Show in Columbus; about three hundred and sixty conservation talks before mass meetings, housewives' leagues, women's study clubs, normal-school classes, and other groups. The summer volunteer work in the cities was organized through the University and the Women's Committee of the Ohio Branch of the Council for National Defense. In most cases it was conducted through boards of education and their corps of teachers. Summer classes were held in some twenty cities of the State. Pledge-card campaigns were conducted. Professor Anna R. Van Meter made a number of investigations suggested by conservation needs. The Home Economics Extension Service and the Council for National Defense, Professor Edna White and other representatives of the College of Agriculture being members of the latter, sent out 75,000 canning bulletins, 95,000 recipe bulletins, and 50,000 food leaflets, of which the subject matter had been prepared by members of the department. Professor White gave half of her time daily to the work of the Federal Food Administration in Ohio, which was executive. She prepared a series of ten conservation lecture outlines for use in all Ohio colleges, so that the women of the graduating classes might be ready to assist in food work.

The freshman classes in home economics were given laboratory instruction in surgical dressings. The juniors were organized into classes for Red Cross work and taught, and a course in Red Cross dietetics was offered. This work was supplemented by garment making under the supervision of Professor Maude Hathaway throughout the year.

Red Cross activities outside of the University were also promoted. Professor Grace Walker of the Domestic Arts Department took charge of garment making and surgical dressing for the Columbus Chapter of the Red Cross during the summer months. In December, 1917, outlines of fifteen lessons on the conservation of food were prepared for the use of the American Red Cross, as also ten lessons on canteen cookery, giving instructions and recipes for preparing food in quantity and a plan for serving soldiers in transit and in camps. Some of these activities were prompted by Red Cross needs, Professor White being chairman of the Dietitians' Committee of the national organization.

On October 18, 1918, the Home Economics Department was notified that, on account of the outbreak of influenza, there was a considerable number of students in the Military Hospital on the campus. These young men belonged to the Students' Army Training Corps. Investigation showed that the hospital was intended for twenty patients, but had one hundred and seven of them needing attention. Equipment was hastily moved over, and, with the aid of trained volunteers from the department, the food situation was cared for adequately.

The fluctuations in student attendance in home economics during the war years are more surprising than in any of the other departments of the Agricultural College, especially as its students were women. Starting with eleven hundred and twenty-five in 1916-17, the number dropped to less than four hundred the next year, then rose to over seven hundred in 1918-19.

The Rural Economics Department gave two of its staff to civilian service in April, 1917; another enlisted in October; the Federal Food Administration in Ohio took part of the time of two others during 1918; and a sixth man enlisted in March of the same year. Since only juniors and seniors took courses in rural economics, the attendance was lower in this department than in most of the others where the younger students were to be found. In 1916-17 the registration was slightly over five hundred and eighty, while in 1918-19 it was only two hundred and forty-two. It declined only five in the year following. Three classes were discontinued on account of the small enrollment and the depletion of the teaching staff.

As in other departments so also in zoology and entomology the number of students declined before hostilities were declared. Of course, this decline continued during the war years. The following table tells the story:

Year	1916-17	1917-18	1918-19
Number	1,510	1,140	1,082

The insistent call for men from farm and factory was early felt. After this came the call to military service, which was responded to by many of the older students. In the introductory course in entomology, a sophomore study, there were over one hundred students in September, 1916. A year later the number had dropped to less than half, and in another year to only twenty-eight. Among the advanced graduate students the reduction was very large. Many of the younger instructors were of draft age and were anxious to enter the service. Their minds were more or less diverted from their college duties. This condition also prevailed among the older students, not only in this department but in all of the departments on the campus. Eventually two instructors and all the older students of the Zoology Department did enlist. A number of them entered the Sanitary Corps, where their training in biology and entomology afforded them opportunities for special work.

At the Lake Laboratory the classes were almost extinguished during the war, being made up of advanced and graduate students only. During several years before hostilities the attendance had averaged twenty. In 1918 it fell to two students, both of whom happened to be undergraduates. In the autumn of 1919 the attendance in this and all other departments on the campus showed a marked increase.

The following is a list, by departments, of members of the teaching and extension staffs of the College of Agriculture who entered military service:

Agricultural Chemistry and Soils
  John L. Hutchinson
  Thomas G. Phillips
  John J. Riggle
  Charles Thrash

Agricultural Engineering
  Norman S. Fish
  Richard C. Miller
  Virgil Overholt
  Walter Pettit

Animal Husbandry
  Cecil Bayes

Botany
  Paul B. Sears

Dairying
  William D. Axtell, Jr.
  Elmer Helbig

Horticulture and Forestry
  Francis E. Allen
  Frank H. Beach
  Brooks D. Drain
  Philip H. Elwood, Jr.
  Harry W. Lutz
  Lloyd W. Wise

Rural Economics
  Golden N. Dagger
  Donald G. Hughes

CHAPTER XI

THE COLLEGE OF ARTS, PHILOSOPHY, AND SCIENCE

Like the College of Agriculture, the College of Arts, Philosophy, and Science contains a large proportion of women among its students. The number of women increased in the college during America's participation in the war, while, as was to be expected, the number of men declined. Near the end of the conflict, however, a notable change took place in this respect, the men making a much larger gain in number than the women. In the fall of 1916-1917 the total enrollment in the college was 1,305, of which 902 were men and 403 were women, not counting the 110 in the arts-education course of whom 80 were women and 30 were men. In the following spring the enrollment in Arts had declined to 1,221, the loss being chiefly among the men; while the arts-education course had 112 matriculates, about 16 per cent being men.

By the middle of May, 1917, 273 male students withdrew from the Arts College to do farm work and 79 to enter military service. Of the arts-education students nine went into agricultural pursuits and only one into military service. Although war preparations were under full headway in the fall of 1917, the Arts College made a slight gain in attendance, the enrollment rising to 1,243. This is explained by the increase in the number of women to 452, albeit the number of men had declined to 791. Eighty-six women and 18 men had registered in arts-education. In the spring of 1918 the enrollment in the Arts College rose to 1,324 students. Of this number 840 were men and 484 were women.

The dean of the college reported at the end of June, 1918, that the enlistments of arts men in the Army then totaled 222, in the navy 47, and that 48 of the former and three of the latter were granted their degrees at the recent Commencement, since they were within less than half a semester of completing the curriculum. He added that the figures given did not include withdrawals for service in the Y. M. C. A., the Red Cross, or other forms of work incidental to the war. Of these there was a considerable number.

The corresponding figures in arts-education were 108, 17 being men and 91 women. When the Students' Army Training Corps was established in the autumn of 1918, the total enrollment in Arts leaped to 2,142, of which 638 were cadets, paid and equipped by the Government, 1,003 were other male students, and 505 were women. The increase in the number of male students who were not in the S. A. T. C. was due, no doubt, to the requirement of two years of Arts College work for admission to the College of Law, which went into effect at this time, and to the operation of a similar requirement for entrance into the College of Commerce and Journalism. The arts-education course, however, experienced a decline of more than 40 per cent in the fall of 1918, its attendance of both women and men dropping off materially. The enrollment in the course at this time was only 60, two being S. A. T. C. cadets; four, male students in the regular course; and 54, women.

The signing of the Armistice in November, 1918, and the withdrawal of 417 cadets in the following month on the disbandment of the Students' Army Training Corps, caused the Arts College the loss of more than one-fifth of its total enrollment. Two hundred and twenty-one cadets continued in the college after demobilization. At the opening of the spring semester, 1919, it gained more than 100 students over its number immediately after the demobilization of the S. A. T. C. It now had 1,849 students, of whom 1,278 were men and 571 were women. The arts-education course rose to 65 students, 7 being men and 58 women. It had had 60 students. It now had 59. In the fall of 1919 the College of Arts leaped forward at one bound, regaining many of its former students, as well as many others whom the war had kept away from the University. Its increase was more than 1,100 students or over 94 per cent, carrying its total up to 2,318. Of this number 1,549 were men and 769 were women. The arts-education course gained only four, three of whom were men and one, a woman.

The summer sessions of 1917, 1918, and 1919 show an increasing enrollment in the Arts College, but not in the arts-education course:

Summer, 1917

Arts College
Men, 7
Women, 124

Total, 206

Arts-Education
Men, 7
Women, 25

Total, 32

Summer, 1918

Arts College
Men, 112
Women, 156

Total, 268

Arts-Education
Men, 3
Women, 13

Total, 16

Summer 1919

Arts College
Men, 244
Women, 180

Total, 424

Arts-Education
Men, 5
Women, 14

Total, 19

The effect of the war on the enrollment of the various departments in the Arts College is shown in the accompanying table:

Departments	Before the War			During the War		After the War
	1914-15	1915-16	1916-17	1917-18	1918-19	1919 (1st Sem.)
American History	535	840	1121	965	734	847
English	4131	4097	4955	4295	4522	3828
European History	753	917	1042	1025	1604	771
Geology	830	874	823	652	419	569
German	2291	1583	1538	654	149	187
Greek	77	96	69	13	34	26
Latin	265	307	286	242	175	101
Philosophy	303	416	524	445	534	356
Political Science	208	295	359	329	293	250
Romance Languages	1560	2396	2785	3237	4502	3086

In the above table the figures of the Department of German have a peculiar significance, for they correspond with certain historical events in the relation between the United States and Germany. In France, Belgium, and England the war stimulated the study of the German language, according to the testimony of competent witnesses. The reverse was true in the United States. In April, 1916, the American Government warned the German Imperial Government that it would sever diplomatic relations, unless the latter abandoned its ruthless methods of submarine warfare. In the previous May a German submarine had sunk the *Lusitania*, causing the loss of 114 American lives. The German Department, which had nearly 2,300 students in 1914-1915, dropped to less than 1,000 in the next year. It lost 45 more in 1916-1917. When the University resumed its activities in the fall of 1917, that is, six months after the United States had entered the war, the German Department found its enrollment was only 654 or nearly 900 less than in the previous year. It reached the bottom in 1918-1919 with 149 students, the period in which our Government declared hostilities against Austria-Hungary. The loss since the college year 1917-1918 was over 500 students. In the fall semester of 1919 the Department of German showed a gain of 38 students, which brought its enrollment up to 187.

As a certain minimum amount of foreign-language study is required of all students in most of the colleges of the State University, those who manifested their hostility towards the Central Powers by dropping German displayed their friendliness to the Associated Powers by substituting one of the Romance languages, French, Italian, or Spanish, the last-named language having come into favor in recent years because it is supposed to be of commercial value. In 1914-1915 the Department of Romance Languages had 1,560 students. Its gain in the next year was 836 and in 1916-1917, 389 more. After the United States went into the struggle, the Romance group acquired over 450 new adherents, and in our second year of the war it gained 1,271 students, reaching a total of 4,508. This record is the more remarkable in view of the fact that the general attendance of the University had been steadily declining during the war period. With the great increase in numbers that came in the fall of 1919, the Department of Romance Languages was almost swamped by the enrollment of 3,086 students for the first half-year alone.

The Department of European History sustained an increased attendance during the war not on account of a new hostility to any other study, but on account of a livelier interest in the European belligerents. Starting with 753 students in 1914-1915, this department made a gain of 164 in the next year and of 125 more in 1916-1917. It lost only 13 in the year after the United States entered the conflict and then gained 579 in the second year of the war, reaching a maximum of over 1,600 students. In the fall of 1919 its enrollment fell off about thirty. Besides the larger number of freshmen electing the general course in the department, more advanced students than usual were attracted by the courses dealing with Europe since 1815, Europe and Turkey, the Far East, and especially by the history of France. This last course was elected by 52 students in 1918-1919, or more than double the number ever electing it before. The course was repeated the following year, when it had 38 students. Inasmuch as a course in War Issues was required by the Government of all cadets in the Students' Army Training Corps who were without an equivalent, the teachers of European history had to discontinue three advanced classes in October, 1918, in order to instruct 20 sections in the required subject. In 1919-1920 the department gave a course on the World War, which was elected by 75 students of sophomore or higher rank. This course also drew 24 auditors. Developments in Russia and the Balkan peninsula led to the offering of a course on Slavic Europe in 1920-1921.

Before the United States entered the war, the Department of American History grew more rapidly than that of European History. In 1915-1916 it made a gain of more than 300 students over the previous year, and in 1916-1917 it added about 280 more; but in 1917-1918, under war conditions, it lost about 155 students and in the following year about 230 more. Ten sections of the War Issues course were taught by members of this department in the fall of 1918, besides four sections of S. A. T. C. cadets who were taking the introductory course in American History. Thus, a total of 48 sections of the S. A. T. C. men were provided for by the two history departments, leaving as many more to be taught by teachers drawn from the Law School and other departments.

About 1,950 cadets were enrolled in these sections, the syllabus of which was prepared by a committee of instructors representing the two history departments under the chairmanship of Professor E. H. McNeal of the European History Department. Professor G. W. Knight of the American History Department was the director of the War Issues course. Three advanced courses in American history were discarded to make room as far as possible for the new sections. The organizing of the War Issues course for the S. A. T. C. cadets soon created a demand among the unenlisted students, including the young women, for a similar course. This new course was started on November 19, 1918, the public being admitted. At the outset the attendance ran as high as 300, seven sections being required. Credit was allowed for the course to students in the Colleges of Agriculture, Arts, and Education. Professor H. C. Hockett of the Department of American History was in charge of the course and secured the assistance of other members of that department, as also of the Departments of European History, Political Science, Economics, Sociology, and perhaps others.

The Departments of Philosophy and Political Science were both promoted by the war. It is true that none of the courses in political science was open to freshmen and that oll of them were more freely elected by men than by women, and yet such topics as the governments of Europe, problems in international politics, and international law could not but make a special appeal in wartime. Starting with 208 students in 1914-1915, the Political Science Department gained 87 the next year and 64 more the next. It lost 30 when we entered the war, and in 1918-1919 it lost 36 more. Despite these losses, the department came through at the end with about the same enrollment it had in 1915-1916. In the fall of 1919 it had about 100 more students than in any single semester during the war period.

For several years before the United States went to war the Department of Philosophy had been winning adherents at rates varying from 20 to 37 per cent *per annum*. The war appears to have accelerated this tendency. In 1915-1916 the department gained 113 students over the 303 it had in the previous year, and it gained 108 more in 1916-1917. As soon as we entered the war, withdrawals began from the advanced courses taken by seniors and graduate students. In 1917-1918 the attendance fell off to the extent of 79 students. However, this loss was more than recovered in the next year, the figure reaching 534, and in the fall of 1919 a considerable increase was made. The general conclusion to be drawn from these figures is that the war stimulated interest in philosophical questions, and it may be added that this interest was shown especially in ethics and social philosophy.

In the Departments of Geology, Greek, and Latin the attendance, as the table on page 149 indicates, was cut unevenly year by year from 1916-1917; but in the autumn of 1919 geology received a large influx of students, while the classical departments received relatively smaller ones. Besides cutting down the enrollment of the Department of Geology, the war deprived the department of part of its staff of teachers. Professor Thomas M. Hills had become interested in the relation of geography to the campaigns of the war and had given two lectures on this subject to his classes within a few days before the United States had entered the conflict. When the School of Military Aeronautics was established on the campus, in May, 1917, Professor Hills was selected to teach the course in aerial observation, for which maps and a miniature artillery range, with its scenic battlefield for practice in shell spotting, were devised by him. Professor Charles St. J. Chubb of the Department of Architecture, and Mr. Kenneth Cottingham and Mr. Arthur Bevan of the Geology Department assisted Professor Hills in preparing these accessories and in giving the course. At the close of the School of Military Aeronautics,

August 31, 1918, Mr. Cottingham entered military service at Camp Dick, Texas, with the rank of lieutenant. Meantime, Professor J. Ernest Carman of the Department of Geology had secured leave of absence and gone to Lake Geneva, Wis., in order to prepare himself for war work in the Y. M. C. A. In July, 1918, Professor Carman was sent to France, and from September 25 to December 10 he served as athletic secretary at Base Hospital No. 8 on the Loire River, near St. Nazaire. During the next six months he was connected with the educational branch of the Y. M. C. A., doing lecture-service work in France and western Germany. After 13 months abroad Professor Carman returned to the University.

The instruction ordinarily given by Professors Carman and Hills was carried on by Professors M. M. Leighton and W. M. Tucker, respectively, but when the Students' Army Training Corps was started in the fall of 1918, these two men, together with Professor Hills, were appointed to give the military work of a geological nature to the cadets in the new organization. The S. A. T. C. greatly increased the enrollment in the Geology Department; but the attendance of the cadets was very irregular, and their preparation was poor. They were much interested in the military phases of their training and not at all in geology.

The marked reduction in the enrollment of the Department of Latin during the war made possible the giving of a smaller number of courses and the combining of sections of lower classmen, thus enabling two of the instructors, Professors Wallace S. Elden and Arthur W. Hodgman, to devote about half of their time to teaching French. The failure of a number of former students to return in the fall of 1919 resulted in smaller advanced classes, but the lower classes showed an increase in numbers over the previous year amounting to more than 100 per cent, thus promising well for the future.

The Department of English derives its constituency from all the undergraduate colleges, as well as from the Graduate School. Its enrollment ranged from 4,100 to nearly 4,960 students during the war period, a large proportion of these being women. As compared with 1915-1916 the department recorded a gain of about 860 students in 1916-1917. When the war overtook us, English suffered a loss of 660 but recovered more than a third of this number in the year 1918-1919. With the great influx of new and war-belated students in the fall of 1919, the enrollment in the English Department was more than 3,800.

The effect of the European conflict upon the attendance of students and upon the courses of instruction offered by departments was much the same in the summer sessions as in the regular sessions. The enrollment of Arts College and arts-education students in the summer sessions just before, during, and after the war is given in the following tables:

ENROLLMENT IN THE COLLEGE OF ARTS, PHILOSOPHY, AND SCIENCE

	Men	Women	Total
Summer Session of 1916	157	113	270
Summer Session of 1917	82	124	206
Summer Session of 1918	112	156	268
Summer Session of 1919	244	180	424

ENROLLMENT OF THE ARTS-EDUCARION COURSE

	Men	Women	Total
Summer Session of 1916	15	14	29
Summer Session of 1917	7	25	32
Summer Session of 1918	3	13	16
Summer Session of 1919	5	14	19

Several points in the former of these two tables are deserving of comment. While the men lost 75 in number from the summer of 1916 to that of 1917 due to the war, the women made an appreciable gain. The men regained part of their loss in enrollment in the summer of 1918, the gain being 30. This time the women increased notably, that is, to 156. But in the summer of 1919, after America's share in the war had become a matter of history, the large increase was on the side of the men who gained 132, while the women only added 24 to their number of the previous summer. The increased attendance of male students was due to the return of young men from service to take the "make-up" courses that were offered in the summer of 1919 for their benefit. It should be added that pre-medical students utilized this summer session in meeting new requirements imposed by the American Medical Association.

The arts-education course is one of those intended for prospective teachers. The tabulation for this course shows that the number of men in it declined year by year, while the women gained 11 the second year but lost the succeeding two years. Obviously, war conditions were not favorable to young people going into teaching. In order to meet the need for enlightenment regarding world problems, Professor Frank J. Klingberg, who was temporarily connected with the Department of European History, gave a valuable course in the summer session of 1917 on the expansion of Europe since 1785, which, among other things, dealt with the rivalries of European Powers; it was attended by 75 or more students and auditors. During the latter part of July, 1917, the Department of American History offered three public lectures, two on the origin of American democracy and the third on the reasons for defending democracy. Patriotic education was the motive of these addresses, which were heard by 75 persons on the average. In the summer session of 1918 the Department of European History offered among its regular courses one on modern history from 1500 A.D., in which especial attention was given to the causes and events leading to the World War and another on the history of modern France. Both were unusually well attended for summer courses, the former attracting 35 students and the latter 60. The Department of American History gave a special course of 20 lectures, semi-popular in character and open to the public, on "The United States and the World War." One hundred and ten students enrolled for this series, which was also attended by about fifty visitors. The *Bulletin* of the summer session of 1919 contained the announcement of two new courses suggested by the war, one in American history and the other in European. The former was entitled "Some Revisions of American History" and dealt in particular with restatements concerning the relations of England and the United States at critical periods of the latter's history. It was given by Professor A. M. Schlesinger. The other course, called "Problems of World Peace and Reconstruction," was conducted by Professor G. A. Washburne of the Department of European History, with the assistance of certain members of other departments. The social, economic, and political conditions in the European countries at the signing of the Armistice, the work of the Peace Conference, the readjustment of international relations, etc., were among the topics considered. The course was semi-popular in character and was attended by 85 students and auditors.

Concerning the condition of the College of Arts as a whole during the war period something should be said. "As in all other colleges," wrote Dean J. V. Denney, "the work of the year 1917-1918 was prosecuted under serious difficulties. Chief of these was the unsettled condition of mind among students and faculty. Withdrawals of students were so numerous as to be noticeable in many classes. Changes of teachers were so frequent as to impair the quality of the work in several departments. Added to this was the physical discomfort in some buildings owing to inadequate heating and the uncertainty as to the continuance of college. All of these conditions were borne with good spirit, for the most part, as unavoidable in time of war and public excitement." During the summer and early autumn of 1918 the number of teachers and laboratory assistants, as well as students, going into war service was much increased, leaving certain departments short-handed. This condition was made decidedly worse in October, 1918, by the assignment of many instructors for most or all of their time to the teaching of classes in the Students' Army Training Corps, so that unavoidably many had to be transferred from certain departments to others, and new instructors had to be employed as fast as they could be obtained. Despite all these efforts to meet the situation, the educational work of the fall semester suffered seriously because of the disparity of military and academic authority in the S. A. T. C., the neglect of supervised study by the cadets, the interference of military duties with class attendance, and the wholesale "cutting" of classes by the cadets. The lack of sufficient fuel to heat some of the buildings adequately and the visitation of the influenza caused the irregularity, and at times the cessation, of the classes of the regular students.

After the signing of the Armistice in November, 1918, the demobilization of the S. A. T. C., and the return of a number of members of the Faculty from war service, the pressure in certain departments was relieved during the second semester. "Great commendation," said Dean Denney, "is due to those members who willingly undertook extra burdens of teaching during the war, as well as to those engaged directly in the service. The spirit of the faculty rose to all the requirements of war sacrifice."

By the authority of the University Faculty the executive committee of the Arts College granted credit to a maximum of eight semester hours to students returning from war service. This credit applied in substitution for elective work mainly. In pre-medical courses, however, it applied in substitution for any work excepting the sciences and English. Other universities also granted war credits, the amount of these credits varying in different institutions. For special technical work in military service a common practice of the universities, including Ohio State, was to determine the amount in each case by the departments concerned. In the College of Arts and the other colleges of the University S. A. T. C. credits were also reported by departments in the usual manner, the total actually obtained not exceeding in any case 14 hours and in the majority of cases not exceeding nine hours.

Practically all of the members of Arts College staff were engaged in patriotic service of one kind or another, many of them while attending to their regular duties in the University. The following statement is intended to be a complete enumeration of those who were granted leave of absence for the purpose of engaging in war work, or of entering the service.

COLLEGE OF ARTS 159

The services of Assistant Professor Walter T. Peirce of the Department of Romance Languages and Assistant Professor Albert A. Chandler of the Department of Philosophy, which were rendered in France and Italy, respectively, under the auspices of the American Red Cross and, in the case of Dr. Peirce, under those of the headquarters of the A. E. F. and the Peace Conference, have already been sufficiently noted in Chapter IV of this volume.

Mr. Theodore F. Kotz, instructor in German, who had returned from military service on the Mexican Border at the beginning of April, 1917, entered Camp Benjamin Harrison, Indiana, and enlisted in the 146th Motor Ambulance Company, 37th Division, 5th Corps, First Army. He was stationed at Camp Lee, Virginia. After November 1, 1918, he was with the 37th Division in France and Belgium, seeing service on the Lorraine and Argonne fronts and at the Army School at Langres, France. He received his discharge at Camp Sherman, April 12, 1919.

On September 1, 1917, Dr. Clarence E. Andrews of the Department of English was engaged as aeronautical engineer in the office of the chief signal officer in Washington, D. C. Five weeks later he was commissioned as a first lieutenant in the Air Service and continued in Washington as officer in charge of observation training and later of navigation. In August, 1918, he sailed for France, where he was detailed as information officer at the headquarters of the chief of the Air Service and later at the headquarters of the Air Service of the First Army at the front. In February, 1919, he was attached to the Balkan Division of the American Commission to negotiate peace, with which he remained connected until May, 1919. From this time to September Lieutenant Andrews served as an officer of the American Relief Administration in Serbian Macedonia and had the opportunity of traveling through the Balkan States. He spent the summer in organizing food relief in Macedonia. He was discharged from the service, October 15, 1919.

Dr. William E. Bingham, formerly assistant professor of

philosophy, enlisted in the Navy at the outbreak of hostilities as an ensign. In October, 1917, he was ordered to sea. While crossing Tangier Harbor, Morocco, in a small boat with six other men, December 2, 1918, the boat was swamped and Ensign Bingham was drowned. His sister, Miss Winnie Bingham, was one of the passengers on the *Lusitania* who lost their lives. Mr. Bingham had four brothers in the British Army, one of whom was killed in France.

Walter French of the Department of German, who received his degree of Ph.D. in June, 1918, enlisted as a private in the Infantry and was sent overseas in July. Later he became a sergeant in the Provisional Supply Company, Commissary Officers' Depot. At the end of April, 1919, he was at Gondrecourt, on the Meuse River in France, and was discharged from the service on the 24th of the following July.

After serving with the Home Guards in Columbus from the beginning of the war, Professor Berthold A. Eisenlohr, also of the Department of German, was appointed an assistant in the American Legation at the Hague, Holland, and left the University for his post, August 14, 1918. He remained on duty at the Hague until in April, 1919, when he was sent to Berlin, Germany, as a member of the American Mission. He left Berlin, July 18, 1919, and on his return to Holland was permitted to sail for the United States on a visit. He is still "visiting."

Professor Henry R. Spencer of the Department of Political Science, who was acting dean of the Graduate School at the time, sailed for France about December 1, 1917, in the service of the Y. M. C. A. From December 13 to the middle of the following February he was with the American Expeditionary Force and the French Fourth Army. He was then transferred to duty with the Italian Third Army, serving at Bologna and Mogliano. On July 1, 1918, he was made regional director of the Y. M. C. A., being stationed at the headquarters of the Third Army, about ten miles north of Venice, until Trieste and Trent were occupied by the Italian forces, November 3, 1918. From that time until the termination of his service a month later his headquarters were at Trieste. He returned to the University early in January, 1919.

Professor Charles A. Bruce of the Department of Romance Languages obtained a leave of absence from the University at the beginning of February, 1918, and entered the Educational Department of the Y. M. C. A. to teach French to the soldiers at Camp Sherman, Ohio. After less than two months of teaching he fell sick with a severe cold, about March 24, and returned to his home. Pneumonia developed, and he died on April 3. From the time of his graduation from the Ohio State University in 1895 Professor Bruce had been a teacher in Romance languages, with the exeception of a year spent in study in Paris and the brief period he was permitted to devote to the cause of his country.

Mr. Homer C. Haddox, another member of the Department of Romance Languages, after receiving training at Camp Sherman, Ohio, and Camp Merritt, New Jersey, was sworn in on May 8, 1918, as a private in the Medical Detachment of the 308th Regiment of Engineers, being attached to headquarters of the Eighty-third Division. In the following month he went overseas, and during the next 10 months he saw service in France, Belgium, Luxemburg, and Germany. In France he served with his regiment in the Aisne-Marne, Oise-Aisne, and Meuse- Argonne offensives. During the first half of February, 1919, he was in an evacuation hospital and until March 21 in Base Hospital 81. He was discharged from the Army, May 14, 1919.

Mr. Alexander P. Moore, also of the Department of Romance Languages, joined the Thirty-fifth Regiment of Engineers early in February, 1918, as civilian interpreter and served at Mimes, France, from April 15, 1918, to January 10, 1919. He returned to the United States and was discharged late in February of the latter year.

Several members of the instructional force of the College of Arts who enlisted were disappointed in not getting into the war. Assistant Professor Wilmer C. Harris of the Department of European History and Mr. Louis M. Eich, instructor in the Department of English, went into training at Camp Gordon, Georgia. The latter was promptly sent home on account of physical disability. Later he was drafted and again discharged for the same reason. The former spent several weeks in the strenuous life of the camp, only to have his hopes blasted by the signing of the Armistice. He resumed his duties in the University in January, 1919. Mr. Erwin A. Esper of the Department of English was sworn into the service in May, 1918, received his training at Camp Lee, Virginia, became a private in the Quartermaster's Department, Ship Repair Shop Unit No. 301, was promoted to sergeant, served at Hoboken, N. J, and was released, November 23, 1918. Mr. Sidney E. Mix, assistant in geology, entered the service as a private and was promoted to a second lieutenancy before his discharge. Mr. Waldo Schumacher, graduate assistant in political science, had been at several camps when the war closed.

A considerable number of the members of the Arts College Faculty rendered civilian service of various kinds during specified periods. Professor M. Blakemore Evans of the German Department was a special investigator in the United States Food Administration in Ohio during the summer of 1918. Professor J. R. Taylor of the Department of English, Professor E. H. McNeal of the Department of European History, and Professor H. C. Hockett of the Department of American History were assistants in the Sugar Division of the Food Administration. The members of the Romance Languages and German Departments, together with individual members of the Philosophy, English, European History, Greek, and Latin Departments, formed an organization under the chairmanship of Professor M. B. Evans at the request of the postoffice to read foreign-language newspapers. Only one of these Government translators was given an opportunity to perform a task of importance, namely, Professor George M. Bolling of the Department of Greek, who spent about 100 hours in reading a set of Lithuanian newspapers published in the United States.

Other members of the Faculty of the College of Arts,

Philosophy, and Science who were engaged in military or civilian service were Professors William McPherson, William L. Evans, and James R. Withrow of the Department of Chemistry; James E. Hagerty and Matthew B. Hammond of the Department of Economics and Sociology; Major George L. Converse of the Department of Military Science and Tactics; Professor E. F. McCampbell of the Department of Preventive Medicine; Professor Frederick C. Blake of the Department of Physics; Professor George F. Arps of the Department of Psychology; Professor Osman C. Hooper of the Department of Journalism; Professor Victor A. Ketcham of the Department of English, and Professor John H. Nichols of the Department of Physical Education. As these gentlemen were members of one or another of the other college Faculties, their special services are briefly chronicled in other chapters. No attempt has been made here or elsewhere in this volume to set down the long list of the names of those members of the Faculty who participated in the Liberty Loan and similar campaigns, or in some other forms of service incidental to the war. A complete enumeration of such activities would be impossible.

Several members of the Arts College staff wrote and spoke on various themes connected with the war. Mr. John R. Knipfing, who became an instructor in European history in the fall of 1917, was pursuing graduate study in Germany when the United States entered the conflict. In various trips about the German Empire he had collected considerable data in regard to the conditions prevailing in that country. Having secured permission to leave Germany, he proceeded to Copenhagen and there entered the service of the American consul-general as a translator of the editorials contained in representative German newspapers concerning the action of the United States Government. His translations were cabled to the secretary of state at Washington. After Mr. Knipfing associated himself with the Department of European History, he was several times called on to address audiences at the University, in Columbus, and elsewhere on war conditions in Germany, and two or three of his communications on the same topic were printed in the *New York Times*. In the summer of 1917 Professor Joseph A. Leighton of the Department of Philosophy had an article in the *Scientific Monthly,* in which he dwelt upon the opportunity of the United States to do more than any other country toward founding a new international order.

Professor J. V. Denney of the Department of English wrote for the *Ohio State University Monthly* of April, 1918, a paper on "War and Poetry," in which he characterized the verse inspired by the World War as a poetry of ideals rather than of the old "drum and trumpet" kind, a fact which he attributed to the presence of many poets, artists and university men in the armies of the Allies and also to the large number of reading and thinking men in those armies. Professor Denney maintained that the Germans, aside from their "Hymn of Hate," produced a "literature of release," the object of which was "to take the mind off the war" for "despotism has yet to find a poet to sing its praises."

Professor Clarence E. Andrews, also of the Department of English, while serving as a first lieutenant in the Aviation Section of the Signal Reserve Corps, compiled a volume of trench poetry which was published by D. Appleton & Co. in the summer of 1918. It was entitled *From the Front* and contained for the most part poems by authors who had never written verse before. Some of these poems were written in camp, billet or dugout, in the trenches, under fire or in the convalescent hospital. Among the better-known poems included in Professor Andrews' collection are: Rupert Brooke's "The Soldier," Alan Seegar's "I Have a Rendezvous with Death," Robert W. Service's "Rhymes of a Red Cross Man," Sergeant J. W. Street's "The Undying Splendor," and Lieutenant Colonel John McRae's "In Flanders Fields." The royalties from the sale of the book went to the British Red Cross fund.

During July and August, 1918, the weekly Convocations of the students of the summer session were addressed on subjects suggested by the war, as follows: "Gas Warfare," by Professor C. W. Foulk; "Woodrow Wilson," by Professor Wilbur H. Siebert; "Education and the War," by Professor J. H. Coursault, and "Educational Problems of a Nation at War," by President W. O. Thompson.

Professor Wallace C. Sabine, B.A. '86, physicist at Harvard University, rendered a greater variety of important war services than any other graduate of the University. His opportunity came through his being appointed by the Harvard authorities as exchange professor to deliver the Sarbonne Lectures at the University of Paris. His subject was Acoustics, of which he was the recognized authority. He and his family sailed in July, 1916, and had scarcely reached Paris when both Professor and Mrs. Sabine were asked by the Rockefeller War Relief Commission to engage in the work it had in hand, with headquarters at Berne, Switzerland. Sabine's first war work kept him in Berne two months, looking after the hospitalization of hundreds of Belgian children and sending condensed milk to Polish and Serbian babies. Then he was transferred to France to investigate tuberculosis. Late in September he sent off his report on this subject to the Rockefeller Foundation in New York City. In this report he called attention to the fact that at the beginning of the war there was more tuberculosis in France than in any other country of western Europe, and that it had greatly increased under war conditions. Furthermore, France had but few hospitals for the treatment of tubercular patients, and these few were of low standards of practice. The situation must be handled diplomatically so as not to offend the French, and therefore Sabine recommended the study of the situation by a small international commission which might not only serve France but also find the best method for any national endeavor against tuberculosis.

As a result of this report the Rockefeller Foundation sent over a representative to establish in France, in cooperation with the French Government and the medical profession, a dispensary, publicity, and training demonstration for the purpose of helping to control tuberculosis. Hitherto there had been only twelve tuberculosis dispensaries. During the next six years these were increased to one hundred and sixty-eight. "Subventions were granted for the building of sanatoria, training-schools were conducted for public health visitors, offering a two-years' course, and a graduate course in tuberculosis was completed by 175 dispensary physicians. The work of the Foundation was transferred to the French Government in 1922."

Sabine's Sarbonne Lectures began late in February, 1917, and ran into May. At their cessation he was asked to help in the Information Bureau of the United States Navy in Paris in finding ways of detecting approaching submarines. At about the same time he became adviser to the French *Bureau des Inventions* on the submarine problem and on the scientific instruments used in airplanes. He was also placed at once on the staff of the Bureau of Research of the Air Service of the American Expeditionary Force, becoming an assistant to Colonel E. S. Gorrell, assistant chief of staff, who was then in charge of the Technical Section of the Air Service. Simultaneously Sabine received a request from the British Munitions Inventions Bureau to come to England for consultation on some problems in acoustics.

He first went down to Toulon, the Mediterranean base of the French fleet, where he descended in a submarine and discussed with the high authorities the problem of detecting enemy submarines at a distance. He made another descent in an Italian submarine at Spezia, where he continued his experiments in sound detection. Having been authorized by Colonel Gorrell to travel through Italy, France, and England in order to learn all he could concerning the technical features of and air service in wartime, and being invited by the Italian authorities, Sabine made several flights in bombing-planes over the Austrian lines in the Trentino. With a special camera devised by him, he took numerous photographs of the enemy's works. One of these disclosed thirty-two hitherto unknown Austrian hangars. In the late summer of 1917 Sabine was in the great Italian offensive on the Isonzo—the Carso—with the shells flying overhead in both directions. He was also in a great bombarding aeroplane over the Adriatic and Trieste. On September 3 he went out over the Mediterranean in a dirigible and shortly thereafter he flew out from Genoa in a hydroaeroplane. Every facility was given him in Italy to study the problems which had been submitted to him.

Sabine next went to England in answer to the invitation of the Munitions Inventions Department. The first problem given him was the failure of the English anti-aircraft shells to explode in the air when fired at enemy planes crossing the English Channel. The shells exploded along the coat, inflicting terrific damage. Sabine found two things to be the matter: (1) that the internal mechanism was set at too high a speed, and (2) that the powder did not explode during the flight of the shell because it was pressed between the seams. The shell burst only when it struck the ground. He was at once attached to the Aviation Section of the Signal Corps and served part of the time on the Bolling Aircaft Commission.

While thus engaged, Sabine found that military etiquette was preventing the mutual understanding of complicated problems between the Air Services of England, France, and Italy. Having won the confidence of those high in authority in the three countries by his practical, scientific ability, he was given the initiative as "an uncommissioned confidential liaison agent" to arrange conferences between them. He thus facilitated a direct exchange of technical information and the discussion of their common military problems.

Colonel A. D. Butterfield has characterized Sabine as "the eyes and ears of the Technical Section of the Air Service" of the American Expeditionary Force. His service to the Allied cause lasted during seventeen months. His last conference before sailing for Boston, in Septemb, 1917, was with the authorities at the "American Front."

He brought back a number of official papers entrusted to him by the Allied Governments and carried them immediately to Washington, where he also made a report of conditions as he had found them. The great value of his information was appreciated, and he was desired to give it to Colonel E. A.

Deeds, chief of the Equipment Division of the Aviation Section of the Signal Corps. After hearing him, Colonel Deeds immediately made Sabine a member of his staff and gave him a desk in an adjoining office. However, Sabine refused a lieutenant colonel's commission. He passed upon all cablegrams regarding apparatus, kept the Allies informed of the progress in the Air Service of the United States, and interpreted their development to the high officers of ours. He was soon made the final authority on the selection of instruments for production from those received from abroad, and he sent to those particularly interested the confidential, technical information arriving from many sources after having sifted it.

During the winter of 1917-1918 Sabine made frequent official trips from Washington to the Wright Flying Field at Dayton, Ohio, in connection with experiments on airplanes and aircraft equipment, despite the poor state of his health during this period. Nevertheless, after the separation of the Air Service from the Signal Corps in the spring of 1918, he was appointed director of the newly created Department of Technical Information in the Bureau of Aircrafe Production and organized the department. In this capacity he was responsible for the securing, collating, and distributing of the technical data received from the British Ministry of War and Munitions; the British, French, and Italian War and Aviation Missions; the scientific attaches accredited to the American Embassies in London, Paris, and Rome by the National Research Council; and a special Mission sent abroad by the Bureau of Aircraft Production. He also cooperated closely with the Naval Aviation Information and with the National Advisory Committee for Aeronautics. Sabine's extensive acquaintance among French, Italian, and English officers and with the leaders in the American Air Service enabled him to gather practically all information of value for distribution.

During the entire period of his service in Washington Sabine was teaching his classes at Harvard during a part of each week. He arrived in Cambridge from Washington at eight o'clock on Tuesday morning and devoted himself to his university work until he was ready to return on the midnight train on Thursday. A School of Aviation was then in progress at Harvard, and Sabine realized that its students needed to know something about the laws of shell flight and the effect of the density and piling up of the air in front of moving projectiles. He therefore gave them a course on aviation ballistics, inducing Professor William F. Osgood to present the mathematical aspects of the subject.

During the summer of 1918 Sabine experienced an alarming return of his kidney trouble, but would not give up and submit to a surgical operation. "Not while the War is on and other lives are in danger," he said. However, he could not see his way clear to going back to France "to become the head of a bureau of technical information, which should serve as a clearing house for the aeronautical service of the United States and of the Associated Governments.

Sabine continued to perform his duties in Washington until the Armistice, November 11, 1918, relieved him of them. His connection with the Bureau of Aircraft Production had already terminated. By the end of November he completed his work in Washington and sent in his resignation to Secretary of War Baker as one of the representatives of the War Department on the National Advisory Committee for Aeronautics. He was still the editor-in-chief of the Specification Section of the Experimental Engineering Department, and as such his duty was to record the development of engineering work in the Bureau of Aircraft Production. After the Armistice he served on the Committee of Science and Research and Aeronautical Development, which was a subcommittee of the Board for the Organization of the Air Service on a peace basis. He wrote the report containing important recommendations as to the steps and organization for the proper development of aeronautics and its promotion for commercial purposes.

At length, in December, 1918, Sabine underwent a preliminary operation in Boston, which afforded him temporary relief. On January 5, 1919, he returned to the hospital and had the major operation. His reserves of vitality had been so impaired by his unstinted services since the summer of 1916 that he survived only a few days, his death occurring on July 10.[1]

Mr. Halbert E. Payne, Arts '87, joined the group of Ohio State workers in Washington, D. C., March 1, 1918, and was later commissioned a captain in the Aviation Section, Signal Corps. His work was especially concerned with the materials for airplane production. In the spring of 1918 Henry L. Rietz, '99, professor of mathematics at the University of Illinois, was called to Washington for special war work in the Quartermaster Department under General G. W. Goethals. Arthur F. Graves-Walker of Baltimore, a former member of the class of 1905, was chosen by the United States fuel administrator, Dr. Harry A. Garfield, as chief of the Division of Manufacturing Fuels, with headquarters at the national capital. His task was to supervise the use of all fuel in the country, except that used in firing steam boilers. He had under his direction a large force of engineers as plant inspectors to promote the conservation of coal.

The Washington colony of Ohio State graduates was not without its women members. Miss Thelma L. Lyons, Arts '17, was employed in the Executive Division, Military Intelligence Branch of the War Department, and Miss Katherine Krauss, Arts '91, served as library assistant in the Division of Military Aeronautics.

After having been engaged as a civilian during the summer of 1918 in the Quartermaster's Department, Mr. Carl E. Steeb, '99, business manager of the University and secretary to the Board of Trustees, was commissioned a major in the same department late in September. He served as liaison officer at headquarters in Washington, where for a period he was in charge of quartermaster training. He also saw service at Camp Johnson, Florida, and at Camp Meigs, in the District of Columbia. He was discharged in December, 1918.

---

[1] The above account of Sabine's war services has been taken from the volume, *Wallace Clement Sabine, A Study in Achievement*. By William Dana Orcutt. Plimpton Press, Norwood, Mass. 1933.

A class in trap-shooting, Army School of Military Aeronautics

Professor H. C. Lord conducting a class in aids to flight

Graduating Exercises of a Unit of the Army School of Military Aeronautics

A University wartime parade passing the State House, Columbus, Ohio

CHAPTER XII

THE COLLEGE OF COMMERCE AND JOURNALISM IN WARTIME

The academic year 1916-17 marked the entrance of the Department of Journalism into the newly organized College of Commerce and Journalism. Undoubtedly the war greatly reduced the attendance in the new college, inasmuch as it was a senior college in which only third- and fourth-year students were enrolled. In the fall of 1916 the registration was 77 and in the following February, 82. Almost a third of this number withdrew in the early part of May, 1917, when 16 students left the University to go into farm work and 9 others, into military service, under permission from the Faculty. In September the college enrolled 97 students; but five months later the attendance fell to 64, a drop of $33\frac{1}{3}$ per cent. In the fall of 1918 the number of regular students in the college was 62, to which should be added 16 cadets of the Students' Army Training Corps, making a total of 78. The spring semester, following the signing of the Armistice in November, was marked by the return of a number of men and the registration of a few new students, bringing the enrollment up to 103, and when the college opened in September, 1919, it jumped to 251. Similar conditions are revealed in the number of students in Commerce and Journalism attending the summer sessions of 1917, 1918, and 1919, namely, 7, 9, and 41, respectively.

From the time of its completed organization the College of Commerce and Journalism comprised only two departments, namely, (1) Economics and Sociology and (2) Journalism. The former of these departments drew students from several colleges, besides that of Commerce and Journalism. Its attendance was, therefore, a reliable index of the general attendance in the University. The enrollment of the first semester of 1917-18 in economics was 1,097 and in sociology 411, making a total enrollment of 1,508. But this was 200 less than the enrollment in the year 1916-17, and reflected the reduced enrollment in the University at large for the former year.

The Department of Journalism experienced a progressive decline in attendance during the years of the war, a part of this attendance coming from the College of Arts, Philosophy, and Science. The total number of students in journalism for the year 1916-17 was 319; for 1917-18, 239; for 1918-19, 173, and for 1919-20 it rose to 210.

When the Faculty order dismissing students to enter productive or military service went into effect, May 1, 1917, it took about three-fourths of the young men of the department; but classroom and laboratory exercises were carried on with those remaining. In the fall of 1917 the department suffered a greatly reduced enrollment as to men, although a considerable number registered while awaiting the call to service. Most of these dropped out within a month or two. All courses of instruction were maintained throughout the academic year 1917-18, despite the reduced attendance. In the fall of 1918 the enrollment in journalism reached its lowest point, the record for the beginning course being indicative of the others. In this course 17 men registered, and 20 women, whereas in previous years the enrollment had been about 75 per cent men. Of these 17 men 10 withdrew to enter the Students' Army Training Corps, or other war service. The advance courses were very small, and what few men remained were either ineligible to service, or were awaiting a call to the Navy. The *Ohio State Lantern,* the University daily paper, for the first time in history was conducted largely by women students, who held several responsible positions on its staff, including that of business manager. Even the carriers were women. The half-year following the signing of the Armistice saw the return of a number of men to journalism, some of whom had started in it the preceding September. The effect of the war on the upper classes in journalism is shown in the number of graduates in the subject during this period. Instead of eight or ten graduates in 1918, the first year the degree in journalism was conferred, there were only two, one a woman, and the other a man who went into service on Commencement Day. In 1919 three received degrees, one being a man who normally would have graduated in 1918.

During the first half-year of 1918-19 many of the courses in the College of Commerce and Journalism were omitted, on account of the absence in war work or military service of a large number of the teachers. Out of a staff of 23 instructors 17 were engaged in war service of one kind or another, some giving continuous service almost from the beginning of our entrance into the conflict, and others giving their full time during only a part of the war period. With the return of several of the absentees for the second half-year of 1918-19 and the employment of new teachers, all but a few of the courses in the college were carried on during the second half-year.

The attempt is made below to present the record of those members of the college staff who engaged in war work; but it should be remembered that the others who remained at their posts were rendering an important service, which was expected by the Government and the State, albeit a less conspicuous one. At the organization of the Columbus Chapter of the Red Cross in the spring of 1917, Dean James E. Hagerty was appointted chairman of the Civilian Relief Committee and as such became chairman of the Home Service Subcommittee. He directed the work of material and advisory aid of the families of soldiers and soilors, giving to the men needed information before going to camp and after discharge, and to their families information and aid of various kinds until the readjustment to industrial and community life was complete. He organized a corps of investigators which was aided by a Consultation Committee that met at stated intervals to consider the more difficult problems. Professor Osman C. Hooper of the Department of Journalism served on this committee.

At the invitation of the National Red Cross Dr. Hagerty

organized at the University a Home Service Institute for the training of investigators and office managers in civilian relief work, and this institute was conducted under the joint auspices of the National Red Cross, the Columbus Chapter of the Red Cross, and the University Department of Economics and Sociology. Three classes were instructed, one in 1917 and two in 1918, each doing six weeks of classroom and field work, the latter in connection with local philanthropic organizations. Some of the students became volunteer workers in the Civilian Relief Department of the Columbus Red Cross Chapter, while others returned to the counties from which they came to render similar service. A number of permanent social workers came out of these classes.

Dean Hagerty served as an adviser to the Federal Food administrator in Ohio, chiefly on problems of marketing, from September, 1917, until February, 1918. He was then granted leave of absence from the University and gave his whole time to the food administration as head of the Division of Marketing, which exercised general supervision over price fixing and middlemen's margins. This involved the regulation and control of margins on feeds, grocers' and jobbers' margins, the fixing of prices of bread and ice, the maximum prices of seed corn, and the prices of milk until the Ohio Milk Commission was formed. As deputy food administrator Dr. Hagerty served on a committee that visited Camp Sherman in July, 1918, to see to what extent food conservation was practiced there and secure the cooperation of the officers in charge of the camp in preventing waste of foods of all kinds. As the camp accommodated 40,000 soldiers, and its officers pledged their support to the Food Administration in this matter, Dr. Hagerty's committee was successful in its mission. Professor Joseph S. Myers, head of the Department of Journalism, gave much time to war work, while carrying a full schedule of teaching in the University. He acted as publicity agent for the first Red Cross drive and was a member of the campus branch of the American Protective League and of the executive committee that conducted the campus campaign for the

Community War Chest and the Liberty Loan drives. He also served as a member of the Red Cross committee that made a survey of the supply of nurses in Franklin County. In the summer of 1918, when there was a pressing need for nurses, a campaign was organized in Columbus for the enrollment of graduate nurses and of young women willing to take the training necessary to become nurses. Professor Myers was chairman of the committee that opened headquarters at the Deshler Hotel and in two weeks succeeded in enrolling 203 nurses and 126 young women willing to take the training. His work on the committee that visited training camps to obtain for the University records the names of Ohio State men in the service is referred to elsewhere.

Professor M. B. Hammond's first war work began on April 23, 1917, when he was released from the University to organize employment offices in Springfield, Hamilton, and Washington C. H. as part of the plan of the Ohio Branch of the Council of National Defense for fourteen new employment offices, in addition to the seven already in existence. All of these offices were to be utilized in mobilizing the labor forces of the State. After a few weeks Dr. Hammond was asked to extend his field of operations so as to include southeastern Ohio, where offices had been opened by other organizers at Chillicothe, Athens, Marietta, Steubenville, and Portsmouth. These employment offices were usually established by the joint action of the State and the municipality concerned, the latter supplying suitable rooms, furniture, and the other accessories, while the former paid the salaries of the superintendents and clerks. It was the function of Dr. Hammond to pay weekly visits to the offices within his territory, in order to give supervision and direction to their work. He continued to act as supervisor until June, 1917, when his task was assumed by the regular supervisors of the State Employment Service. At this time the fuel situation in Ohio was threatening to become acute. As a member of the Ohio Coal Mining Commission of 1913, Professor Hammond had gained some insight into the economic and social conditions of the coal-mining industry.

He was therefore requested by the Council of Defense to investigate and report on the conditions in eastern Ohio that were retarding coal production in that region. After this had been done, Dr. Hammond served on as secretary of Governor Cox's Special Coal Committee, with some of the leading coal operators of the State, in formulating plans for improving the coal situation in Ohio. The labors of this committee ceased in July, 1917, when the United States Fuel Administration was established.

At the end of the month just named Dean David Kinley of the University of Illinois, director of the Research Department of Economics and Politics for the Carnegie Endowment for International Peace, invited Professor Hammond to prepare a preliminary study of British labor conditions during the war, the work to be carried on as far as possible in Washington. Accordingly, Dr. Hammond pursued investigations in the Library of Congress during August and September and again during the Christmas holidays, and completed his monograph nearly a year later. This work, which numbers 350 pages, has since been published by the Carnegie Endowment under the title *British Labor Conditions During the War*.

During the early part of 1918 Dr. Hammond was, among others, called to Washington to attend a conference of the Advisory Committee of the United States Department of Labor, then formulating plans for the organization of the United States Employment Service. In June of this year Dr. Hammond was granted leave of absence from the University, in response to a request from Mr. Herbert Hoover, director of the United States Food Administration, that he be permitted to serve on the National War Labor Policies Board. This board was composed of one representative from each of the following departments: War, Navy, Agriculture, the United States Shipping Board, the Emergency Fleet Corporation, the Food, Fuel, and Railroad Administrations, and the War Industries Board. Heads of various bureaus of the Department of Labor also sat with the War Labor Policies Board and served on its committees. The work of this board dealt chiefly with securing coordination and introducing a uniform labor policy among those departments of the Government that were employing labor in productive operations on a large scale, especially the Ordnance and Construction Divisions of the War and Navy Departments and the Emergency Fleet Corporation. Dr. Hammond served on committees on industrial furloughs, standardization of wages, cost of living, employment service policy, agricultural cooperation, and also on the committee that devised the plan for requiring centralized recruiting of unskilled labor by public and private employers through the United States Employment Service and secured deferred classification for industrial registrants under the Second Selective Act whose services would be of more value in industry than in the Army. The work of this last committee was particularly important, and may probably be regarded as one of the most significant contributions of the War Labor Policies Board in solving war problems. Its recommendations were adopted by the War Department and incorporated in the Second Selective Service Act and in the rules adopted for the enforcement of that act.

On his arrival in Washington in June, 1918, Professor Hammond became not only the representative of the Federal Food Administration on the War Labor Policies Board, but also the labor adviser to the Food Administration itself by Mr. Hoover's appointment. The heads of all divisions of the Food Administration were instructed to transmit their labor problems through Professor Hammond as head of the Labor Division. These problems came up from the employers of labor in all the various food-producing industries. The solving of these questions occupied more of Dr. Hammond's time and attention than did the business that came before the War Labor Policies Board. The most important work of the Labor Division was in discovering and making available new sources of labor and in suggesting more effective ways of using the labor power already existing. With the help of technical experts of the Food Administration, the Labor Division prepared *A List of the Most Important Occupations and Employments in the Food Producing Industries under the Supervision of the United States Food Administration.* This list made a pamphlet of sixty pages, which was sent to all District Draft Boards, the federal food administrators of the various States, and the United States Employment Service examiners. The object in preparing and distributing this pamphlet was to assist the District Draft Boards and others in determining what were the essential occupations in the food industries, so that the highly skilled men engaged in these occupations might be granted deferred classification for military service and thus kept in the industries. As a further means of safeguarding the essential industries the adjutant general's office was authorized by the general staff of the Army to issue indefinite furloughs to approved industrial applicants. No industrial furloughs in the food-producing industries were granted, except on recommendation of Dr. Hammond, who was appointed certifying officer in the Food Administration and passed on hundreds of applications for such furloughs. The Labor Division also assisted in securing the temporary release from Army camps of hundreds of men whose services were greatly needed in the harvesting of crops.

During December, 1918, Dr. Hammond gave much of his time to the planning of normal courses for the training of examiners in the offices of the Federal Employment Service, who, in turn, were to instruct the local examiners in the various States. Although released from service at the end of December, he remained in Washington during the following month, still engaged in this work and also in serving as assistant director of the course given to nearly a hundred examiners from the northeastern group of States. Dr. Hammond returned to his duties at Ohio State University, February 1, 1919.

Assistant Professor Carl E. Parry of the Department of Economics and Sociology served as secretary of the Committee on Patriotic Education, Ohio Branch, Council of National Defense, from November, 1917, until January 1, 1919. During the months from February to June, inclusive, of 1918, he was on leave of absence from the University for this purpose. For one month, July 15 to August 15, 1918, Dr. Parry was secretary of the Speaking Division of the Committee on Public Information at Washington. During most of his period of service Dr. Parry's principal duties were those connected with the direction of the Speakers' Division of the Ohio Branch, Council of National Defense, mainly in cooperation with the Speaking Division of the Committee on Public Information. The primary purpose of the Speakers' Bureau was to promote the understanding of the war on the part of the general public. The bureau made use of but few Ohio speakers, for it had the opportunity of employing the services of French and Italian officers who knew intimately conditions in Europe. Among these were Lieutenant Paul Perigord of the French Army and Lieutenant Bruno Rosselli of the Italian Army.

The Speakers' Bureau, under Dr. Parry's supervision, also cooperated with the Federal Food Administration in Ohio to the end of carrying its message into all parts of the State. Its functions in this connection were: (a) the scheduling, routing, and management of special food speakers supplied by the Food Administration at Washington; (b) the enrollment and assignment of Ohio speakers for addresses in various localities; and (c) the preparation of bulletins and information sheets for the use of local speakers on food subjects throughout the State. Perhaps the most comprehensive speaking program carried out in Ohio during the war was that filled by six outside speakers, who were sent into the State by the Federal Food Administration in March, 1918, and spoke in some eighty towns and cities. They traveled about 2,000 miles in Ohio and addressed approximately 40,000 auditors. All of the cities of the State with a population of 20,000 or over and about half of the smaller cities that are county seats were visited at least once by some speaker furnished by the Speakers' Bureau. In the summer of 1918, through an arrangement with the Chautauqua Bureau, two food experts were sent over addresses and demonstrations to large assemblies. The gencircuits, by which they were enabled to give more than fifty eral result of all this effort was, no doubt, to help impress on the minds of the people of Ohio the need of economy in the use of foods and especially to increase the popular understanding of the European peoples and of some of the issues involved in the war.

On October 2, 1917, Dr. Cecil C. North, assistant professor in economics and sociology, was granted leave of absence and was engaged in war work during the next thirteen months. Dr. North organized the War Camp Community Service at Louisville, Kentucky, and had charge of it for eight months. He also directed similar work in El Paso, Texas, for two months and in Detroit, Michigan, for three months.

After six months' service at the head of the Civilian Relief work at Camp Sherman, Mr. Roderick D. McKenzie, instructor in economics and sociology, became a special investigator in the Division of Prices of the Food Administration in Ohio, May 1, 1918. Mr. Shirley J. Coon of the same department at the University became associated with Mr. McKenzie in a similar capacity on June 6, 1918, having served for two months of the previous summer in the Ohio Branch of the Council of National Defense. The aim of the investigations of these two economists was to keep the Food Administration informed in regard to the war prices of food commodities, with a view of insuring "fair and reasonable" prices. The passage of the Food Control Act in August, 1917, resulting in the establishment of the Federal Food Administration and its State branches, supplied adequate authority and the centralized agencies for this purpose. In order to exercise this function properly, the Federal Food Administration in Ohio organized its Division of Prices, October 1, 1917. Mr. McKenzie remained connected with the division until September 7, 1918, and Mr. Coon until September 21 of the same year, "by which time much of the pioneer work had been completed."

Miss Mary Louise Mark, instructor in economics and sociology, was the statistical adviser to the Food Administration in Ohio from December 27, 1917, to January 15, 1919. Assistant Professor Henry F. Walradt of the same department served as an assistant in the Sugar Division during the summer of 1918, as did his associate, Mr. Donald R. Taft. During the first half-year of 1918-19 Dr. Walradt was absent from the University on leave while in the employment of the United States Shipping Board in Washington.

Another member of the Department of Economics and Sociology who was connected with the Shipping Board was Professor Clyde O. Ruggles. In August, 1919, Dr. Ruggles was called to Washington to direct an investigation into the terminal charges at the ports of the United States. The investigation included all charges incident to the coordination of rail and water carriers, and involved some examination of port terminal services as affected by private ownership of port terminal facilities and the absence of any Government control; the industrial use of a port; exclusive contracts between ocean and rail carriers, and lack of coordination among rail carriers themselves or between rail and water carriers. The work was completed in January, 1919, the results being embodied in a published report of 180 pages, entitled *Terminal Charges at United States Ports*. Under Part I it deals with such subjects as general characteristices of port terminal charges, methods of investigation, comparison of charges at various ports, advances in port charges during the war, and consequences of present policies concerning port charges and services. Under Part II is given a general description of terminal facilities and port charges at ten principal ports, a comparative view of important charges in these ports, and an account of terminal facilities and port charges at other ports. The report recommended the establishment of a bureau of the United States Shipping Board to deal with port terminal charges and service. The duties of such a bureau would be to collect the latest information concerning port charges and services and, in cooperation with the Interstate Commerce Commission and local port authorities, to enforce equitable charges and require such joint use of port facilities and such coordination of rail and water carriers as would prevent congestion in ports and resulting embargoes upon the railroads leading thereto.

Professor Oliver C. Lockhart of the Department of Economics and Sociology was on leave of absence in New York City during the year 1918-19, and was engaged in war work there. Mr. William F. Bloor, instructor in the same department, spent the summer of 1918 in the office of the Federal Trade Commission in Washington. Other instructors who were absent from this department were: Mr. George Gephart, who gave a year's service in 1917-18 in the office of the State Draft Headquarters; Mr. Harry E. Shepperd, who was employed in the same office for several months; Mr. Herman C. Miller, who left to enter the Navy at the beginning of September, 1917; Mr. George W. Eckelberry, who departed in the winter of 1917-18 to enter the Air Service; Mr. Horace B. Drury, who served from May, 1918, until after the end of the war in the Marine and Dock Industrial Relations Division of the United States Shipping Board in Washington; and Mr. Warner E. Gettys, who resigned to go into the Medical Service with a base hospital.

It is not known how many students and graduates of the College of Commerce and Journalism enlisted in the Army and Navy, but undoubtedly the college was represented in the armed forces of the United States by its full proportion. This is suggested by the fact that records in the possession of the Department of Journalism show that nearly a hundred of its students were in the service during the war. One of these, Lawrence C. Yerges, died of wounds received in action; another, Carl A. Geiger, died of disease contracted in a training camp; and a third, William Paul Bancroft, died after the war from causes directly traceable to service in the Army.

CHAPTER XIII

THE COLLEGE OF DENTISTRY, THE DENTAL CLINIC, AND MILITARY SERVICE

The College of Dentistry, like the other colleges in the University, felt the ill effect of the war before the United States entered the conflict in April, 1917. This ill effect was shown most clearly in the reduction of the enrollment during the year 1916-1917. At the beginning of the first half-year the number of students in the college was 162; at the beginning of the second it was 157. When the University Faculty excused young men from all the colleges to go into agricultural or other Government service in the early part of May,, 1917, seven dental students withdrew to engage in farm work and two to enter military service. The participation of the United States in the war lowered considerably the number of students enrolling in the fall of 1917, this number being only 133. The same number registered in February, 1918. This maintenance of numbers is explained by two things. In the first place, Congress enacted a law, October 6, 1917, permitting all dental students to become members in the Medical Enlisted Reserve Corps, Dental Section. This enabled them to remain in college to complete their studies. Those who were twenty-one years of age or over and physically fit availed themselves of this opportunity. The number entering the reserve corps was 83. However, such students were sent into active service whenever their marks fell below a certain grade. In the second place, during the year 1917-18 former students who were already in active service were sent back by the Government and allowed to enter the reserve corps, so that they might fit themselves for better service. The establishment of the Students' Army Training Corps at the University, October 1,

1918, brought 82 cadets of that organization into the Dental College, in addition to the regular students, and sent the enrollment to 196. In February, 1919, that is, after the signing of the Armistice and the demobilization of the S.A.T.C., the enrollment dropped to the low level of 85. Before the close of this half-year two seniors and three sophomores returned from active military service. Conditions became normal in September, 1919, when 166 students were registered in the college. The changing conditions of the war period were reflected in miniature in the attendance of dental students at the summer sessions of 1917, 1918, and 1919. In the first of these sessions only 3 students enrolled; in the second, 13; and in the third, 9.

During the first week in May, 1917, the Faculty of the College of Dentistry passed resolutions in favor of the dental colleges of the country offering their services to the Government and proposing that all dental students joining the Dental Section of the Officers' Reserve Corps should take a course in military dentistry at one of these colleges. It was recommended that some of the instructors in dentistry at Ohio State enlist in the Officers' Reserve Corps in anticipation of giving dental treatment to recruits at the college clinic. In truth, while Camp Willis was at Upper Arlington in the summer of 1916, the dental clinic of the University had treated hundreds of the men who were stationed in the camp until they should be sent to the Mexican Border. This experience had not been confined to the College of Dentistry in Columbus, and there was, therefore, a general movement among dental colleges and individual dentists to respond promptly to the needs of American soldiers and recruits in case the United States went into the World War. This general movement resulted in the organizing of the Preparedness League of Dental Surgeons in the spring of 1917. As a participant in this league the College of Dentistry was in a position to open its clinic and give free dental services to "the recruits, the selected men from the draft, and the National Guardsmen" who were mustered into the federal service. During the spring, summer, and fall of

1917 about five hundred young men were treated at the clinic before being sent to their cantonments. This clinical work was done by the members of the senior class of the college under the supervision of their instructors. Most of the other dental colleges of the country were giving similar services to the Government.

After the establishment of the Dental Section of the Officers' Reserve Corps, June 1, 1917, by the Federal Government acting through the surgeon general's office, some five thousand dentists enlisted in this organization and received commissions as lieutenants, captains, and majors. About half of these were sent into active service. In round numbers, one hundred and twenty graduates of the College of Dentistry in Columbus entered the Officers' Reserve Corps, Dental Section, of whom three-fourths saw active service.

In accordance with the action taken by the Dental Section of the Council for National Defense at Washington in the middle of May, 1917, the Faculty of the College of Dentistry decided to continue the work of the college all summer to help in standardizing dental instruments of all types in order to simplify instruction and enable the War Department to buy instruments in great quantities, and to offer advanced courses from two to eight weeks long in military dentistry. These advanced courses were opened to graduates of the college, practicing dentists, and advanced undergraduates. Sophomores and juniors were encouraged to take advantage of the summer opportunities thus afforded, not that they might graduate the more quickly, but that they might become more proficient for military service through practice and clinical work. A number of the graduates in dentistry availed themselves of this instruction.

On October 1, 1917, the Faculty voted to grant students the privilege of enrolling late on account of war conditions, and to assist them as much as possible in their studies. On November 12, the Faculty decided to give examinations to such students as should be called into service before the close of the semester, with a view to their receiving credit for the half-year's work. The Faculty also voted that, as it was desirable to have all students continually at work in order to perfect themselves for Government service, the Thanksgiving, Christmas, and Easter holidays would be considering shortened, and that the laboratories and clinic should remain open during the pause between semesters.

During the spring of 1918 the National Dental Educational Council classified the dental colleges of the United States and placed the College of Dentistry in Class A, along with fifteen others. Under the surgeon general's ruling this entitled the graduates of the college to the ranking of officers in the Army and Navy.

In July, 1918, the College of Dentistry, like the other colleges of the University, was placed in the group of those educational institutions whose professors and instructors were entitled to be classified as "essential teachers," that is, engaged in training men for war service. The Faculty members of the College of Dentistry were not only engaged in preparing men for such service, they were also acting as dental examiners for the local draft board. This list of essential teachers was drawn up late in September, 1918, and duly sent on to Washington. With the establishment of the Students' Army Training Corps at the opening of the following month, the Dental Section of the Medical Enlisted Reserve Corps became a part of the new organization.

Three members of the teaching staff were released to go into active service. These were Dr. John W. Means, Dr. Frank C. Starr, and Dr. Louis E. Reif. Dr. Means began his service at the Columbus Barracks in April, 1917. Thence he was ordered to Philadelphia to take a course of instruction in oral and plastic work, but later returned to the Columbus Barracks for a brief period of duty. Dr. Means was subsequently assigned to Base Hospital No. 22 in Milwaukee and went to France with that organization. This hospital was stationed at Beau Desert, Gironde, France. Dr. Means, who became a major in the Medical Corps, did both maxillo-facial and general surgery until his return to this country and was discharged from the Army in April, 1919. Dr. Frank C. Starr entered the service in August, 1917, as a first lieutenant in the Medical Corps. He left almost immediately for France and was assigned to civilian relief work among the French people. He also served at headquarters, 26th Division. Later he was connected with the Red Cross Military Hospital in Paris, where he remained until the hospital was closed in February, 1919. He was then assigned to duty as a major with the headquarters base, Section No. 1, at the port of embarkation at Saint-Nazaire. He returned to the United States in June, 1919, when he received his discharge. Dr. Louis C. Reif entered active service in the Medical Corps, Dental Section, in September, 1917, and was assigned to duty as a captain in the 85th Division at Camp Custer, Michigan. In July, 1918, he was sent overseas and spent much of his time in an advanced area. On his return to the United States he served at General Hospital No. 36 at Detroit, Michigan, where he remained until his discharge.

The vacancies created by the absence of Captain Reif and Majors Starr and Means were filled voluntarily by other members of the Faculty, who carried on the work of the absentees in addition to their own. Dean H. M. Semans was appointed by the surgeon general as one of the examiners of applicants for membership in the Officers' Reserve Corps, Dental Section. This service was rendered from June 1, 1917, until September of that year, after which he became one of the Committee on Mobilization of Dental Education.

According to records in the possession of the College of Dentistry, 99 of its graduates were in active service in the war, not counting the members of the classes of 1917 and 1918, who graduated after the United States was drawn into the vortex. All but five of these 99 were sent overseas, most of them serving in France and at least one in Germany. Four others were on duty in the Philippine Islands, three in the Hawaiian Islands, and one in the Canal Zone. Of the 25 members of the class of 1917 who were in service at least eight went overseas, one of these being in Germany, one in Italy, and one in Siberia. Of the 29 members of the class of 1918 in active service four were overseas.

The war records of the college show that 29 undergraduates joined the Medical Enlisted Reserve Corps, Dental Section, at the University, and that 82 undergraduates, including many of the M.E.R.C. men, enlisted in the Students' Army Training Corps when it became a part of the University organization in October, 1918. All of these undergraduates belonged to the classes of 1919 to 1922, inclusive.

Ninety-four of the 99 graduates of the Dental College were given commissions, 45 being appointed first lieutenants; 20, captains; 26, majors; and 3 lieutenant colonels. The class of 1917 alone had not less than 19 first lieutenants.

Two of the dental graduates died in the service, namely, First Lieutenant Alexander H. Jones in France, October 1, 1918, and Captain Hal Wright at Fort Oglethorpe, Georgia, October 17, 1918.

CHAPTER XIV

THE PSYCHOLOGICAL AND OTHER SERVICES OF THE COLLEGE OF EDUCATION

The College of Education is largely a woman's college. Nevertheless, it lost in number of students during the war period, as did the men's colleges on the campus. Even before the United States declared war, the enrollment began to fall off. In November, 1916, it was 528, and in February, 1917, it was 60 less. On the release of male students for agricultural and other war service in May of this year, 21 young men withdrew, two-thirds of these to do farm labor and the other third to go into military service. In the fall the attendance was down to 433, and in the next spring it was 48 less. At the opening of the first semester of 1918 it recovered somewhat, rising to 438, partly through the registration of 24 cadets of the Students' Army Training Corps. The second half-year saw its enrollment fall once more, this time to 378, but with the restoration of normal conditions it ascended to 440, which was a score or more below the number of students just before the declaration of hostilities, in April, 1917. For the summer sessions of 1916, 1917, 1918, and 1919 the enrollment figures were 402, 320, 266, and 260, respectively, showing a rapid decrease.

The effect of the war upon the enrollment of departments listed in the College of Education is given in the following tabulation:

Departments	1915-16	1916-17	1917-18	1918-19
Art	602	909	703	669
History and Philosophy of Education	260	270	307	213
Industrial Education	60	85	58	57
Principles of Education	195	191	250	236
Psychology	1,751	2,030	1,734	1,586
School Administration	196	185	86	162

In the Departments of Art, History and Philosophy of Education, and Psychology the figures are disproportionately large for a college with the number of students of the College of Education. It should be remembered, however, that the departments named received students from other colleges and courses of the University.

Undoubtedly the Department of Psychology was more affected by the war than any other department in the College of Education. Its enrollment was not only about four hundred and forty less than at the beginning of the war, but it also suffered more changes in personnel; it was called upon to do research work in cooperation with various war agencies; and, both during and after the war, it found the student body and public taking a lively interest in the applied aspect of psychology. Five members of the teaching staff of the department left the University to enter Government service. Professor George F. Arps was commissioned a captain in the Sanitary Corps in February, 1918, and served at Camp Greenleaf, Georgia, until the following April. He was then sent to Camp Sherman, Chillicothe, Ohio, as chief psychological examiner, where he remained on duty until November, 1918. While at this camp Captain Arps organized the morale office, which supervised the Red Cross, Y.M.C.A., Knights of Columbus, and all other agencies having to do with the morale and welfare of the soldiers of the camp. Promoted to the rank of major, Dr. Arps was next ordered to Camp Custer, Michigan, as special psychological examiner of the Reserve Officers' Training Corps, and later was transferred to the United States General Hospital No. 36 at Detroit, Michigan, as chief educational officer in charge of the work of re-education and rehabilitation of disabled soldiers. This work was conducted through four divisions, namely, (1) Psychology and Statistics, (2) the Technical Division, (3) the Academic Division, and (4) the Division of Occupational Therapy. When Major Arps took hold of this work, there was no equipment for it in the hospital. At the time the hospital was demobilized the Educational Department possessed property valued at $80,000. Besides serving as chief educational officer, Major Arps held other appointments in the hospital. As chief morale officer he exercised supervision over the entertainment of the soldiers. He was chairman of the hospital welfare board, which attended to the distribution of the numerous deliaccies and tokens of appreciation sent to the hospital. He was the supervisor of the *Detroit Az-u-wer*, and as such developed the organization that issued the hospital newspaper. Major Arps was also chairman of the board of recommendations, which passed on all applications for discharge and classified the men for recommendation in and out of the hospital. As hospital publicity officer Major Arps dealt with reporters of the daily press, special correspondents, and feature-story writers, and on occasion lectured before various clubs and organizations in the interest of the Academic Division. After serving for eighteen months, Major Arps was discharged at the Columbus Barracks, August 14, 1919.

Professor Rudolph Pintner served as civilian psychological examiner at Camp Lee, Petersburg, Virginia, from September to December, 1917. He was among the first of those sent into the field to establish the validity of psychological group tests in the Army. After this had been accomplished, the whole organization was put on a military footing. During the spring of 1918 Dr. Pintner conducted psychological tests of the aviators in the ground school at the Ohio State University. This work was done for Professor E. L. Thorndike of Columbia University. From May until September, 1918, Dr. Pintner was a member of the Trade Test Division at Pittsburgh, this division being a part of the Committee on Classification of Personnel in the Army. The work at Pittsburgh consisted in standardizing trade tests on civilian tradesmen. Later on these tests were used to measure the trade ability of the men in the Army.

Dr. James W. Bridges was appointed civilian psychological examiner in the Medical Department, in September, 1917, and sent to Camp Zachary Taylor, Kentucky, to assist in the try-out of psychological tests, which was being conducted in four cantonments. In the following December he was ordered to the surgeon general's office at Washington to assist in revising the test methods in the light of the results from the four camps. His especial problem was to arrange a program for the individual examination of recruits who failed in the group tests. The solution of that problem resulted in shortening the standard Binet-Simon tests and in choosing and standardizing a group of performance tests for illiterate subjects. During his connection with the surgeon general's office Dr. Bridges was sent on psychological duty to Camp Lee, Virginia; the port of embarkation at Newport News, Virginia; Milwaukee, Wisconsin; and other places. In November, 1918, Dr. Bridges was appointed supervisor of personnel methods, Students' Army Training Corps, under the Committee on Education and Special Training, his duties including intelligence rating of S.A.T.C. cadets in District No. 10. Dr. Bridges was released from service at the end of December, 1918.

Dr. Harold E. Burtt was chairman of the original Psychology Subcommittee on Aviation of the National Research Council. This subcommittee gave a wide range of tests to cadets in the School of Aeronautics at Massachusetts Institute of Technology, with a view of predicting a man's flying ability before he was sent into the air. After these men had been at the flying fields for a few weeks and the data as to their ability in the air had been collected, the subcommittee compared these data with their test results in order to obtain a set of crucial tests. This set of tests was given a trial at one of the flying fields, and a combination of tests was thus determined which was adopted by the Air Service. On October 22, 1918, Dr. Burtt was commissioned a captain and assigned to the Personnel Unit, School of Military Aeronautics at Princeton, New Jersey. He was discharged on December 24, 1918.

One other member of the Department of Psychology went into war work, namely, Miss A. C. Bowler, who resigned her position as instructor and entered the service of the Red Cross.

Some research was conducted by members of this department in connection with the Psychological Division of the surgeon general's office and the Trade Test Division of the adjutant general's office and in cooperation with Professor E. L. Thorndike of Columbia University, as already noted above. While the individual research of members of the department was necessarily interrupted by the war, the department was able to carry on satisfactory work with its graduate students, who were not much diminished in number.

The war greatly stimulated the interest both of the public and the student body in the applied aspect of psychology. In the first half-year of 1919-20 the enrollment of students in the department was 1,479, as compared with 1,058 in the corresponding period of 1917-18. This notable increase in number of students reflects not only the general increase in the University as a whole, but also the added interest in psychology in particular. Besides the students, the faculties and administrative officers of universities have developed a new interest in the subject. Impressed by the psychologist's methods of intelligence testing in the Army, they have applied these methods to the student body in order that they might compare the results thus secured with those obtained in the usual examinations. Industries and commercial organizations have also sought assistance, asking the help of the psychologist in solving questions of personnel, labor, vocational guidance, and educational surveys. In general, the tendency has been pronounced in the direction of practical applications as contrasted with theory. In this respect psychology is following the development of the older sciences.

Two members of the Department of Art entered war service. Professor Charles F. Kelley had charge of the County Organization Division of the Federal Food Administration in Ohio from November, 1919, to February, 1919. Aside from the staff of the Food Administration in the office at Columbus, the Food Administration in Ohio consisted of county committees in the eighty-eight counties of the State and eighteen city committees. The rules and regulations of the Food Administration were carried out by these local committees, upon whose organization and efficiency depended the success of the Food Administration. Professor Kelley exercised supervision over all the county committees. He and his assistants visited these committees at least once, and in some cases several times, a year, helping them perfect their local organization, construing rules and regulations for their benefit, assisting in hearings of violators, and suggesting proper penalties. Professor Kelley also rendered valuable service by lecturing in many places on food conservation, especially in 1918, during the first nine months of which he gave on the average three addresses each week.

Dr. Erwin O. Christensen of the Department of Art was sent to the Ground School of Aerial Photography of Cornell University for a course in aerial photography, observation, and map-making, enlisted in the National Army on June 3, 1918, and served at the School of Aerial Photography at Rochester, New York, until September 4; then at Cornell University, Ithaca, New York, until November 11; and finally in Aerial Photography Sector 84 at Camp McClellan, Alabama, until January 16, 1919, when he was discharged.

Mr. Anthonio Marino, assistant in the history of education, was called into military service.

Dean George W. Knight of the College of Education became the director of the course on War Issues, which was required of all cadets in the Students' Army Training Corps, from the inception of that organization on the campus, October 1, 1918, until its demobilization in the following December. This course was handled in more than forty sections, the administration and supervision of which centered in the dean's office, being carried on through a committee of those teachers in the University who were directly in charge of the sections.

Finally, it should be said that the College of Education, in response to the appeal of President Wilson for the efficient maintenance of public education, encouraged and assisted its students to find positions in the schools, which were suffering from a shortage of teachers. Of the graduating class in 1918 a larger proportion than of any former class rendered a needed service to the country by going into teaching, despite the low salaries prevailing at the time.

CHAPTER XV

THE COLLEGE OF ENGINEERING AND TECHNICAL WAR SERVICE

The College of Engineering comprised the following fifteen departments: Architecture, Astronomy, Ceramic Engineering, Chemistry, Civil Engineering, Electrical Engineering, Engineering Drawing, Industrial Arts, Mathematics, Mechanical Engineering, Mechanics, Metallurgy, Mineralogy, and Physics. It will be seen at a glance that not a few of these departments teach technical subjects that bear directly upon important phases of modern warfare, being conversant with engines, minerals, chemicals, railroad construction, gas production, etc. Furthermore, these departments are manned by engineers and scientists at whose disposal are well-equipped laboratories in which definite problems are subjected to careful methods of solution by means of experiment. The advanced development of technical education in Germany enabled that country to display a material resourcefulness in fighting such as the world had never witnessed before, and such as could only be counteracted by calling in experts capable of improving on the devices and methods of the enemy. Wherever technical and scientific men of standing could be found in the United States ready to turn their attainments to public use, their services were at once accepted by the Government for the purpose of winning the war at the earliest possible moment. It was this need of the Government for technical experts and for the technical training of numbers of young men who were preparing to enter special branches of the service which gave the College of Engineering, along with many other technical schools, its opportunity to do valuable war work.

In their counteroffensive against Ypres in the spring of 1915 the Germans struck consternation into the Allied troops by releasing a cloud of greenish vapor, April 22, which a gentle breeze wafted toward the Allies' trenches. This vapor proved to be chlorine gas, which chokes and asphyxiates those who inhale much of it and produces violent coughing in the case of those who get but little of it. This novel and diabolical form of attack, for which the Allies were wholly unprepared, caused the French troops holding the line north of Ypres to break and flee, the town being saved only by the dogged resistance of Canadian troops. From this time on throughout the war the Germans made use of poisonous gas of one kind or another, thus introducing a change in the methods of warfare greater than any since guns and cannon were developed into fairly effective weapons back in the fourteenth century.

After some weeks without protection against the drift gas, the Allies improvised cloth hoods impregnated with chemicals to absorb the chlorine, from which they later evolved the respirator, consisting of a mask with a connecting tube and canister filled with a quantity of neutralizing chemicals. As chlorine gas is two and one-half times as heavy as air, some of it was apt to settle in the trenches after a vigorous gas attack. Hence, the Allies resorted to spraying the lurking places of their trenches with liquids that would absorb the chlorine, or to mechanical devices that would drive it out. The heaviness of the drift gas caused a considerable quantity of it to land in the immediate front of those using it. This fact led the Germans to employ gas shells which, on impact, threw a spray of very volatile liquid over the enemy. Chlorine gas is said to have been responsible for 35 per cent of the casualties suffered by those under attack.

Among the many war gases used by the Germans were phosgene, chlorpicrin or "tear" gas, and mustard or blistering gas. Like chlorine, phosgene is a poisonous gas. It is reported to have a severe, delayed action upon the heart, which often proves fatal after the immediate effects have apparently disappeared. It is estimated to be five times as deadly as chlorine.

It penetrated the ordinary gas mask and could be kept out only by a filter of paper or some other impervious material. Such a filter was invented in April, 1918, in the form of a complete outer covering for the canister. This was followed by the "Connell mask," an American device, the canister of which inclosed a filter that completely strained out the phosgene. In July, 1917, began the use of the most painful of the gases, namely, mustard gas, which blistered the skin through the clothing as readily as it burned lungs and eyes, and it destroyed the shoes and clothing of the soldiers. A man who had been severely affected by this gas found himself incapacitated for three months. The casualties due to mustard are reported to have been fourteen times as many as those produced by all the other kinds of gas, and a certain percentage of the injured died, the inhalation of this gas producing inflammation of the lungs. Chlorpicrin or tear gas was not only a strong lachrymotor, but also a deadly gas. Of the 275,000 casualties suffered by the American troops on the field of battle, 75,000 are attributed to war gases.

The Germans had been using these gases for two years when the United States entered the war, and the chemists of the country fully realized that their aid was needed to answer the challenge of the German chemists. It was not enough to be satisfied with defensive measures against the enemy's gas attacks, it was also necessary, as the Allies had already discovered, to develop a gas offense in order to maintain the morale of the troops who had to face the lethal vapors emitted for their destruction.

Already in the early part of February, 1917, the American Chemical Society offered its services to President Wilson, reaffirming its offer by resolution of April 11. On March 6 the Faculty of the College of Engineering adopted a resolution to communicate with the Council of National Defense, the Advisory Commission of that body, and the National Academy of Science and offer their services, in so far as their duties and responsibilities permitted, in industrial research for the United States Government and to send a copy of this resolution to the President of the United States. This action was approved by the Board of Trustees of the University on April 3, 1917, three days before the United States declared war on the German Imperial Government. Early in May President Thompson received a letter from Mr. Van H. Manning, director of the Bureau of Mines, Department of the Interior, at Washington, explaining that work had already been started in the bureau on the investigation of problems pertaining to gases in warfare, this work being conducted under the auspices of the National Research Council in cooperation with the Army and Navy. Mr. Manning went on to say that it was recognized that independent chemists, as well as those in universities and research institutions, were desirous of assisting in the efficient waging of the war, and that some of them could spare the time and facilities for work on specific problems in need of solution in connection with the use of gases; that in order to prepare for defense against the new gases continually encountered at the front, it was essential that every substance conceivably available should be studied and its offensive possibilities accurately determined; that a large force of chemists was at work in the Gas Service organizations of England and France; and that the Bureau of Mines would like to know whether the Ohio State University had men and facilities available for the kind of tasks indicated. If so, specific problems would be assigned in proportion to the facilities and time that could be devoted to them. Mr. Manning added that Mr. George A. Burrell had been placed in general charge of this research work, and that in carrying on investigations at the University or elsewhere every effort would have to be made to insure secrecy.

Mr. Burrell, whose appointment as chief of the Research Section of the Chemical Warfare Service of the United States Army was thus first communicated to the University, had been a student at Ohio State during the years 1902-4 and had spent the next two years as chemist in the United States Geological Survey office at the St. Louis World's Fair under Professors N. W. Lord and E. E. Somermeier of the old Department of

Mining and Metallurgy in the University. During the years 1906-8 Mr. Burrell remained connected with the Geological Survey, after which he spent eight years in charge of gas investigations at Pittsburgh, Pennsylvania, under the United States Bureau of Mines. In 1917 he was employed in directing research on war gases in the Bureau of Mines for the Army.

On May 10, 1917, the letter from Director Manning of the Bureau of Mines was placed in the hands of Professor William McPherson, who at once called a meeting of the chemists of the various departments of the University, at which it was decided to cooperate with the bureau in every way. On the next day Dr. McPherson sent President Thompson a letter for transmittal to Mr. Manning, expressing the desire of the committee thus formed to assist the Government on any of its problems that might fall within the domain of chemistry. A few days later a telegram was received from Mr. Burrell, stating that Dr. W. K. Lewis would be in Columbus on the following day to assign problems in connection with gas warfare. In addition to the members of the Department of Chemistry, representatives of the Departments of Physics, Metallurgy, and Mineralogy were summoned to meet Dr. Lewis, who addressed the group informally upon the problems to be dealt with in gas warfare and left certain problems to be distributed among the members. At a meeting held on May 18 a formal organization of the Ohio State University War Chemical Association was effected, with Professor McPherson as chairman and Professor Charles W. Foulk as secretary, and the problems were assigned. On June 7 Secretary Foulk forwarded a report of progress to Mr. Burrell, in which he said that nearly all of the chemists in the University would give considerable time during the summer to their problems and named the personnel of the group as follows: Professors William McPherson and W. L. Evans and Assistant Professor C. E. Boord in organic chemistry; Professor W. E. Henderson in physical and inorganic chemistry; Professor J. R. Withrow and Dr. O. R. Sweeney in industrial chemistry;

Professor C. W. Foulk, Assistant Professor H. L. Olin, and Mr. Marion Hollingsworth in analytical chemistry; Professor Dana J. Demorest in metallurgical chemistry; Professor W. J. McCaughey in mineralogy and assaying; and Professor J. R. Lyman in agricultural chemistry. Secretary Foulk added that other men were also available and had signified their intention to help. He enclosed reports on problems from Professor Evans, Assistant Professor Boord, and Dr. O. R. Sweeney.

During the summer of 1917 representatives of the Chemical Warfare Service made frequent visits to the University for conference. The Department of Chemistry withdrew its graduate thesis men from problems previously under investigation and set them at others relating to gas warfare. Indeed, Faculty members, assistants, graduate students, and even advanced undergraduates gave much of their time to answering the questions propounded by Colonel G. A. Burrell and his staff at the American University Experiment Station at Washington. For example, Professor Withrow devoted his laboratory, assistants, and advanced and graduate students to the solution of problems connected with canisters, gas masks, charcoal, soda-lime permanganate, and a long series of other things involved in gas warfare. Until the summer of 1918 his laboratory was operated as a field station of the Chemical Warfare Service, and the expense for the chemicals and other supplies was borne by the University, or by Professor Withrow himself. The total number of reports issued by Dr. Withrow and his immediate associates from May 15, 1917, to October 10, 1918, amounted to nearly three hundred and represented the work of sixty-three men, some of whom were outside chemists who were not graduates of Ohio State University but of other institutions. All of these persons served as volunteers and gave weeks and months to the work. In a few cases the work was privately done for Dr. Withrow.

Already in the latter part of July, 1917, Professor McPherson had gone to Washington to serve as chemical adviser to Captain E. J. W. Ragsdale, head of the Trench Warfare

Section of the Army. Professor McPherson was commissioned a captain in the United States Reserve Corps on July 30, was called into active service on August 22, and assigned to office work as a member of Captain Ragsdale's staff. At this time the work was not organized, but little was known of the details of gas warfare, and not much progress was being made. In truth, little could be accomplished until the research undertaken by the Bureau of Mines under the management of Mr. Burrell had obtained certain results. At first Mr. Burrell and his assistants had offices in the new building of the Department of the Interior in Washington, the investigations being conducted at different universities throughout the country. More concentration of the work of research at the national capital seemed necessary, and arrangements were therefore made with the American University in that city whereby the Government agreed to take over its buildings, besides erecting new ones adapted to the work. Inasmuch as the research was of primary importance, Captain Ragsdale, at Mr. Burrell's request, assigned Captain McPherson temporarily to the work at the American University, and he was soon placed in charge of the production of toxic gases on a semi-commercial scale. Accordingly, he proceeded to bring together a staff of assistants, which included several of his colleagues from the Ohio State University. In August, 1917, Dr. O. R. Sweeney joined Captain McPherson's staff. At the end of the following September Professor Withrow became consulting chemist to the Trench Warfare Section and spent a part of each week in Washington until June, 1918, after which time he was there almost continuously until his discharge early in January, 1919. Professor W. L. Evans, who had been conducting investigations in gas warfare at the University with a group of his graduate students, was called to Washington near the end of October and carried on research during several weeks under the direction of Captain McPherson.

As yet the American University was not supplied with the necessary apparatus for the production of gases on a semi-commercial scale. Hence, it became necessary to secure the cooperation of a number of chemical manufacturing plants. This task fell to Captain McPherson. It required a great deal of traveling and proved to be difficult, since all the reputable firms were already overwhelmed with orders and did not care to undertake work of such dangerous character as the manufacture of poisonous gases. Indeed, it soon became evident that the Government would not be able in this way to obtain all the toxic gas desired. The only method left was for the Government to build gas-producing plants of its own, especially in view of the fact that by November 1, 1917, the methods of producing phosgene and chlorpicrin in large quantities had been developed by research.

It was therefore decided to construct such plants in connection with the United States Shell-Filling Station, which was being rapidly built on Gunpowder Reservation, Edgewood, Maryland, about seventeen miles east of Baltimore. The whole project centering here was afterward known as Edgewood Arsenal and included a works laboratory for which plans were being formed by the Trench Warfare Section in the middle of November. On the twenty first of this month Professor Evans, who had received a captain's commission in the Ordnance Officers' Reserve Corps upon his entrance into the service, was assigned the duty of building, equipping, and directing the laboratory at Edgewood and of organizing its personnel. With so many chemists already in the service, or engaged in necessary war industries, it was no easy matter to bring together a strong scientific organization.

On December 1 the decision was reached to include the manufacture of toxic gases at Edgewood. This immediately widened the scope of the proposed laboratory. As many chemical problems were pressing for solution at this time, it became necessary for Captain Evans to organize several provisional laboratories for this work, in addition to the existing field stations. One of these was set up in the east basement of Lord Hall on our campus, where three different war gases were under study. In one room a complete experimental plant for the manufacture of phosgene was installed. In another room the properties of chlorpicrin were determined. Work with mustard gas occupied two more rooms. Captain John A. Wilkinson of the class of 1903 and later a member of the Department of Chemistry, who had joined Captain Evans' staff, was in charge of the experimentation from February 15 to May 15, 1918. Among the score of officers and men who were under the direction of Captain Wilkinson, seven or eight universities and research institutions were represented. The Ohio State men connected with this gas laboratory were T. G. Phillips and J. L. Hutchinson, instructors in the Department of Agricultural Chemistry; Joseph T. Parsons, '17; and Charles E. Mack and D. Roy Virtue, both former members of the class of '18. Of the three gases mustard gas was the most dangerous to handle. All of the men who worked with it were burned so badly that they were incapacitated for a period of from several days to three months. A member of the laboratory group asserts that about one-quarter of the detachment was always in the University Hospital while the work on mustard gas was being prosecuted. Some of the most important investigations dealing with the manufacture of war gases were conducted by the detachment of chemists in Lord Hall.

Of three other provisional laboratories organized by Captain Evans early in 1918 one was located for a few weeks at the Carnegie Geophysical Laboratory in Washington under the direction of Captain Ralph E. Hall, who had received his M.A. from Ohio State in 1911 and had been an assistant in the Chemistry Department of the University. Many difficult problems were placed in the hands of Captain Hall at this time and later for solution. This officer contributed not a little by his sound advice to the success of the work undertaken.

Until April 9 Captain Evans was busily engaged with all the details preliminary to the construction of the laboratory, besides directing a large volume of chemical work of both a research and a routine kind. His headquarters were then transferred to Baltimore. Construction of the laboratory began April 7, and actual chemical work was started in it on June 18. From that time on the chemical laboratory at Edgewood Arsenal was kept running day and night until the signing of the Armistice in November, 1918. Captain Evans was promoted to the rank of major in the Chemical Warfare Service on July 13.

The laboratory personnel was divided into two major groups, the one devoted to research and development, the other to routine and control. The routine work consisted of the chemical inspection of all raw materials received at the arsenal, while the control work involved the chemical analysis of the gases at the various stages of manufacture. With the encouragement of Major (afterward Lieutenant Colonel) Chance, Major Evans planned his works laboratory so that it could handle not only the routine and control tests, but also the problems that would arise in connection with plant operation. This proved to be an important part of the laboratory's functions, for the officers in charge of the chemical plants early began to propound to Major Evans questions involving chemical research. At first such problems had been worked out at the provisional laboratories established at Ohio State University and several other institutions. Later a great deal of investigation was accomplished at the Edgewood laboratory. The personnel of this laboratory numbered 238 chemists at the time of the signing of the Armistice.

The laboratory organization comprised eleven subdivisions, as follows: Analytical, Physical-Chemical, Chemical Engineering, Organic, Gas Analytical, Mustard Gas, Gas Shell, Special Problems, Power House Control, Inspection, and Chemical Supply. The last three subdivisions belonged to the routine and control group. Of the Ohio State men in charge of one or another of the eleven subdivisions, Corporal D. Roy Virtue was placed in complete charge of the Chemical Supply Division; Lieutenant Edgar W. Fasig was connected with the Inspection Division; Captain H. L. Olin, formerly assistant professor of chemistry in the University, with the Special

Problems Division; First Lieutenant Lowell H. Milligan, '16, in charge of the Chemical Engineering Division; Captain R. E. Hall, M.A., '11, in charge of the Physical-Chemical Division; and Captain J. A. Wilkinson in charge of the Analytical Division. The following list gives the names of the enlisted men from the Ohio State University who were members of the works laboratory organization. All of them, like the officers named above, deserve mention:

Maynard Brown, '17	Alton Mitchell
Raymond Brown, '09	Angus H. Orr
William I. Burt, '17	Joe T. Parsons, '17
H. J. Darby, '12	William M. Reese, Jr.
Howard A. Durham	Henry J. Schleich
L. C. Flickinger	Martin O. Shafer
Paul H. Groff	Frank L. Sinks, '17
G. H. Hufford	R. H. Smith, '14
P. H. Hugus	C. L. Thrash, '17
Leon B. Komisaruk, '18	D. Roy Virtue, '19
Charles E. Mack, '19	Spencer G. Weber, M.A., '18

J. D. Wright

During September, 1918, the duties of the laboratory were increased by the addition of a newly formed Inspection Division. This division became responsible for seeing that all material used in filling gas shells was in accordance with specifications, that shells were filled to the proper weight, and that they were properly painted, marked, and tested. One of the capable men in this division was Lieutenant Fasig, who helped to make it one of the most efficient groups in the laboratory organization.

After the signing of the Armistice, November 11, 1918, the laboratory continued its regular work until Thanksgiving Day. Then Major Evans and his staff began the task of invoicing and checking up. This was done so rapidly that by Christmas nearly all of the enlisted men of the laboratory had been discharged from the service. Under the able management of Major Evans, whose title was director and officer in charge of the Laboratory and Inspection Division, Edgewood Arsenal, Offense Division, results of great value were obtained. He was discharged on January 4, 1919, after a little more than fourteen months in the service. Eight months later he was offered the commission of lieutenant colonel in the Reserve Corps but was unable to accept it, much to his regret.

In mid-January, 1918, Captain McPherson was promoted to the rank of major in the National Army, and in the following spring, when Colonel W. H. Walker was made commanding officer of Edgewood Arsenal, Major McPherson was placed in charge of all outside plants. As head of the Chemical Supply Section, he was concerned with the purchase of all chemicals used in the manufacture of toxic gases. Since many of these chemicals were not made commercially, methods for their production had to be developed and firms interested in undertaking their manufacture.

On June 28, 1918, the Chemical Warfare Service was created as a distinct branch of the Army, in addition to the Infantry, Artillery, and Aviation branches. This change was effected by General Orders No. 62 of the War Department, which stated the functions of the new branch or arm of the service to be "operating and maintaining or supervising the operation of all plants engaged in the investigation, manufacture, or production of toxic gases, gas-defense appliances, the filling of gas shells, and proving grounds utilized in connection therewith, and the necessary research connected with gas warfare." This action brought the gas research work of the Bureau of Mines, which was under Colonel G. A. Burrell whether at the American University or the field stations; the Edgewood Arsenal with its laboratory and plants for the development of gas production for defense and offense, which had been under the control of Colonel W. H. Walker of the Ordnance Department of the Army; the outside plants engaged in the manufacture of toxic materials under the supervision of Major McPherson; and the development work of the Bureau of Mines at Cleveland under Colonel Frank A. Dorsey, all into one military organization under the command of Major General William L. Sibert.

Under the new arrangement Colonel Burrell remained at

the head of the Research Division, which comprised seven hundred chemists at work on all the problems connected with gas warfare, such as new processes of gas production, protection against toxic gases, design of gas masks, smoke funnels, screens, and grenades, gas projectors and flame throwers, colored rockets, gases for balloons, etc. This body of chemists had over one thousand helpers in the way of clerical force, engineers, electricians, photographers, mechanics, and laborers. It has been said that Colonel Burrell, as chief of the Research Section of the Chemical Warfare Service, made the American University in Washington "the greatest research organization ever dreamed of," and that its work covered the exhaustive investigation of more than four hundred materials. Colonel Burrell is credited with having located the supply of helium gas in Texas, on which the Government spent $10,000,000. Its importance lies in the fact that it was developed as a noninflammable substitute for hydrogen for filling balloons, thus reducing the dangers and increasing the usefulness of this accessory to warfare. At the close of hostilities Colonel Burrell was awarded the Distinguished Service Medal. In June, 1918, he received the degree of Chemical Engineer from the Ohio State University in recognition of his achievements in the scientific world.

On July 13, 1918, Major McPherson was promoted to the rank of lieutenant colonel in the Chemical Warfare Service, with headquarters at Baltimore, and remained in charge of the outside manufacturing plants until October 2, when he was ordered overseas as representative of the Chemical Warfare Service to the Inter-Allied Conference on Gas Investigations, held in Paris beginning October 25. He was also instructed to visit the various commercial plants for the production of toxic gases in France and England. Embarking, October 9, he reached Paris on the 24th and after the conference, which lasted a week, was ordered to the French headquarters for further conference and then to England to visit various manufacturing plants. In this way it was intended to maintain cooperation among the different governments in all matters pertaining to the manufacture of toxic gases. While Lieutenant Colonel McPherson was in England the Armistice was signed, and all plants used in manufacturing gases were closed. He therefore returned to the French headquarters and thence home, under orders, to assist in closing up the work at Edgewood Arsenal. Arriving in New York, December 11, he remained at Edgewood until March 24, 1919, when he secured his discharge.

Professor Dana J. Demorest of the Department of Metallurgy at Ohio State had been called to Washington by Professor McPherson in December, 1917, to attend to toxic gas production. He was commissioned a first lieutenant in the Trench Warfare Section, Ordnance Department, and was instructed to design a method for manufacturing pure carbon monoxide on a large scale and, in collaboration with Mr. (later Major) F. C. Frary, to design a phosgene plant, since phosgene was at this time the most destructive gas employed in warfare. With the rapid growth of the United States Army's gas program, it became necessary to provide a commercial-sized plant at Edgewood for the production of oxygen, besides other plants for the manufacture of chlorpicrin, the liquefying of mustard, sulphur chloride, and chlorine. As the officers who were charged with planning these chemical activities were given no definite gas program, they had to anticipate the huge demands that finally developed, and they succeeded in doing so through the visualizing faculty of Major E. M. Chance and the information supplied by the reports of officers with the French and other Associated armies.

The organization formed by Professor Demorest, who was soon promoted to be major, and by Major Frary to design, equip, and operate the chemical plant under their care, included the following Ohio State men: Dr. O. R. Sweeney, who had been commissioned a first lieutenant and attached to Professor McPherson's staff in August, 1917. He was now placed in charge of the design, erection, and operation of the chlorpicrin plant. Lieutenant William A. Mueller also helped in designing the chemical plant. Captain F. M. Demorest was made responsible for the inspection, storing, and recording of all materal shipped to the plant. In other words, he became the officer in charge of the property section. Captain Dale M. Boothman was the drafting and maintenance officer. Lieutenants P. D. Helser and F. R. Henniger were employed in the manufacture of carbon dioxide (CO_2) and Captain William A. Mueller in that of mustard gas. Lieutenant G. G. Rosino was placed in general charge of the production of oxygen (O_2). Gaylord T. Stowe entered the service on February 13, 1918, and was with the Engineer Bureau, Ordnance Corps, at Washington, until June 24. He was then assigned to Company K, 3d Battalion, at Edgewood Arsenal. On August 1 he was promoted to master engineer, junior grade, and was commissioned a second lieutenant in the Chemical Warfare Service on September 4, He remained at Edgewood Arsenal until his discharge on December 18, 1918. All told, there were more than fifty officers and several hundred enlisted men in the chemical organization, Major F. C. Frary being in charge of chemical technology. For most of the time after their erection, Major Demorest was commanding officer of the toxic gas plants at Edgewood.

While part of the equipment was being designed by Major Demorest's fellow-officers, he arranged in January, 1918, for the shipment of two gas generators, with all the structural steel, blowers, scrubbers, etc., that went with them. Owing to freight congestion the shipment did not arrive until early in February. A similar delay occurred in securing the carbon dioxide equipment. Despite these annoying postponements, a new and urgent need arose for a large plant to produce oxygen, and Major Demorest entered into a contract with a company to install a plant with a capacity of 95,000 cubic feet per day. He also began negotiations for additional plants.

The erection of buildings to house the chemical processes at Edgewood was started in January, 1918, and was carried on with surprising speed in view of the fact that the labor market was almost exhausted, and that Edgewood was described as a dangerous place to work in. As it was impossible to secure enough labor to satisfy all demands at the arsenal, soldiers were put on the installation of inside apparatus as fast as they could be procured, but after July the number of enlisted men was inadequate for both the installation work and the operation of the plant at full capacity.

The chlorpicrin plant under Major O. R. Sweeney started production, June 9, 1918, and thereafter continued in successful operation, except when prevented by shortage of picric acid and bleach. Indeed, few plants adopting a new process have run more smoothly than this chlorpicrin plant. The first unit of the phosgene plant did not reach production until July 5, and regular twenty-four hour production was not attained until ten days later. The other units, three in number, were started as fast as finished, the last on October 12. The mustard plant in Building No. 605 began producing on August 1, 1918. After continuing in an irregular way for three weeks, some necessary changes were made and production was resumed. From September 11 until the outbreak of the influenza epidemic, early in October, the output was ten tons of mustard gas a day. By October 3 a new unit was started, which had a capacity of twelve tons per day. A third unit was put in operation on November 6. Three days later the entire mustard plant was shut down because every available mustard container was full. The signing of the Armistice closed all the chemical plants at Edgewood. At that time they were in condition to produce per day thirty-five tons of phosgene, twenty-five of chlorpicrin, and thirty of mustard, or a total of ninety tons of toxic gases per day.

In following the fortunes of the chemists of Ohio State University who went to Washington to do research for the Bureau of Mines, or to become officers in the Trench Warfare Section of the Ordnance Division until all of them were incorporated in the Chemical Warfare Service of the Army, we have lost track of those men who were dealing with gas warfare problems as members of the field station at the University. Despite the departure of Professors McPherson, Evans, and Withrow, and Dr. O. R. Sweeney in the summer and fall of

1917, gas problems were taken up with renewed energy following the opening of the University in September, 1918. A number of graduate students elected special problems in organic chemistry and were given investigations relating to gas warfare under the direction of Assistant Professor C. E. Boord.

During October and November close contact with the experiment station at the American University in Washington was lost. The rapid growth of the Gas Warfare Section of the Bureau of Mines and the lack of clerical help in Washington rendered it difficult to maintain connection with outlying laboratories. In December, however, this connection was re-established when a representative of the bureau visited the University for conference. As a result of this conference the Ohio State University Field Station, Offense Division, Organic Chemical Research, of the Bureau of Mines was instituted with Dr. Boord as chemist in charge. Hitherto all expenses for materials and equipment used in the gas warfare investigations at Ohio State, with a few exceptions, had been borne by the University, but henceforth they were met by the Government. In fact, the new field station was an integral part of the Gas Warfare Experiment Station at the American University. This official relationship made it possible for military and civilian chemists to be detailed to our University station by the Government. The problems were assigned by the chief of the Organic Section, Offense Division, at the American University, and reports of progress and an exchange of views concerning the problems were frequent until the close of the local field station. In all, some twenty complete detailed reports were forwarded to the American University station. One of these was an efficiency study relating to the production of ethylene by the contact catalysis process in the manufacture of mustard gas. This study was eventually incorporated in a monograph issued by the Chemical Warfare Service concerning the production and properties of mustard gas. During the early months of 1918 a series of experiments was carried on which gave a product called selenium mustard. Samples were sent to the American University for toxicological study. The measurements of the toxicity of this new gas proved to be so interesting that the investigations were pushed to completion, a method being developed for preparing the product in a very satisfactory yield. Under date of July 30, 1918, Colonel Burrell specially commended the work of our University Field Station to Major General William L. Sibert, director of the Chemical Warfare Service, and stated that "a new gas has been investigated by Mr. Boord which promises to be of great importance." He also referred to the research conducted by Dr. Boord and his staff in Volume II of the *Journal of Industrial and Engineering Chemistry*, where he says concerning the selenium derivatives of mustard gas, they "threatened to displace mustard for a time, so it will be appreciated how important this laboratory was and how interested we were in their work." The work upon selenium mustard was, without doubt, the most important contribution from the Ohio State University Field Station.

The last problem attacked by Dr. Boord and his associates was undertaken at a late date, after it had developed that the earlier methods used in the production of mustard gas were unsatisfactory. The handling of this problem was giving every promise of disclosing a new and better method of manufacture of the gas when the Armistice was signed.

On January 28, 1918, Captain Paul M. Giesy, who received the degree of Chemical Engineer from Ohio State in 1912, reported to Dr. Boord for duty, having been detailed to the field station. With the gradual militarization of this unit, Captain Giesy became the ranking military officer and had charge of all matters pertaining to the military personnel. In March Dr. Boord had under his direction the following graduate students: Messrs. Lorin B. Sebrell, Carl E. Frick, William W. Bauer, and Clyde S. Adams. Mr. Frick severed his connection with the University in February and accepted an appointment as junior gas chemist with the Bureau of Mines. He was transferred to the Gas Warfare Division and placed

Officers of the Laboratory and Inspection Division, Edgewood Arsenal, Maryland, under Major W. L. Evans. (In the front row are seven Ohio State University men.)

The Chlorine Plant, Edgewood Arsenal, Maryland

Airplane view of the toxic-gas buildings at Edgewood

Tear-Gas Plant at Edgewood, designed and erected
by Major O. R. Sweeney

on gas-mask research under the direction of Mr. A. C. Fieldner, '06. On March 1 Mr. Sebrell also became a junior gas chemist, but continued as a member of the field station. A few days later Private J. J. Loudermill was detailed from the American University in Washington to duty at the Ohio State University station. In April Mr. Sebrell was transferred to the American University to help out in the gas-mask research under Mr. Fieldner. During May and June Messrs. W. W. Bauer, C. S. Adams, and C. E. Curran received their appointments as junior gas chemists with instructions to continue their duties at Ohio State. With the general militarization of the work in the fall of 1918, the three men last named were commissioned second lieutenants. Private Loudermill was promoted to the rank of sergeant and would doubtless have received his commission had it not been for the extreme slowness of promotions in the enlisted group. Following the signing of the Armistice, the field station was closed, December 31, 1918, with a letter of thanks and appreciation from Colonel Burrell for the assistance which the University had given. The military group was discharged during January, 1919, and all material on hand was either returned to the American University, or purchased by Ohio State for the use of the Department of Chemistry.

A large number of Ohio State men were engaged in the Chemical Warfare Service and materially assisted in making the Edgewood Arsenal "the greatest chemical plant in the world." Ohio State University and the Massachusetts Institute of Technology divided the honors in having the largest numbers of representatives at Edgewood. Another but much smaller group of Ohio State men was in the Zone Supply Office at Baltimore, Maryland, only a few miles from the Edgewood Arsenal. In December, 1918, this group included Captain Charles F. Johnson, '02, and Lieutenants O. R. Crawfis, '11; R. L. Lazarus, '12; S. C. Dildine, '17; G. R. Carmack, J. E. Patrick, and S. L. Van Orman. In the winter of 1918 these loyal sons of the University, together with the other Zone

Supply and Port Storage officers, held their first annual banquet.

Only an hour's ride distant in the city of Washington was located still another colony of Ohio State alumni, many but not all of whom had been students or professors in the College of Engineering. Many of these were connected with the American University Research Station under Colonel Burrell. For example, Mr. Arno C. Fieldner, '06, who was in charge of the gas-mask section at the American University and was made a major in August, 1918, directed the investigations of some of his college mates, including Messrs. Parker K. Baird, Carl E. Frick, and Lorin B. Sebrell. Other men who were stationed at the American University were Charles F. Rudmann, '15; Carlos I. Reed, '15, instructor in the Department of Physiology, who was engaged in research work on poisonous gases from July 1, 1918, until his discharge, and who in September of the year named received a commission as second lieutenant; Lee Irvin Smith, '13 and '15, second lieutenant in the Chemical Warfare Service, who was transferred from Cambridge, Massachusetts, early in 1918 to Washington; and Harold K. Baumgardner and Merle L. Bundon, assistants in the Department of Chemistry. John A. Vander Werf, another assistant in chemistry, was sworn into the Chemical Warfare Service early in November, 1917, and was assigned to duty at the American University Experiment Station. Later he was promoted to a second lieutenancy and became head of the chemical laboratory at Edgewood Arsenal, Stanford, Connecticut.

Other members of the College of Engineering, who served part or all of their time in Washington, D. C., were Professor Alfred D. Cole of the Department of Physics, Professor Alan E. Flowers and Assistant T. O. Farmer of the Department of Electrical Engineering, Professor Frank E. Sanborn of the Department of Industrial Arts, and Dean Edward Orton, Jr., '84. Dean Orton's activities in connection with the passage of the National Defense Act have already been set forth in Chapter I of this volume. Throughout his student days Mr.

Orton served in the University Battalion, part of the time as a member of the band. During two years of this period he was also connected with the Ohio National Guard. From that time on he was a thorough believer in military training. In the summer of 1916 Dean Orton attended the United States Army Training Camp at Plattsburgh, New York, and on January 5, 1917, was commissioned a major in the Quartermaster Officers' Reserve Corps. In the following May he was assigned to the Motor Transport Repair Shops at San Antonio, Texas, as assistant to the commanding officer, with the duty of preparing engineering studies and calculations of the repair shop equipments needed for motor transport companies for various military units. He also served as personnel officer. Early in June, 1917, Major Orton was transferred to the Transportation Division, office of the department quartermaster, Fort Sam Houston, Texas, as assistant in charge of tests and reports on motor equipment in the Southern Department. Remaining at Fort Sam Houston, he was transferred to the Motor Truck Group for the purpose of preparing himself to take command of it on the departure of the regular officer, then in command. On August 18 Major Orton was ordered to Washington, D. C., where he served as assistant to Lieutenant Colonel Chauncey B. Baker, an Ohio State man of the class of 1881, who was chief of the Motor Transport Division, Quartermaster Corps, and who set Major Orton at work studying the organization and operation of the Engineering Section. A few days later Orton was placed in charge of this section, including the corps of automotive engineers engaged in designing standardized military trucks.

During the Mexican Punitive Expedition and Border operations of 1916-17 the United States Government had experienced great difficulties in maintaining a fleet of commercial trucks of many different makes. In order to reduce and simplify repairs as far as possible, it was proposed to design and build for the Army three or four types of completely standardized trucks suitable for the severest military service. Each model was to be the super-truck of its class in power, reliability, and ability to go under any conditions, and the parts of any machine were to be interchangeable with the corresponding parts of any other of the same model. This ambitious plan had been on paper for some months and had the backing of many of the leading members of the Society of Automotive Engineers.

When Major Orton took charge, between thirty and forty of the best truck engineers and designers and a number of draftsmen were scattered about in several offices in Washington, wherever they could find room. During the five weeks they had been at work they had made little progress, owing to lack of organization and direction. The new officer was given full authority to get results, regardless of obstacles. The progress soon made was remarkable. Between July 25, 1917, and January 25, 1918, or a period of six months, the corps accomplished a huge task of designing, building, and testing three truck models, or a model every two months. The significance of this achievement will be better understood when it is stated that ordinarily the time required to design, build, and test a single model is about eighteen months.

Besides building these models, the engineering work relating to all the other varieties of motor transport vehicles had to be carried on. For this purpose there were only three or four men available in August, 1917. Within six months this section had grown to large size.

Simultaneously with the designing and testing of the military trucks and motor transport equipment of all sorts, an organization had to be provided for producing these things on a large scale. By January, 1918, the pressure was shifted from engineering to production. Preliminary to this final stage, an automotive expert of great reputation was secured to go over the work of the preceding months with exactness, and the Engineering Section was reduced to its normal place.

Late in February, 1918, Major Orton was transferred to the Maintenance Division and given duties, chiefly executive, in connection with designing and building motor transportation repair shops of very large size and procuring equipment for them. He was sent to secure a site for large repair shops in San Antonio, Texas and got the purchase confirmed by the authorities in Washington, the expenditure being the lowest for any shop in the series. He then went to Baltimore and Atlanta to report on the condition of the shops under construction there.

Near the end of May, 1918, the Motor Transport Division of the Quartermaster Corps was abolished, and the Motor Transport Service was created, a radical change being made in all the higher officers. Major Orton was the senior in service and rank of any officer retained from the old organization. He became the chief of the Overseas Liaison Branch of the new service. His new duties required him to conduct all correspondence with the overseas branch of the Motor Transport Service, to see that all cablegrams relating to the matters under his jurisdiction went to the right place for attention, to compute all requirements for the service, and to calculate the proper rates of completion and delivery of all vehicles and equipment. A new organization had to be created, while the work to be done daily was very complicated and urgent, the cablegrams betraying a constantly growing anxiety and tension overseas. As senior officer of the old division, the responsibility rested upon Major Orton during the next three months to keep things going, until the new men in charge could get an organization together and learn their duties. This was an unusually trying period.

On August 20, 1918, the Motor Transport Service was supplanted by the Motor Transport Corps, independent of any other corps. All the officers who had been displaced in May now returned, Major Orton being retained and made chief of the Service Division. His duties were to prepare the requirements calculations, as before, besides keeping at hand all statistical data, making efficiency studies of the corps' operations, conducting an inventory of all corps property, writing a history of the organization, and acting as morale officer. A staff of officers and clerks for each of these activities was collected, instructed, and their work supervised. Early in November Major Orton was promoted to lieutenant colonel. After the Armistice the inventory section had to be developed under great pressure and came to include about 125 officers, 75 enlisted men, and as many civilians. Six months were required to prepare the inventory. The historical section had a personnel of six officers and several civilians.

On May 19, 1919, Lieutenant Colonel Orton was directed to report to the office of the Secretary of War to receive a Distinguished Service Medal upon the following citation:

>   Lt. Col. Edward Orton, Jr., M. T. C., Formerly in charge of Service Division M. T. C. His untiring energy and splendid judgment were displayed in the efficient organization of the Engineering Division of the Motor Transport Corps, in bringing about standardization of equipment and supplies, and in efficiently directing the forces of the motor industry to the mutual advantage of the Army and the Industry itself.

On June 1, 1919, Lieutenant Colonel Orton was discharged from the service and near the close of the following September was commissioned colonel, Quartermaster Section, Officers' Reserve Corps, United States Army.

Among the Ohio State men who served with Orton in standardizing military trucks were Captain William C. Britton, '02, and Captain Allando A. Case, formerly instructor in the Department of Industrial Arts. After serving successively as unit organizer, shop engineer, and engineer officer, Captain Case was appointed, April 23, 1919, a member of a committee of three to draft courses of instruction for Motor Transport Corps Training Schools, to be conducted in connection with the shops for the intensive training of men as ignition experts, electricians, battery repairmen, blacksmiths, truck drivers, etc., so that the Army might have a highly skilled body of men for its Motor Transport Service. At the end of May Captain Case was ordered to Camp Holabird, Baltimore, Maryland, to organize a school for enlisted men. This was the first school of the kind in the Army. A few days later he was appointed educational director and constructive engineer of this school, being promoted to the rank of major on July 22. In the fall of 1919 Major Case also sat one day each week on the Civil Service Board for Motor Transport Training School Instructors at Washington, D. C. On November 1 he was sent to Camp Jesup at Atlanta, Georgia, to open a school there. That he did not overlook Ohio State men in choosing his instructors is shown by the fact that in January, 1920, he had six of them on his staff and was expecting to take on two more in a short time. Among these men were C. R. Upp, '03, and R. S. Richards and Fay Dunn, both of the class of 1900. Mr. Dunn was made head of the Engineering Section, and the other two men were in the machine department. Victor Darnell of the class of 1900 was in charge of tool installation at Camp Holabird. At the end of the year 1919 the school here had 650 students and was expected to graduate 1,500 students a year. Other schools for enlisted men were established at Camp Normoyle and Camp Boyd, Texas, and one for the training of Motor Transport Corps officers was formed at the Georgia School of Technology.

In October, 1918, Mr. Bertram S. Stephenson, '01, was summoned to Washington by the War Industries Board as an expert on pig iron.

Professor Alan E. Flowers of the Department of Electrical Engineers and a member of the Graduate Council entered the service, April 3, 1918, as a captain in the Radio Development Section of the Signal Corps at Washington, being placed in charge of the power supply equipment for all Army radio sets under development. He was discharged, March 8, 1919. Troi O. Farmer, assistant in Electrical Engineering, enlisted in Company B, 48th Regiment, Engineers, on May 17, 1918 and was in training at Fort Benjamin Harrison, Indiana, until the end of June, when he was transferred to the Signal Corps and was engaged in electrical research at the Bureau of Standards in Washington until August 1, after which he was connected with the Air Service in the national capital, being concerned with aircraft production. His whole term of service was seven months. Professor Frank E. Sanborn of the Department of Industrial Arts became a captain in the Sanitary Corps at the end of August,

1918, and for nearly three months thereafter was in charge of the Educational Department of the United States General Hospital No. 31 at Carlisle, Pennsylvania. He was then made assistant director of Occupational Therapy and head of the Technical Department in the Walter Reed General Hospital in Washington, D. C. Professor Alfred D. Cole of the Department of Physics spent the summers of 1917 and 1918 in radio development work in the Government laboratories in Washington: the first summer in the United States Naval Laboratory studying the use of electron tubes as receivers for wireless telegraphy, and part of the second in similar work in the Radio Division of the Bureau of Standards. A considerable portion of this summer was devoted to writing part of a manual on wireless telegraphy, which the Signal Corps of the Army had requested the experts of the bureau to prepare for use in military camps and training schools. A number of men cooperated in the preparation of this book in order to get it out quickly. The chapters on the use of electron tubes as receivers, amplifiers, and generators of radio signals in both telegraphy and telephony were the sections prepared by Professor Cole. Professor Samuel J. Barnett, also a member of the Department of Physics, attended the Submarine Conference, held in Washington in June, 1917, and gave some time to work on instruments and methods for the detection of submarines.

With so many loyal Ohio State people in and about Washington, it would have been strange, indeed, if they had not found the time for an occasional social gathering. The prime movers in bringing about the first of these meetings were Ralph H. Brown, '16, and L. H. Hart, '10, a visit of President W. O. Thompson to the city on war business furnishing the occasion. A notable dinner was given in Dr. Thompson's honor at Harvey's Restaurant, February 19, 1918, Colonel Chauncy B. Baker of the Quartermaster's Corps, who had recently returned from France, being another distinguished guest. One hundred alumni of the University, two-thirds of whom were in uniform, attended the function and listened attentively to President Thompson's stirring remarks on "The University and the War." He declared that practically all the buildings and grounds of Ohio State were devoted to war purposes, and that there was scarcely a student within the draft age who had not joined the forces. Others who responded were Major Edward Orton and Captain William C. Britton, both of whom were engaged in perfecting motor trucks for the Army; Colonel George A. Burrell, head of the gas and flame investigations of the Government, who spoke of what had been accomplished by the engineers in his section, many of whom were Ohio State men as has been already noted; Major William McPherson; Major David S. White, who was helping to organize the Veterinary Corps; Captain William L. Evans; Professor Henry L. Rietz; Dr. W. J. T. Duvel of the United States Department of Agriculture, who left immediately after the banquet for Australia on a war mission for the Government, and Willard Kiplinger, '12, correspondent for the Associated Press.

The gathering was so successful that a second one was arranged for April 1, notice being given that all Ohio State men in or near Washington would be welcome and might obtain information from Ralph H. Brown, who was called on to act as secretary of the local group or association. As the number of Ohio State people increased in and near Washington a series of Saturday night dinners was provided for at Cushman's Café on 14th Street, near F. The members gathered about the tables at 6 o'clock and afterwards adjourned to the club rooms on the fourth floor for a meeting. As there were three hundred or more alumni in Washington in the fall of 1918, the attendance was usually large until it was reduced greatly by the influenza epidemic. On the return of President Thompson from France, the association tendered him a big reception.

Although the College of Engineering had large groups of its teachers and graduates engaged in war work in Washington and Edgewood, as well as in the laboratories of the University in Columbus, its representatives were to be found meeting the public needs of the hour in other localities and in a variety of ways, for which they were especially fitted. Professor Franklin A. Ray, '87, of the Department of Mining Engineering was in Russia for several months in 1916-17, investigating the coal deposits, mining conditions, coal reserves, etc. In April, 1917, he made a report on these matters to the War Department, besides furnishing military information of value on Russia to the chief of staff of the United States Army. He also served on the Conservation Advisory Board of the Federal Fuel Administration in Ohio and as a district conservation engineer for central Ohio from August 20, 1918, to March 1, 1919. Professor Horace Judd and Instructor Paul Bucher, both of the Department of Mechanical Engineering, were members of a subdistrict conservation committee of the Federal Fuel Administration in Ohio from November 5, 1918, to January 1, 1919. Professor Karl D. Schwartzel, '93, of the Department of Mathematics served with the Committee on Education and Special Training as assistant educational director for Ohio, Indiana, and West Virginia. Associate Professor Edmund S. Manson, Jr., of the Department of Astronomy attended the United States Army Training Camp at Plattsburgh, New York, in the summer of 1916, was sworn into the service in the middle of May, 1917, and received three months more training at Fort Benjamin Harrison, coming out a first lieutenant. He served in the adjutant general's department at Camp Sherman, Ohio, besides attending the School for Personnel Adjutants at Camp Meigs, D. C., in the spring of 1918, was promoted to a captaincy early in October, 1918, and was discharged, September 6, 1919.

Not all of the representatives of the College of Engineering who were in the Chemical Warfare Service were stationed at Columbus, Edgewood, and Washington. At least a few in this branch of the service were to be found at other places. Thus, Lieutenant David R. Mellon, graduate assistant in chemistry in 1916-17, was stationed at Niagara Falls with the chemical detachment, being assistant production manager of the Government toxic gas plant, which was a part of the Oldbury Electro-Chemical Company at that place. First Lieutenant Claude P. McNeil, '14, was connected with the Chemical Warfare Service Gas Mask Chemical Plant at Long Island City. Sumner B. Frank, '11, enlisted as a private in the Chemical Warfare Service and was stationed in the Offense Laboratory at Cleveland, Ohio. Dean O. Crites, assistant in chemistry, became a second lieutenant and was at the United States Bureau of Mines at Pittsburgh.

Other kinds of war work were performed by members of the College of Engineering. Earle C. Smith, instructor in 1916 in metallurgy, who was at first on the inspection force of the Signal Corps, was later transferred to the Pittsburgh office of the Bureau of Aircraft Production, his entire term of service being from August, 1917, to January, 1919. Samuel S. Withrow, assistant in engineering drawing, served in the Ordnance Department as assistant ballistic engineer on Browning Machine Gun testing at the Frankfort Arsenal in Philadelphia. Hugo Diemer, '96, professor of industrial engineering at Pennsylvania State College, entered the service in July, 1917, and was commissioned major in the Ordnance Department, his first assignment being to the Frankfort Arsenal, Philadelphia. After two months there, in which he familiarized himself with the various operations of cartridge making, he was selected to represent the Ordnance Department at Lowell, Massachusetts. Very soon all Lowell and vicinity were added to the territory under his charge. Thus he represented the Government at the plants of the Newton Manufacturing Company and the International Steel Ordnance Company. He was then transferred to the staff of General Dickson, which had charge of all Army work at the Bethlehem Steel Company at Bethlehem, Pennsylvania.

Charles E. Skinner, M.E. '90, directed much of the investigation undertaken during 1918 in the Research Division of the Westinghouse Electric and Manufacturing Company at East Pittsburgh in connection with war problems. Ralph D. Mershon, also of the class of '90, resident in New York City and distinguished as an electrical consulting engineer, was appointed on the Naval Advisory Board at the beginning of the war and by the signing of the Armistice had been promoted to a lieutenant colonelcy. In June, 1918, Tufts College in Massachusetts conferred upon him the honorary degree of D. Sc., in recognition of his notable record. Benjamin G. Lamme, '88, was made a member of the Naval Advisory Board by Secretary Josephus Daniels in 1915. In that position during the war he made important contributions to the Allied cause. In the business world Mr. Lamme was widely known as the chief engineer of the Westinghouse Electric and Manufacturing Company, a place he held from 1903 until his death. At the annual meeting of the American Institute of Electrical Engineers in New York, May 16, 1919, he was awarded the Edison Medal in recognition of his notable service in developing electrical machinery. On this occasion also an address was read on "The Achievements of Benjamin Lamme." In the early summer of 1918 Herman Gamper of the class of 1899 was appointed power engineer for the new Emergency Fleet Corporation, his headquarters being in Philadelphia. Archibald C. Huston, '16, was commissioned a second lieutenant at the beginning of the war on the recommendation of Captain George L. Converse, commandant of the University Battalion. He received his training at Fortress Monroe, Virginia, was promoted to the rank of first lieutenant and in September, 1918, to that of captain. A little later he was placed in command of Fort Pickens, a coast artillery post outside of Pensacola, Florida. On the entrance of the United States into the war Paul M. Lincoln, '97, received a commission as captain in the United States Officers' Reserve Corps. Late in May, 1918, Carl B. Harrop, assistant professor of ceramic engineering at Ohio State University, entered upon important work for the Government at the Bureau of Standards in Pittsburgh.

Captain Gerald E. Tenney, B.M.E. '16, was stationed at the Springfield Arsenal, Massachusetts, in the Ordnance Department of the Army during the war. Under his supervision hundreds of thousands of rifles were manufactured. At mid-March, 1919, he sailed from San Francisco to report to the commanding officer of the Manila Arsenal, having been appointed in the Regular Army. He was one of three, out of fifteen, whose recommendation was approved in Washington.

A notable service was rendered to the Government by F. M. Craft, '05, and C. P. Cooper, '07, two graduates in electrical engineering. At the time the United States entered the war Mr. Craft was in charge of inside plant engineering work for the Chesapeake and Potomac Telephone Company at Baltimore, while Mr. Cooper was division superintendent of plants for the New York Telephone Company at Albany. With the declaration of hostilities the demands for telephone facilities in Washington became pressing. The entire resources of the great Bell system in personnel, money, and materials were placed at the disposal of the Government; and engineers, traffic experts, maintenance and construction men, and operators were brought to Washington to handle the situation. It was not until near the end of 1917, however, that it became apparent that the surpassing needs of the emergency demanded other than the ordinary organization methods, and it was then determined to equip the national capital with adequate telephone service. It was at this juncture that Mr. Craft was asked to organize and direct an engineering department recruited from the Bell companies throughout the East to perform the engineering work, while Mr. Cooper was assigned the task of constructing and maintaining the telephone plant as plant superintendent.

The magnitude of the work entrusted to these gentlemen will appear from the following statements: At the time the United States entered the World War the Bell Telephone property in the District of Columbia was valued at $6,500,000 and served about 60,000 telephones, of which 4,600 were for the use of the Federal Government. During the period of belligerancy the value of the District establishment was increased to $14,000,000. Over 73,000 telephones were installed, most of them for Government use. A nine-story office and equipment building was erected in record-breaking time at a cost of $1,350,000. Prior to April 1, 1917, a switchboard requiring less than thirty operators sufficed to handle the local toll business. By the time of the signing of the Armistice a central toll office equipment requiring about two hundred operators was partially completed. Within the same period a complete new local central office was placed in service, and two others were constructed and ready for installation. Large service extensions of the six existing central offices were made, requiring in two cases additions to the buildings. Subways were built and cables laid in numerous instances in sections which before the war were public parks, and on which acres of temporary buildings were erected for Government use. One hundred and fifty miles of underground cable ducts were installed.

Private branch exchange switchboards were put in place for the Government departments, in many instances comparable in size with those of small cities. Not a few of these equipments were soon outgrown. In the case of the War Department five different switchboards were installed, the last of these being the largest private branch exchange in the world. It afforded accommodations for seventy-five operators and cost over $400,000. This board was capable of handling 8,000 private exchange stations and was actually serving 5,000 at the time the Armistice was signed. It was housed in a building erected by the Government but planned and supervised by the telephone company.

Mr. Craft and Mr. Cooper continued their service until hostilities ceased, when the special organization was abandoned, and Washington became again one of the divisional units of the Chesapeake and Potomac Telephone Company.

A few members of the teaching staff and many of the graduates and students of the college saw active service overseas. Something of the record of this service has been told in another chapter. Suffice it to say here that Grover C. Seegar, '17, instructor in civil engineering, enlisted at Camp Sherman, Ohio, late in April, 1918, as a private in the Transport Battalion, 158th Depot Brigade, and was later transferred to the Machine Gun Corps, 322nd Battalion, 83rd Division. In July, 1918, he landed in France, where he served in the Le Mons area until September, 1919. From that time to the end of October he was on duty in the Paris area, receiving his discharge October 30, 1919. Meantime, he had been promoted to the rank of sergeant. Thomas C. Coleman, assistant in the Department of Industrial Arts, received his training at Camp Devens, April 28 to July 5, 1918, and went to France with the United States Engineers, 29th Regiment, 74th Division, where he landed on July 17. During a period of more than seven months, that is, until February 28, 1919, he saw service at Angers, Fort St. Menge, Toul, and St. Nazarin. About a month later he was discharged at Camp Devens. William E. Davis, '04, went to France with the Canadian railway troops. He was advanced to the rank of major and in October, 1918, was awarded the Distinguished Service Medal of Great Britain for brave conduct under heavy shell fire, while supervising the construction of a railroad near the front in the previous August.

The Effect of the War on the Departments of the College of Engineering

It scarcely needs to be said that certain general departments named in the above list, such as astronomy, chemistry, mathematics, and physics, draw numbers of their students from other colleges than that of Engineering and that in the case of the departments just named the enrollment figures given under the years 1917-18 and 1918-19 indicate withdrawals of students and the decline in registration extending throughout the University in those years.

The first withdrawals from the College of Engineering, as from the other colleges, due to the war took place in the third week of April, 1917, when within two days 373 students withdrew from the University as a whole, at least ten of these being from the College of Engineering. This departure of young men from the campus was but the forerunner of the withdrawal of nearly three times as many less than a month later, when the University Faculty gave its sanction to students leaving for the purpose of going into agricultural and military service. This time 101 engineering students withdrew to go to work on farms and 29 more to enlist in the Army. Many who did not leave with the crowd during May 10-15 entered the service during the summer months, and the enrollment of the College of Engineering was down to 855 when the University opened in the autumn of 1917. During the following months 149 more students withdrew from the college to enter some branch of military service. Under the Selective Service Law 63 students enlisted in the Engineer Enlisted Reserve Corps and thereby obtained a re-classification by which they were permitted to complete their studies before being drafted. Twelve of the fourth-year electrical students entered the Signal Corps by completing a wireless course, which was prescribed by the office of the Signal Corps, War Department, and given by Mr. Roy A. Brown, instructor in the Department of Electrical Engineering, assisted by Professor Alfred D. Cole of the Department of Physics. When the second half-year began in February, 1918, the number of engineering students was found to be 693, or 162 less than in the previous fall.

When the University resumed its activities in the following September, the enrollment in the College of Engineering jumped to 1,236, the large increase being due to the Students' Army Training Corps. Of the number given 834 were inducted into the S.A.T.C., while another group withdrew on account of their failure to qualify. Only 379 were regular students. On the demobilization of the S.A.T.C. in December most of the S.A.T.C. cadets and many of the first-year students left the University, the latter because they had found conditions for study unsatisfactory under the congested conditions then existing.

Remembering that the United States declared war on Germany, April 6, 1917, one can note the effect of the war on the enrollment of the departments in the College of Engineering in the following table:

College of Engineering

Departments	1915-16	1916-17	1917-18	1918-19
Architecture	354	510	330	192
Astronomy	148	145	118	107
Ceramic Engineering	262	255	165	126
Chemistry	3,316	3,371	2,853	3,736
Civil Engineering	881	876	637	615
Electrical Engineering	442	559	284	310
Engineering Drawing	1,661	1,683	1,550	1,508
Industrial Arts	937	1,164	743	574
Mathematics	1,722	2,111	1,762	1,377
Mechanical Engineering	756	740	479	441
Mechanics	346	353	254	222
Metallurgy	162	286	197	213
Mineralogy	76	74	64	52
Mine Engineering	111	82	87	74
Physics	980	1,308	999	1,001

The fluctuations in enrollment during the years 1917-18 and 1918-19 are exhibited in the following table:

Departments	1917-18 1st Sem.	1917-18 2nd Sem.	1918-19 1st Sem.	1918-19 2nd Sem.
Architecture	44	59	23	23
Architectural Engineering	23		36	18
Ceramic Engineering	62	53	39	31
Chemical Engineering	173	146	213	134
Civil Engineering	140	118	242	119
Electrical Engineering	206	156	269	153
Mechanical Engineering	164	130	269	146
Mine Engineering	30	18	32	23
General Engineering	11	7	9	16
Special	2	2	2	..
Unclassified	..	4	55	23
Totals	855	693	1,189	686

Some of the old students, who had been mustered out of service, reappeared with the opening of the second half-year in February, 1919, the enrollment being at this time 685 and approximating closely what it had been just a year before. The number of students receiving engineering degrees in June was 62 and was made up largely of men who at the beginning of the year were enlisted in the Engineers' Reserve Corps of the Army. Most of the senior electrical engineers had previously enlisted in the Signal Reserve Corps. If these men had not thereby received exemption from the draft as being already in the service, the list of graduates would have been very small.

That the war made deep inroads on the Faculty of the Engineering College, as well as on the number of its students, during the year 1917-1918 is shown by the records of the Board of Trustees for that year. Seven leaves of absence were granted and thirteen resignations were accepted by the Board during the period mentioned, the result being that the Department of Chemistry lost nine instructors; the Department of Civil Engineering, three; the Department of Metallurgy, two; and the Departments of Astronomy, Ceramics, Physics, Electrical Engineering, Mine Engineering, and Engineering Drawing, one each, within a few months.

Meantime, the School of Military Aeronautics had been inaugurated on the campus late in May, 1917, three other United States military schools being opened in rapid succession and continuing to various dates in the summer of 1918. As the courses of intensive training in all of these schools involved the teaching of various specialized, technical branches, several departments of the College of Engineering were called upon to supply instructors and even administrative officers. For example, the Department of Mechanical Engineering furnished six instructors; the Department of Astronomy, two; the Department of Industrial Arts, two; and the Departments of Architecture and Electrical Engineering, one each. The Department of Physics supplied for a part of the time the president of the Academic Board, and the Department of Mechanics supplied an assistant in his office. As we are here concerned only with the College of Engineering, it is unnecessary to refer to the number of instructors provided for these military schools by the other colleges of the University.[1]

Although certain parts of the present chapter have been

in the nature of a commentary upon the effects of the war on those engineering departments most deeply involved in its prosecution, yet it seems desirable to set before the reader more directly and specifically the wartime experiences of these departments, in order that he may appreciate as fully as possible the reflex influence of the unique episode upon the educational units of the University.

THE EFFECT OF THE WAR ON THE DEPARTMENT OF CHEMISTRY

None of the departments in the Engineering College was more affected by war conditions than was the Department of Chemistry. This was due to the predominant part played by chemistry in the World War and the great demand for trained chemists in the service of the Government, as also in many of the industries that took on Government contracts. Conditions preceding the entrance of the United States into the war had stimulated interest in chemistry and increased the attendance of the department. For several years chemical industries in this country had been expanding at a rapid rate, and very attractive positions were open to competent chemists. As a result it had been difficult to maintain an efficient staff of instructors, while at the same time the body of students was growing rapidly.

The declaration of hostilities by the United States made an immediate and heavy call upon the teaching staff of the department, for the only reserves of trained chemists in the country were in the college faculties. Three of the six professors at once entered the Chemical Warfare Service, and soon after a fourth arranged to be absent in Washington as a consulting expert, returning once a week for a day of concentrated lectures. Of the force of nearly twenty-five men of lower rank about one-half left in rapid succession to enter either munition plants, the Chemical Warfare Service, or the Government Research Laboratory at the American University

[1] On the participation of the staffs of the different colleges and departments in the instructional work of the Army military schools, see Chapter II, pp. 17-40.

in Washington. The number was somewhat further reduced as time passed, until not more than eight or nine remained. Those who did remain devoted a considerable part of their time to war problems in cooperation with the Government Research Laboratory

A limited number of new instructors was secured by filling vacancies with satisfactory high-school teachers, persons of physical disability, and well-trained women. The earnestness and devotion of this reduced and altered staff maintained the standard of instruction to an unexpected degree.

The immediate effect of the war upon the enrollment of the department was seen in a great reduction in numbers. The more advanced students were rapidly absorbed into the Chemical Warfare Service and the arsenals, and many in the lower classes enlisted or dropped out to fill well-paid positions. In the fall of 1918 nearly all of the members of the newly established unit of the Student's Army Training Corps, numbering finally a little more than 2,000 cadets, elected chemistry. This large election was due in part to the emphasis that had been put upon the shortage of chemists in the public prints and in part to the impression prevailing that students in chemical classes would not be drafted. The organization of the technical courses in the S.A.T.C. was delayed by the Government for a time after the arrival of the cadets; and when, at length, the program of intensive training in chemistry was ready to be put into effect, it had become apparent that the novice could not hope to attain chemical proficiency before he would be called into service. Consequently, the S.A.T.C. enrollment in the department dropped to about eight hundred, a number that was within the staff's ability to handle with some degree of success.

The presence of the S.A.T.C. caused a number of senior chemical men, who had been drafted, to be returned to the University, and some who had escaped draft also returned. This enabled the Department of Chemistry to maintain a small group of senior engineers for intensive training. The junior and sophomore classes were reduced to relatively small numbers.

Notwithstanding the changes in program and in the personnel of the instructional staff, the spirit of the chemical students was very good, but the plan for intensive training was of little avail owing to the lack of any real coordination between the military instruction and the academic instruction. This lack was largely due to the inexperience of the military officers of the S.A.T.C.

The sudden ending of the war, so soon after the reorganization of the chemical work on the intensive basis, occasioned a new dislocation and necessitated another reorganization. Through the remainder of the year 1918-19 old students were returning to re-enter their classes, for it was evident that the industrial demand for chemists would continue, and the students were anxious to lose no time in completing their preparation to take their places in the industrial world. During the second half-year and the succeeding summer session the chief effort was directed to completing the course for the advanced students and fitting the less advanced men into normal courses. By the opening session of 1919-20 the readjustment was accomplished.

The Department of Chemistry, like the University as a whole, experienced an unprecedented enrollment after the termination of the war. In the autumn of 1919 the enrollment in freshman chemistry was over 2,100, and all advanced classes were largely increased. The large body of Ohio State graduates in chemistry that was brought together in the Government Research Laboratory in Washington and in the arsenals called attention to the training afforded at the University, and advanced students from other colleges entered for work in chemistry.

In apparatus and equipment the department suffered considerable deterioration on account of the war. Under the heavy load of teaching imposed on the depleted staff, and with much inexperienced assistance, proper care of equipment was impossible. The substation for Government experimental work maintained on the campus drew heavily on the department's resources of apparatus, and although the attempt was made to keep accurate account of loaned apparatus and to secure proper recompense for damages, much deterioration resulted. The plant itself suffered considerably, for repair work was difficult to secure, and a chemical laboratory is always in need of repair. With diminished equipment, partly due to the increased cost of all kinds of apparatus and partly to the fact that some of it was not available in the market, and with increased enfollment, it is clear that the Department of Chemistry felt the effects of the war in a variety of ways, including the temporary reduction of efficiency for advanced work. It is safe to say, further, that no department staff was under more continued strain than that of chemistry. To some extent this strain was offset by the stimulus of new association and cooperation with other chemists, the pooling of knowledge and ideas in a common cause, and the suggestion of new lines of work for research students.

The whole University, as well as the Department of Chemistry itself, may well be proud of the large number of chemists, trained in the department, who played an honorable part in the technical service of the Government. These men, assembled in research laboratories, arsenals, and industrial plants side by side with the graduates of better known institutions, attained a level of accomplishment that redounded to the credit of the institution represented by them and has given the Chemistry Department at Ohio State University an enviable reputation as a place of training for those entering the chemical profession. Certain it is that the department is better known among chemists and employers than it was before the war.

The Department of Metallurgy

It was inevitable, one may say, that the members of the Department of Metallurgy should be called early into war service. Already in the summer of 1917 Professor D. J. Demorest and Instructor Earl C. Smith of this department were summoned to Portsmouth, Ohio, as experts by steel manufacturers who had undertaken Government contracts. In December the department was deprived altogether of its teachers. It was at this time that two members of the departmental staff became connected with Edgewood Arsenal and devoted their best energies to the development of the toxic gas program.[2] The class work in metallurgy was now assumed by Professor William J. McCaughey of the Department of Mineralogy, Professor H. E. Nold of the Department of Mine Engineering, and Mr. J. O. Druffin of the Department of Mechanics, who carried this extra burden in addition to their regular University work.

During the fall of 1917 there was a large attendance of students in the general courses of fuels, iron, and steel, inasmuch as these courses were especially recommended by the Army authorities; but as soon as the Students' Army Training Corps was formed in the fall of 1918 the attendance dropped to 30 or 40 per cent of the previous enrollment. In the other courses in metallurgy the attendance had been greatly reduced and in some entirely eliminated, owing to the fact that every junior and senior mining engineer who was physically acceptable for military service had volunteered. In brief, therefore, the effect of the war on the Department of Metallurgy was to draw into the Army all of the regular teaching staff and most of the students.

After the termination of hostilities, however, the enrollmen in the metallurgy classes greatly increased, to such an extent, indeed, that the department was perplexed as to how to care for the students under its supervision.

The Department of Electrical Engineering

Two of the members of this department went into military service in the spring of 1918, namely, Professor Alan E. Flowers, who was assigned to duty as an officer in the Signal Corps Division of the Army about April 1, and Assistant Troi O. Farmer, who resigned and enlisted in the Engineers' Corps in May. Mr. Roy A. Brown, instructor, was in charge of the

[2] See p. 210, this volume.

radio instruction in the School of Military Aeronautics on the campus from its inception in the latter part of May, 1917, until its close at the end of August in the following year. He also gave the special radio course to the seniors of the Class of 1918. Mr. William R. Alexander, the mechanician of the department, gave half of his time during the summer of 1918 to the manufacture of a bandage-winding machine, which Professor F. C. Caldwell and he developed for the use of the Red Cross workers.[3]

The student enrollment in electrical engineering was less affected by the war than that of many other departments. This was mainly due to the need of the War Department for technical graduates, especially trained as electrical engineers and radio experts. A few of the upperclassmen, however, dropped out to enter service, the junior class losing more than a third of its members. During the spring of 1918 the seniors devoted the greater part of their time to a special course in radio engineering, which was directed by the officers of the Signal Corps at Washington. Ten men, all but two of the Americans remaining in the class of 1918, took this course and went directly after graduation to a radio school, where they completed their training and were commissioned second lieutenants about the time of the signing of the Armistice.

In the fall of 1918 the Students' Army Training Corps further emphasized the need for technically trained men and held a large proportion of the juniors, keeping them so nearly to their regular course that they were able with only slight modification of the usual curriculum to graduate in June, 1919. Twenty-one men completed their work at this time. Seven of those who had withdrawn from the two preceding classes returned to graduate with the class of 1920.

THE DEPARTMENT OF INDUSTRIAL ARTS

Of seven men of the rank of instructor or above in the Department of Industrial Arts four became sooner or later engaged in Government service. Associate Professor William

[3] See p. 55, this volume.

A. Knight served as head of the Departments of Airplanes and Gunnery in the School of Military Aeronautics from May, 1917, to September, 1918; Professor Frank E. Sanborn was commissioned captain in the Sanitary Engineering Corps of the Army in July, 1918; Mr. Allando A. Case, instructor in machine work, became a captain in the Motor Transport Corps in October, 1918, and was stationed at Camp Holabird, Maryland, and Mr. Jacob A. Foust, instructor in forging, was in the service as civilian inspector of forging from July 5 to November 30, 1918.

The effect of the war on the enrollment of the department is shown by the following figures: 1916-17, 1,311; 1917-18, 852; 1918-19, 726.

In the autumn of 1918 ninety-five cadets in the Students' Army Training Corps took shop work.

Due to the fact that the operation of an army now requires so much technical knowledge and mechanical skill and that so many young men received specialized training in mechanical practice of some kind during the period of hostilities, there was developed a new interest and more thorough appreciation of the value and need of practical mechanical training. These conditions were revealed in the increased enrollment of the department in the fall of 1919, which amounted to 860 students, indicating a total for the academic year of about 1,450.

THE DEPARTMENT OF MECHANICS

During the summer of 1917 Professor James E. Boyd of the Department of Mechanics was employed in testing airplane struts at the Bureau of Standards in Washington, and in the following months he spent some time in calculating the results of these investigations. In the second week of July, 1917, Professor Boyd, in company with Professor Edwin F. Coddington of the same department and with Professor William J. McCaughey of the Department of Mineralogy, attended a meeting in Washington which was held in connection with the Council for National Defense. During December, 1917, and the first three months of 1918 Professor Boyd assisted in the office work of the School of Military Aeronautics on the campus. The remaining teacher in the department, Mr. F. O. Draffin, was employed by the Shipping Board during the summer of 1918 in experimental work on concrete ships. In the absence of the teaching staff of the Department of Metallurgy, Mr. Draffin instructed a part of its classes during the spring and fall semesters of 1918, while Professor Boyd conducted a class in mathematics, besides carrying his work in mechanics. In the fall of 1918, Professor Coddington, in addition to attending to his duties as acting dean of the College of Engineering, gave considerable time to the organization of the Students' Army Training Corps.

The decline in the number of students in mechanics on account of the war is shown in the following figures:

1916-17	First Semester	Mechanics 101	184 students
	Second Semester	Mechanics 102	128 students
		Mechanics 104	39 students
1917-18	First Semester	Mechanics 101	144 students
	Second Semester	Mechanics 102	96 students
		Mechanics 104	12 students
1918-19	First Semester	Mechanics 101	101 students
	Second Semester	Mechanics 102	78 students
		Mechanics 104	12 students
		Mechanics 101	51 students

THE DEPARTMENT OF MINE ENGINEERING

Professor Franklin A. Ray of the Department of Mine Engineering was absent on leave in Russia during the fall of 1916 and the first four months of 1917 in the interests of the American steel industries, investigating coal deposits. He was in Petrograd in March, 1917, during the Russian Revolution, and did not leave Russia until May 8. His extensive travels and his contact with men of standing who were not only thoroughly familiar with the conditions prevailing in the country but were also ready to unburden their minds to an American, enabled Professor Ray to impart valuable information to the State Department in Washington on his return. Professor Ray was again granted leave of absence for the second semester of the year 1917-18 and devoted his energies to increasing the coal output and otherwise assisting the Federal Fuel Administration in Ohio, his leave being extended through the fall semester of 1918-19. The other member of the department, Assistant Professor H. E. Nold, remained on duty at the University, conducting the work of the classroom and in addition teaching a large group of students in the metallurgy of iron and steel, on account of the absence of Professor D. J. Demorest.

In the fall of 1917 there were sixty-four men enrolled in the courses offered in mine engineering. During the semester nine of these students withdrew from the Engineering College to enter the service of their country. A number of others did not return, and the second semester opened with only thirteen students, three of these leaving soon for war service. In other words, every student in mine engineering who was an American citizen and physically able enlisted during the year 1917-18 in some form of war service.

THE DEPARTMENT OF ASTRONOMY

Like other departments in the several colleges, the Department of Astronomy was considerably shaken in the middle of May, 1917. Professor Henry C. Lord, as head of the Department of Aids to Flight in the School of Military Aeronautics, was compelled to devote most of his time to the preparation of his lectures on that subject and to the construction of the apparatus needed for their illustration. Professor Edmund S. Manson finished his work in the general and required courses a fortnight earlier than usual and left for Fort Benjamin Harrison. Carl C. Lowe, student assistant, went into agricultural service before enlisting, and some of the students withdrew during May and June to enter military service or take up farm work.

CHAPTER XVI

THE PROBLEMS OF THE GRADUATE SCHOOL

On March 8, 1917, nearly a month before the United States entered the war, the Council of the Graduate School submitted to the University Faculty a resolution, which was adopted and in turn approved by the Board of Trustees on April 3, authorizing President Thompson to appoint a research committee consisting of representatives of the University Faculty engaged in scientific investigations, one or more graduates of the institution, at least one member of the Board of Trustees and the President as chairman, to cooperate with the National Research Committee according to the program of the National Research Council.

The number of matriculates in the Graduate School in the fall of 1916 had been 196, 48 of these being women. In the following spring the enrollment was 191. By the middle of May, 1917, when male students were leaving the campus with the approval of the University and State authorities, five graduate students withdrew for agricultural service and three more for military service. The summer session of 1917 showed a marked decline in comparison with that of the previous year, the drop being from 195 to 155. Of the absent, thirty-eight were men and two were women. During the opening weeks of the autumn session of 1917 the Graduate School temporarily recovered most of its losses, for on November 8 it had an enrollment of 191; but the school was by no means immune from the contagion of the war and lost, during the next three months, fifty-five of its members. Short registration and withdrawals during the spring brought the number down to 123.

Among those who left the Graduate School during the

academic year, 1917-18, were some of those who were entitled to stipends as fellows and scholars. Of ten fellows three found it necessary to resign, September 1, 1917, and three more during the first semester; while out of a total of twenty-five applicants for scholarships who were recommended, two declined appointment, six resigned before the University opened in September, three resigned during the first semester, and two more during the second. Only eleven of twenty appointees to scholarships retained their appointments, these being mostly women. One student, not counted in the eleven, was appointed at the beginning of the second semester. In the light of this experience the Graduate Council declined during the continuation of the war to recommend any applicant for a scholarship or fellowship who was subject to military service.

The enrollment in the Graduate School reached its lowest ebb in the fall of 1918, when the number of students was 96, forty-seven of these being men (three of them in the Students' Army Training Corps).

After the signing of the Armistice and the release of students from obligations imposed upon them by the war, many of them began to arrange their affairs to return to college. Hence, the opening of the second half-year showed a gain of 23⅓ per cent in attendance over the previous half-year, the increase being from 96 to 119 students. In the summer session of 1919 the number jumped to 164, ninety-four of these being men; and in the fall of the same year it rose to 176, the men now numbering 124. In other words, within less than a year after the signing of the Armistice the enrollment in the Graduate School was rapidly getting back to normal, as was also the proportion of male to female students in the school.

The Graduate School not only suffered the loss by withdrawal of more than half of its students during the war; it was also called on to relinquish for the period of hostilities or altogether the services of more than half of the members of its governing board, the Graduate Council. The dean of the school, Dr. William McPherson, was the first to depart, receiving leave of absence at the beginning of September, 1917.

In the absence of Dr. McPherson, Professor Henry R. Spencer of the Department of Political Science was appointed acting dean and served until the latter part of November, when he also was granted leave of absence. As a student of international relations Professor Spencer had been invited to speak before various groups on subjects connected with the war, one of his addresses, "American Neutrality and Belligerency," being delivered on the evening of April 6, 1917, before the Ohio College Association. About December 1, Professor Spencer sailed for France, and, after a short stay in that country, went to Italy, where he became regional director of the Y.M.C.A. with the Third Army. He remained abroad for a little more than a year, returning to the United States toward the end of December, 1918, and to Columbus, on January 4, 1919.

With the departure of Professor Spencer the duties of the acting deanship devolved upon Professor Wilbur H. Siebert of the Department of European History, who served until the end of the academic year 1919. At commencement time, 1917, Professor Siebert had called the attention of the president of the Alumni Association to the importance of gathering and preserving the records of the services of Ohio State men in the war. The matter was taken up with President Thompson, and in the autumn he appointed the War Records Committee, which was provided with a sum of money sufficient to carry forward its work. Professor Siebert was named on this committee, through the efforts of which a large body of early records of the men and women in service was gathered. In February, 1918, Governor James M. Cox appointed the Ohio Historical Commission on the proposal of President Thompson at the suggestion of Professor Arthur M. Schlesinger and Professor Siebert, both of whom were appointed on the commission. The primary object of this commission was to preserve the war records of the State.

On April 1, 1918, Professor Alan E. Flowers of the Department of Electrical Engineering, who was a member of the Graduate Council, resigned to accept a captain's commission in the Signal Corps Division of the United States Army. On the conclusion of hostilities Captain Flowers accepted a commercial position in Buffalo, New York.

Another member of the council who entered the service of the Government was Professor Dana J. Demorest of the Department of Metallurgy.

Needless to say, all the members of the council who did not enter active service participated in the several liberty loan, war chest, and other drives on the campus, and one or more of them contributed to different publications articles relating to the conflict.

Despite all these distractions the Graduate Council issued the first two numbers of the *Ohio State University Studies,* besides a new number of the *Publications of the Teaching Staff* covering the previous five years.

CHAPTER XVII

THE SERVICES OF THE COLLEGE OF HOMEOPATHIC MEDICINE

The College of Homeopathic Medicine made a remarkably good record during the war, despite its small number of teachers and students. The smallest of the colleges of the University in attendance, it had only 35 students in the fall of 1916 and only 32 in the following spring. Like the Colleges of Medicine, Dentistry, and Veterinary Medicine, it was favored by the fact that all of its students who were physically fit were expected to continue their studies as members of the Medical Enlisted Reserve Corps in order to be of greater service when called. The war had little effect on its enrollment until the spring of 1918. In fact, the attendance of the college increased to 37 in September, 1917, but dropped to 28 five months later. With the induction of men into the Students' Army Training Corps, October 1, 1918, the registration jumped to 50, 16 of this number being cadets in the S. A. T. C. The presence of this new organization and the terrible epidemic of influenza seriously interrupted classroom work. The demobilization of the S.A.T.C. in the following December and the failure of eight freshmen out of a class of 17 to return in the second semester explains the drop in the number of students to 25 in February, 1919. Nevertheless, conditions became more favorable at once, and in the autumn 29 students were enrolled. Corresponding fluctuations on a reduced scale appear in the attendance at the summer sessions of 1917, 1918, and 1919. In the first of these sessions the enrollment was four; in the second nine, and in the third, five.

On March 30, 1917, the homeopathic Faculty voted to ask President Thompson to offer the services of the hospital under their care and of the Faculty as well to the War Department and the State of Ohio, in the event of war. Dr. Jay G. Keiser, '06, assistant in surgery, was commissioned first lieutenant, September 18, 1917, in the Sanitary Detachment, 320th Infantry, and later served as battalion surgeon with the American Expeditionary Force. He was promoted to a captaincy at the end of February, 1919, and was discharged from the service on June 26 at Camp Sherman. Professor Fred B. Grosvenor entered the service in February, 1918, as first lieutenant and went to France in charge of the Department of Internal Medicine of Base Hospital No. 48. He became a captain, February 17, 1919, and received his discharge at Camp Dix, April 23 of the same year, after 14 months' service. Dr. Harry M. Sage, an assistant in the college, was commissioned first lieutenant, May 24, 1918, and served with the base hospital at Camp Jackson, South Carolina, where he was discharged, April 26, 1919. On December 16, 1917, Dr. George B. Faulder, a clinical assistant in the college, was commissioned first lieutenant in the Medical Officers' Reserve Corps and was given leave of absence January 1, 1918, He was sent overseas and became connected with Evacuation Hospital No. 6. He also saw service in Germany. He was promoted to the rank of captain, receiving his commission February 22, 1919.

In addition to the military service of the instructors mentioned above, Dean Claude A. Burrett was a member of the State Committee, Council of National Defense and, with Professor J. A. Ferree, served on the medical staff of the Students' Army Training Corps during the influenza epidemic in October, 1918. Professors W. A. Humphrey, A. E. Hinsdale, R. C. Wolcott, and Dr. W. B. Carpenter were all enrolled in the Volunteer Medical Service Corps.

Five of the students were in active military service, namely, Harley W. Clinton, Peter Jaglinski, Chester W. Knappenberger, Frank G. Pettibone, and Harry G. Stack. Sixteen others were members of the Medical Enlisted Reserve Corps.

The war record of the College of Homeopathic Medicine

would not be complete without the mention of the service rendered by the hospital and the nurses' training school. During the time that the United States military schools were in operation on the campus, that is, from May 31, 1917, to August 31, 1918, 55 cadets from these schools were treated as resident patients in the hospital, and over 600 were treated as dispensary patients. During the same period 10 patients, who were chemists connected with the Ordnance Department of the United States Army engaging in research at the University, were treated for burns received while experimenting with poisonous gases. While the Students' Army Training Corps was a part of the University organization, namely, from October 1, to December 14, 1918, 26 cadets were treated as inpatients and 35 as dispensary patients. During this same period four chemists from the Ordnance Department were resident patients at the hospital. A comparison of the above figures for the spring and summer of 1918 with those for the last three months of the same year suggests that the University Hospital's activities were much greater during the year 1917-18 than during the succeeding year. This fact is accounted for in two ways, namely, by the greatly lessened student body during the year 1918-19 and by the absence of the military schools, both of which sources furnished the hospital more than twelve hundred patients. As shown above, comparatively few patients from the Students' Army Training Corps were treated in the hospital.

The hospital staff and the training school for nurses took an active part in Red Cross work. A part of the lower floor of the old hospital building at the corner of Neil and Tenth Avenues was used throughout the winter of 1917-18 as a center for Red Cross activities. Space in the new hospital was also assigned to this work. A class in Red Cross sewing met during the same period in the nurses' home.

The following named nurses, who were also teachers in the training school, left the University and went into Red Cross service: Lois Campbell, Frances Nichol, Olga Johnson, Murriel Key, Rena Daily, and Vera Benjamin.

Owing to the absence from the Faculty in military service of one professor and three assistants, the hospital practice was especially difficult during the year 1918-19. The absence of the younger men placed a greater burden upon the members of the Faculty, and in a measure affected the hospital's work. Professor Grosvenor's classes in physical diagnosis were conducted by Dr. A. B. Schneider as lecturer. In April and May, 1919, several members of the staff who were in military service returned to the college. Captain Grosvenor returned late in April; Captain Faulder and Lieutenant Sage, in May, and Captain Keiser, in July.

One hundred and twenty-three of the alumni of the College of Homeopathic Medicine received commissions during the war, as shown in the muster roll. Of these 123 men 22 saw service in France; six in both England and France; four in France and Belgium; three in France and Germany; one in England, France, and Luxemburg; one in England, France, and Belgium; and one is recorded indefinitely "overseas." Only one of the entire number is definitely given as having entered the naval service, and he became lieutenant commander of the U.S. S.S. *Von Steuben*, a transport between the United States and France. Two of the graduates received military awards for bravery and distinguished service during the war. They were Captain William H. Caine, '16, who was awarded the British Distinguished Service Cross for his services in the battle of Cambrai, and the other was Captain Neil A. Dayton, '15, who received a similar decoration from the British Government "for conspicuous gallantry and devotion to duty" during October 9 to 22, 1918, in the Wervicq-Comines Sector and later in the rapid advances to the River Scheldt. The citation of Captain Dayton says that it was largely due to him that on one occasion a large number of gassed men were removed from an area saturated with gas, and that on another occasion he collected the wounded (some thirty in number) while he was being "subjected to the most harassing shell and machine-gun fire."

CHAPTER XVIII

THE TEMPORARY CLOSING OF THE COLLEGE OF LAW AND ITS LATER SERVICE

Although the College of Law is one of the smaller colleges of the University, its enrollment was more reduced by the war, in combination with other circumstances, than that of any of the other colleges. Its normal number of students before hostilities was somewhat more than 140. Thus, in November, 1916, it had 147 students and in February, 1917, 141 students. In September of the latter year, however, its enrollment was lowered to 81. This was due not only to war conditions, taken in connection with the fact that the College of Law is a man's college, but also to the enforcement of a new rule in September, 1917, requiring a preliminary year of college work for the admission of candidates for certificates in law. Then, in Februay, 1918, another rule went into effect, abolishing certificates in law and requiring two years of college work as a prerequisite for entrance into the law school. All of these conditions operating together cut down the attendance at once to 54. When, in August, 1918, the "man power bill" was enacted by Congress, placing the minimum draft age at eighteen years, no students were left for the College of Law, except those entitled to deferred classification. Hence, the college was not opened during the first half-year of 1918-19, as there were not enough students to justify it. With the American troops just arriving on the Lorraine front and Russia withdrawing from the war, prospects for the prolonged continuance of hostilities were still good in February, 1918. Nevertheless, the law school again opened its doors and enrolled 33 students. It also gave courses of instruction in the summer session of 1919 to 16 men who had returned from military service. It was not until the following September that the College of Law approximated its pre-war registration, with 133 students in its classes.

The largest withdrawal of men from the college took place from May 10 to 14, 1917, after the University Faculty had decided to release male students to go into farm work and military service. Of the 141 students then attending the law school, 11 withdrew for the latter purpose and 33 for the former.

The war services of the professors of law were of various kinds. When the School for Aero-Squadron Adjutants began on the campus in January, 1918, Dean John J. Adams lectured to the adjutants on the law of evidence, and Professors A. H. Tuttle, C. D. Laylin, J. W. Madden, and H. C. Corry gave them instruction in military law. The starting of the School for Balloon Adjutants in the following March called for the same sort of service, in which Professor G. W. Rightmire took part with the others. On March 5, 1918, President Thompson was granted leave of absence by the Board of Trustees in order to make an extended trip through the northwestern States in behalf of the United States Department of Agriculture and the Federal Food Administration; and again about September 1, 1918, he was called away by the Government, this time to report on agricultural conditions in England, France, and Belgium. His absence during this second trip continued until near the middle of November. During these periods of Dr. Thompson's absence Dean Adams served as acting president of the University. From June 18 to September 15, 1918, Mr. Adams was in charge of the Law Enforcement Division of the Federal Food Administration in Ohio. In this capacity he issued licenses to dealers in foods under the proclamations of the President of the United States. During the summer of 1918 Professor Tuttle served in the Quartermaster General's office in Washington, D. C., first as "specialist in orders and regulations," Methods of Control Division, and later as "associate chief" in the Treasury Branch of the same division. Professor Tuttle also served in the Federal Food Administration in Ohio. In the fall of 1917 Professor Rightmire was made a member of the War Records Committee of the University, and in February, 1918, visited Camp Sherman, in company with other members of the committee, in an effort to get as complete a list as possible of the records of the Ohio State University men who were in service. Later he was sent on a similar mission to Camp Sheridan, Montgomery, Alabama, where most of the Ohio National Guard entering federal service were stationed. In the latter part of July, 1918, Professor Corry was given leave of absence. When the Students' Army Training Corps began, October 1, 1918, most of its members were required to take a course in War Issues. This requirement made necessary so large a number of sections that each member of the law Faculty, with one or two exceptions, took over several sections of the new course until the demobilization of the corps in December of that year.

CHAPTER XIX

THE SERVICES OF THE COLLEGE OF MEDICINE

In the fall of 1916 the College of Medicine had 148 students, of whom 138 were men. With the opening of the spring semester in 1917, the total number of registrants was only slightly less than in the previous September, namely, 144. By the middle of May, or three weeks after the United States had declared war, eight medical students had withdrawn for military service, and doubtless others withdrew during the following weeks. When instruction began in the autumn of 1917 the enrollment was down to 120 students, of whom 112 were men. At mid-December the medical colleges of the United States, like the dental and veterinary schools, were placed under the jurisdiction of the War Department, the students in these institutions who were physically fit being enrolled in the Medical Enlisted Reserve Corps to enable them to complete their studies before being called into active service. This wise provision kept many men in the colleges that came within its terms. Nevertheless, another decline took place in the enrollment of our medical college in the spring of 1918, bringing the number down to 107. During the summer the Government announced its plan of organizing the Students' Army Training Corps at selected colleges and universities, including the Ohio State University, and a large number of new students flocked in. Under these circumstances the College of Medicine gained 80 S.A.T.C. cadets early in October, 1918, in addition to its 109 regular students, 106 of the latter being men. With the signing of the Armistice and the consequent demobilization of the S.A.T.C., the bottom was reached, for only 99 students matriculated in the spring of 1919. There had been 15 students in the medical college during the summer session of 1918 and 11 during that of 1919. The opening of the college in the fall of the latter year disclosed the fact that normal conditions had been restored; the attendance rose at a bound to 144, of which number 135 were men.

Among the departments of instruction in the College of Medicine none was more affected by the war than that of public health and sanitation. The total enrollment in the courses offered by the department both on the campus and in the college during the academic year 1916-17 was 370. In 1917-18 it was only 55. After the students were inducted into the Medical Enlisted Reserve Corps in December, 1917, and were assigned to class attendance, the war had little effect on the enrollment. But the absence of Dr. E. F. McCampbell, the head of the department, in military service when the college opened in the autumn of 1917 and the withdrawal of two other teachers, as announced in the *Bulletin* for 1916-17, made necessary the abandonment of the graduate courses. In the second semester of 1918 the department was suddenly called upon to direct the instruction in military hygiene and sanitation in the School of Military Aeronautics. An eight-hour course of seven lectures, with a written quiz and a final examination, was devised and repeated each week throughout the semester. During this period about 800 officers in the "aviation school," as it was commonly called, passed through this course. The Military Department supplied two and later three assistant instructors to Dr. E. R. Hayhurst for the management of this course.

The departure of Dr. R. G. Paterson to enter the Red Cross service in Italy in 1918 reduced the staff of the department to two persons, namely, Dr. Hayhurst and Mr. L. H. Van Buskirk. There was, however, an increase in enrollment in all courses, except graduate work. On the campus the student enrollment was: personal hygiene, 21; industrial hygiene, 58; public health problems, 35, this course being repeated during the second semester with 11 students. In the medical college the numbers were: personal hygiene, 36;

preventive medicine, 17; the Graduate School, one. With the organization of the Students' Army Training Corps in October, 1918, a course in military hygiene and sanitation was given to 215 students, and the work of the course as outlined was practically completed by the time of the demobilization of this unit. The students were divided into seven sections of thirty each. Lectures and quizzes were given daily. The additional work imposed by this course could not be carried by the two remaining men of the department, and Dr. A. M. Bleile, Dr. R. J. Seymour, and Mr. E. P. Durrant of the Department of Phyiology, together with Professors C. B. Morrey and W. A. Starin of the Department of Bacteriology, generously responded to relieve the emergency. In the second semester, beginning in February, 1919, Dr. Hayhurst gave an intensive course of four weeks in industrial hygiene to nine officers detailed to Columbus by the United States Public Health Service.

The effect of the war on the enrollment in the other departments of the College of Medicine are shown in the following table:

Departments	1916-17	1917-18	1918-19
Anatomy	594	671	540
Bacteriology	500	362	280
Medicine	496	287	166
Obstetrics	162	64	57
Pathology	366	121	221
Physiology, Phys. Chemistry, and Pharmacology	1,048	940	...
Surgery and Gynecology	425	269	170

Previous to the declaration of war by the United States six members of the Faculty of the College of Medicine had been commissioned first lieutenants in the Medical Reserve Corps of the Army. These commissions had been held from two to five years. When the United States entered the war the Medical Reserve Corps numbered approximately twelve hundred members. In this list were to be found representatives of practically every Class A medical school in the country. Three days after hostilities were declared the commissioned officers in the Faculty of Ohio State's College of Medicine were ordered to report for duty at the United States Barracks in Columbus, Ohio. These Faculty members were Dr. E. F. McCampbell, Dr. V. A. Dodd, Dr. George C. Schaeffer, Dr. John W. Means, and Dr. Edward C. Ludwig. Dr. Elijah J. Gordon was at that time a member of the Medical Department of the Ohio National Guard and had returned but recently from service on the Mexican Border. He was again ordered to report for duty with the National Guard when that organization was mobilized, July 15, 1917. That thirteen other teachers of the College of Medicine enlisted in the service of their country during the first summer of the war appears from the list of the men on the University staff who were granted leaves of absence at the September and October meetings of the Board of Trustees. Thus, by October 1, 1917, a total of nineteen members of the Faculty of the medical college had withdrawn, the Department of Anatomy losing two; Medicine, three; Obstetrics, Ophthalmology, Oto-Laryngology, and Physiology, each one; Pathology, two; and Surgery, seven. On May 1, 1918, three members of the departmental staff in anatomy left the University, and several more withdrew from other medical departments during the next six weeks. In a word, up to July 18, 1918, twenty-six of the ninety-one teachers of the College of Medicine had been commissioned in the Army. Including others who withdrew, the medical Faculty was reduced fully one-third. Indeed, the depletion of medical staffs not only at our University, but throughout the country also reached such a stage that on July 18, 1918, the Government asked for lists of essential teachers, and from that time on men who were so designated were not permitted to enlist in the medical service of the Army and Navy. The Government recognized the fact that the medical schools of the country were indispensable, that they must be maintained in order that a sufficient supply of medical graduates and medical officers might be forthcoming as needed. In creating these lists of essential teachers in connection with the Class A medical colleges, the United States Government was profiting by the unfortunate experience of England and France, where the members of the medical staffs had gone into the war in such numbers, and the supply of graduate physicians and medical students had been so seriously depleted by heavy casualties, that the civilian populations, as well as the military organizations, were suffering for the need of physicians. It should be said that the service rendered by the essential teachers of the country was in no sense less patriotic than that of the men attached to the various military and auxiliary organizations. Many of them felt the call to active service in the field, but showed their devotion to the duty assigned them by remaining at home to carry on the work of the medical colleges and other activities, such as serving on the draft boards and teaching the cadets in the Students' Army Training Corps.

Professor F. L. Landacre, who was appointed acting dean of the College of Medicine when Dean E. F. McCampbell was given his leave of absence, said that the reduction in the force of teachers necessitated a radical rearrangement in the college and imposed heavy duties on medical teachers who were already overburdened. He also testified that the men remaining on duty rose to the occasion in the very best spirit. He thought that the most serious difficulty in the College of Medicine caused by the war was the cessation of all scientific research, although this advantage was, he believes, offset to some extent by the experience of those who went into Government service.

Of the twenty-six members of the Faculty of the College of Medicine who entered active service, eighteen were commissioned as medical officers in the United States Army, six as medical officers in the United States Navy, one as an officer in the United States Public Health Service, one served as a member of the staff of the American Red Cross, one as an enlisted man in the Army, and another as an enlisted man in the Navy. It is gratifying to be able to record that no casualties occurred among these men. Members of the Faculty of the College of Medicine served in practically every capacity in the various military medicinal organizations. They served as battalion surgeons on the battle line in France, in charge of regimental first-aid stations, in field hospitals, evacuation hospitals, base hospitals, and regimental infirmaries; they served also as sanitary inspectors, camp and division surgeons, members of draft boards, surgeons on transports and combat ships, and as Red Cross relief workers.

With a few exceptions, the members of the Faculty had had little or no military training. A few had previously been in military service, some had taught military sanitation, and in the beginning all except one or two men were commissioned as first lieutenants. Soon after the United States entered the war the Medical Reserve Corps was changed by law to the Medical Sections of the Officers' Reserve Corps of the National Army. Later all distinctions between officers of the National Army, National Guard, and the United States Army were abolished, and all commissions were issued to them as officers in the United States Army. Except in the case of a few of the younger men, all the members of the Faculty in active service were promoted during the months of the war. When the Armistice was signed the College of Medicine could boast of three lieutenant colonels, six majors, four captains, and four first lieutenants in the Army; one commander, two lieutenants (senior grade), and two lieutenants (junior grade), in the Navy; one major in the American Red Cross, and one enlisted man in the Army.

It is not possible within the space available to review the experiences through which all these members of the Faculty passed during the war. One must be content with merely trying to illustrate the variety of the service performed not only by members of the Faculty, but also by some of the graduates.

INSTRUCTIONAL SERVICE IN MEDICAL TRAINING CAMPS

Early in the summer of 1917 the War Department organized two large training camps for medical officers, one located at Fort Riley, Kansas, and the other at Camp Greenleaf, Georgia. Practically all medical officers who were without previous military training were ordered to these training camps. It was recognized that, while such physicians might be well qualified professionally, they stood in need of instruction in military medicine and army regulations. At these camps, therefore, the physicians who had been recently commissioned were given training in military drill, army regulations, and in the various special lines of medico-military service, such as ambulance, field hospital, and base hospital work, besides instruction in certain specialties of medicine in order to prepare them to serve on tuberculosis, cardiacvascular, psychiatric, and other boards.

Later all this instructional work was concentrated at Camp Greenlief, Georgia. Two members of the Faculty, namely, Dr. Wayne Brehm and Dr. Walter E. Duffee, became permanent instructors at this training camp, where they taught drill regulations and military medicine. They were thus occupied throughout the period of their service.

SERVICE IN CAMP ADMINISTRATION AND SANITATION

The only member of the Faculty who served in camp administration and sanitations was Dean Eugene F. McCampbell. After an assignment in the recruiting service at the Columbus Barracks, as an instructor at the Army Medical School at Washington, D. C., and as an officer connected with the office of the surgeon general of the United States Army, Dr. McCampbell was sent into the field as a sanitary inspector for the surgeon general and in this capacity visited most of the large camps in the country. Later he was assigned to deal with the measles and pneumonia epidemic prevailing in Camp Pike, Arkansas. Still later he became successively sanitary inspector, assistant division surgeon, and acting division surgeon of the 87th Division, and when that organization left for France he was appointed camp surgeon of Camp Pike. During the influenza epidemic in October, 1918, Dr. McCampbell also served as camp surgeon at Camp Custer, Michigan, and later in the same capacity at Camp McArthur, Texas. At the time of his discharge Dean McCampbell held the rank of lieutenant colonel in the Medical Corps of the United States Army.

THE UNITED STATES NAVAL RESERVE FORCE MEDICAL UNIT FROM THE UNIVERSITY

In August, 1917, a hospital unit of the United States Naval Reserve Force was organized in Columbus by Dr. Verne A. Dodd, assistant professor of surgery. The commissioned officers of this unit were all local physicians and, with one exception, were members of the Faculty of the College of Medicine. University students and the nurses were also recruited in Columbus. At the outbreak of the war Dr. Dodd was a member of the Medical Reserve Corps. He went on duty at the Columbus Barracks in April, 1917, and, with several of his colleagues, was engaged in examining recruits. In the following August Dr. Dodd was appointed lieutenant commander in the Medical Department of the United States Navy and chief surgeon of the unit referred to. Among the other commissioned officers of the unit were Dr. Frederick O. Williams, a graduate of the College of Medicine in 1893, who was also commissioned lieutenant commander and was made chief of the medical service of the unit; Dr. Arthur M. Hauer, instructor in oto-laryngology, who was commissioned a lieutenant, senior grade, and appointed head of the Department of Eye, Ear, Nose, and Throat Work in the unit; Dr. Jonathan Forman, assistant professor of pathology, who was commissioned lieutenant, junior grade, and appointed pathologist of the unit; Dr. Carl C. Hugger, instructor in pathology, who was appointed a lieutenant, junior grade, and assigned as roentgenologist, and Dr. Philip J. Reel, assistant in surgery, who was commissioned a lieutenant, junior grade, and assigned as surgical assistant. This unit served as the staff of the United States Naval Station Hospital No. 5. The enlisted personnel numbered about forty, and, as previously stated, was largely recruited from among the students of the University. Several young men who had been prominent in athletics and other campus activities were members of the organization. The enlisted men were chosen for their qualifications as carpenters, plumbers, mechanicians, cooks, ambulance drivers, etc. Subsequently seven of them received commissions as officers in the Navy, and five became chief petty officers.

The unit first reported for active duty at Hampton Roads, Virginia, October 15, 1917. Hampton Roads, it will be remembered, was the site of the Jamestown Exposition. This site was purchased for the Navy Department as a permanent base and became later the most important naval base belonging to the United States, and one of the largest and most complete in the world. Here were established for emergency war service a training camp for thirty thousand men and a naval air station.

The hospital to which the unit was assigned was designed to serve this station and camp. Later many patients were received here from war ships and transports entering Hampton Roads Harbor, as well as wounded marines from overseas.

Each regiment of the training station and the air station was provided with a dispensary building, where the medical officers were stationed. These buildings were equipped with about twelve beds each and were thus able to care for minor illnesses and accidents. At the time of the arrival of the unit the hospital was nearing completion, and the first duty was to requisition the equipment and supplies. The unit was placed under the command of Captain F. C. Cook of the Medical Corps, United States Navy, and Dr. Dodd was made the executive officer of the hospital.

The hospital was of the usual emergency construction on the pavilion plan. There were eight wards of forty beds each, administration building, surgical pavilion, nurses' quarters, corps quarters, civilian employees' quarters, galley and mess halls, store house, garage, laundry, chapel, brig, and morgue.

The first patient was received on December 3, and the beds were rapidly filled. The inadequacy of the hospital had been realized before it was ready for the reception of patients, and steps had been taken to increase its capacity. The unit was assigned to the Pine Beach Hotel, a large summer hotel near the hospital, which had been fitted for officers' quarters. Meantime, the Navy Department granted the request for the construction of twelve additional wards. The hotel was later arranged for convalescent patients, and three hundred of them were accommodated in this structure. In the spring of 1918 work began on the new wards, the original group of buildings was subjected to certain alterations, a recreation building and a laboratory building were erected, and other additions were made. The Red Cross provided a recreation center for the nurses also. A patriotic woman of Norfolk, through the Red Cross, gave into the care of the unit her beautiful country home for the use of selected convalescents.

By this time the unit's staff had grown until it consisted of 32 medical officers, 45 nurses, and 200 enlisted men. The average daily number of patients was 750.

After the signing of the Armistice several commissioned officers in the unit were assigned to battleships and transports. Dr. Dodd served as chief surgeon on the U.S. S.S. *Agamemnon*, one of the large transports then plying between New York and Brest. The unit was demobilized in March and April, 1919.

MAXILLO-FACIAL SURGERY

Two members of the Faculty, namely, Dr. John W. Means, instructor in surgery, and Dr. George C. Schaeffer, instructor in oto-laryngology, were assigned to do special work in maxillo-facial surgery, following a period of several months' active duty at the Columbus Barracks in April, 1917. After leaving this post they were ordered to Philadelphia to take a special course of instruction in oral and plastic work and later returned to the Columbus Barracks for a brief period of service. Dr. Means was subsequently assigned to Base Hospital No. 22, which was organized in Milwaukee, and went to France with that organization. The hospital was stationed at Beau Desert, Gironde, France, Dr. Means being its operator in both maxillo-facial and general surgery until his return to this country. In April, 1919, he received his discharge from the Army. Dr. Schaeffer first served in the United States Army General Hospital No. 2 at Fort McHenry, Maryland, after which he went abroad in April, 1918. He was given the opportunity of studying the plastic work being done in the hospitals in England, while the detachment of enlisted men serving with Dr. Schaeffer received special training in the King George Hospital in London. Later Dr. Schaeffer served at the American Red Cross Hospital No. 1 at Neuilly, France, and studied the work of the French plastic surgeons. As a result of four years of war both the French and English surgeons had developed considerable skill in plastic work. At the beginning of the Chateau-Thierry drive Dr. Schaeffer was assigned to hospitals in the advanced section and in the zone of advance, where the field, mobile, and evacuation hospitals, and some of the base hospitals were situated. Dr. Schaeffer was appointed consultant for the various hospitals in these zones for the purpose of organizing and supervising the maxillo-facial work. During this period the St. Mihiel, Argonne-Meuse, and Verdun offensives took place, which provided large numbers of wounded men who required plastic work. After completing his service in France, Dr. Schaeffer was ordered back to the United States Army Hospital No. 2 at Fort McHenry and later was transferred to the Columbus Barracks, where, after his discharge from the Army, he was engaged in completing the plastic operations on a number of cases begun at Fort McHenry.

It may be explained that maxillo-facial surgery includes a wide range of work, generally that of reconstruction, made necessary by severe fractures of the jaw and bones of the face, by the loss of eyelids, lips, or ears, and by deep and deforming wounds. In some of these operations bone grafts are required and in others fat and skin grafts. Fat from the abdomen is used in filling large losses in the cheek and neck. Skin flaps from the neck, chest, abdomen, cheek, forehead, or top of the head are employed in rebuilding lost parts of the face. Cartilage from the end of a rib supplies the material for replacing bones from the nose, the cheek eminences, the angles of the jaw, and the supraorbital ridge above the eyes. Pieces of bone from the tibia, rib, ilium, clavicle, and from the jaw itself are used extensively in bone graft of the jaw. It will be seen that the object of these operations is to replace or rebuild the lost parts of the face and neck, to remove disfiguring scars, and to correct, as far as possible, all defects in the face resulting from wounds. To accomplish these results it is often necessary to subject the patients to repeated operations of short duration.

Service in Evacuation and Base Hospitals

A considerable number of members of the Faculty were assigned to evacuation and base hospitals in this country and in France. In most instances their service corresponded to the specialty they had been teaching in the College of Medicine. Thus, Dr. Hugh G. Beatty and Dr. W. H. Hodges, instructor and assistant, respectively, in oto-laryngology, and Dr. T. Rees Williams, assistant in ophthalmology, were assigned to work in various base hospitals similar to what they had been accustomed to at home. Dr. A. M. Steinfeld, assistant professor of surgery, was given orthopedic work. Dr. H. B. Blakey, assistant professor of medicine, Dr. Samuel Hindman, instructor in medicine, and Dr. S. D. Edelman, assistant in the same department, devoted themselves to work in internal medicine. Dr. W. N. Taylor, assistant in genito-urinary surgery, continued to follow his specialty in the hospitals. Dr. James H. Warren, assistant professor of anatomy, and Dr. J. W. Sheetz, instructor in medicine, were assigned to hospital laboratory work. Dr. Philip D. Wilson, instructor in surgery, after an extended service on an operating team at the battle front, was connected with the surgical service of several hospitals and was finally made chief consultant in amputations for all the hospitals in France. Another instructor in surgery, namely, Dr. E. C. Ludwig, also served on the surgical staff of several hospitals in France. Dr. Fred Fletcher, assistant professor of surgery, who was promoted to the rank of lieutenant colonel in the Medical Corps of the United States Army, was commanding officer of Evacuation Hospital No. 31 at Nantes, France.

A Tuberculosis Unit in Italy

In August, 1918, the American Red Cross organized a tuberculosis unit for service in Italy. Dr. Herbert G. Paterson, assistant professor of public health and sanitation, was assigned to this unit with the rank of captain and placed in charge of the Division of Organization and Education. He left New York with the unit in September and arrived in Rome, Italy, October 6. Dr. Paterson had been identified with tuberculosis work in this country, and especially in Ohio. On the arrival of the Red Cross unit in Italy, it became the Tuberculosis Department of the American Red Cross Commission for Italy. The department was divided for purposes of administration into six main sections, namely, administration, medical service, public health nursing, organization and education, medical inspection of schools, and child welfare, with a chief in charge of each section.

The section of organization and education comprised two bureaus, one being the Bureau of Field Organization, which was in direct charge of the chief, and the other the Bureau of Education, in charge of the assistant chief. In the former bureau there were five American field secretaries; in the latter, three American publicity workers. The equipment, purchased in the United States, consisted of ten automobile traveling dispensaries, seven for tuberculosis work and three for dental work, and a complete motion picture outfit for each dispensary, with an ample supply of films.

Four provinces were organized to serve as models for the remaining sixty-eight. One of the four was in the northwestern part of the Italian peninsula, with the centre at Genoa; one in the interior, with its centre at Perugia; on in Sardinia, its headquarters being at Sassari; and the fourth in Sicily, with Palermo as its base. The plan of organization embraced the formation of an anti-tuberculosis league composed of volunteer members, lay and professional; the employment of a full-time, paid, executive secretary, an Italian; a campaign of health education; the employment of public health nurses; the establishment of diagnostic laboratories under the direction of the provincial departments of health; and the increase of facilities for the care and treatment of children and adults affected with tuberculosis.

Owing to the signing of the Armistice, November 11, 1919, the unit was ordered to discontinue its labors on May 14, 1919. At that time Dr. Paterson was promoted to the rank of major and transferred to the headquarters of the American Red Cross Commission for Europe at Paris, where he remained on duty until his discharge in June, 1919.

Service on the Battle Line

The service of Dr. Philip D. Wilson on the battle front in France has already been referred to. Another member of the Faculty who saw service at the front was Dr. Elijah J. Gordon, assistant professor of medicine. He was the regimental surgeon of the 134th Field Artillery, 37th Division, during the operations of that division in the Morbach, Jannes, and Woëvre sectors. Later he was sent into Germany with the Army of Occupation.

More than seven hundred graduates of the College of Medicine and its antecedent institutions served in the United States Army, Navy, and Public Health Service. A considerable number of these among the recent graduates were in action at the front, one of them, Dr. Guthrie Olaf Burrell, '16, being killed. He was fatally injured by a high explosive shell in the battle of the Argonne Forest, September 26, 1918, and died a few hours later. Another graduate of the same class, Dr. Hadley H. Teter, lieutenant, junior grade, in the United States Navy, by a singular coincidence, lost his life on the very same date, when the U.S. S.S. *Tampa* was torpedoed. How many of the graduates and students of the college died of disease while in the service is not known.

Lieutenant Colonel Harry H. Snively, B.A. 1895, M.D.

1902, M.A. 1903, rendered a wide range of war service, for which his medical training and his long cennection with the Ohio National Guard peculiarly fitted him. He had been a captain and an adjutant in the Fourth Regiment of the State militia in 1903-04 and a major commanding ambulance and hospital companies during the years 1904-16. Early in the spring of the year last named Major Snively was invited by Major General Robert U. Patterson to go as director of the American Red Cross to Kiev, Russia. He sailed with nurses and supplies in March and landed at Petrograd on April 14. He soon proceeded with his party down to Kiev and took charge of a hospital, which occupied a part of the Polytechnic Institute. This hospital then had nine doctors, twenty-seven nurses, sixty-five hospital-corps men ("sanitars"), Russian nurses, clerks, and servants. There were also many military hospitals in Kiev and more than 28,000 wounded soldiers, which had been, and were still being, brought in by special Red Cross trains. Dr. Snively at once made plans to provide for several hundred more patients in the hospital under his care.

On May 13 he went by rail to Luov, Galicia, in response to a telegram to arrange for establishing a small fraction of his personnel near the front in the Carpathian Mountains to operate upon and administer other relief to the wounded who were being brought back from the firing line. He then returned to Kiev, which he did not leave permanently until October 19, when he went on an inspection tour as far as Tabriz, Persia. Early in September the Red Cross Hospital had been removed to Karkov, about 200 miles east of Kiev. While in Russia Dr. Snively was given the rank of a brigadier general in the Imperial Army. By Christmas, 1915, he was home again in Columbus, Ohio.

His medical and military experience in Russia had shown him the great need of a medical regiment, and he proceeded to organize the 112th Medical Regiment of the Ohio National Guard, of which he became the commanding officer. This was the first organization of its kind in the United States. Almost at once the Ohio National Guard was summoned to service on the Mexican Border, and Dr. Snively was with the troops until their return shortly before our entrance into the European conflict. Then he and the 146th Field Hospital Company were sent to Camp Sheridan, Montgomery, Alabama, for intensive training, which they underwent in 1916-17, In the latter part of June, 1917, they embarked for an unrevealed destination. By mid-August they were in France and soon arrived in a "quiet sector," which, however, did not remain quiet long. At one station the buildings in which Dr. Snively had his office had holes torn in them by pieces of shrapnel.

During most of the year 1918 he served as director of field hospitals of the 37th Division. By the end of October he and his outfit were in Belgium, doing hospital work in various convents in a region which had been long occupied by German troops. After being in the attack and capture of Montfaucon, at St. Mihiel, and in the battles on the Lys and Scheldt Rivers, Dr. Snively was called back to direct teams which operated upon severely wounded men. He received the Belgian War Cross for bravery in action. On November 22 he attended the celebration in Brussels of the return of the King and Queen of the Belgians to their capital.

By December 11, 1918, Dr. Snively was at Tours, France, whence he was ordered to Bordeaux as assistant base quartermaster, sanitary inspector, and port supervisor of bathing and delousing American troops preparatory to their embrakation for home. He was assisted by ten commissioned and twenty non-commissioned officers. In February, 1919, he was appointed a lieutenant colonel in the United States Army and stationed at Bordeaux until the following autumn. The capacity of the bathing and disinfecting establishment under his management was 5,000 men a day, but the number treated seems rarely to have reached that figure, if at all. Early in May the rate of treatment had been from 3,000 to 4,000 a day at Bordeaux and the other ports from which our troops were sailing.

In June, 1919, Lieutenant Colonel Snively paid a visit to

Paris, where he learned from his superior officer, Colonel H. L. Gilchrist, that they were being importuned by President Ignace Paderewski to lead a medical expedition to Poland to deal with typhus fever and other contagious diseases then prevalent in that country. Madam Paderewski was in Paris and appealed to the two officers to aid Poland, 300,000 of whose people were suffering from typhus alone, the mortality being 50 per cent. When Colonels Gilchrist and Snively consented, Madam Paderewski gave valuable assistance in effecting the arrangements for their expedition, which was supported by the American Red Cross. As chief of staff of the expedition, Dr. Snively procured 160 large American freight-car loads of the materials needed for Poland, bought 100 Ford ambulances and twenty-five Ford touring cars for the Polish Government, and hired 248 chauffeurs. The first train of fifty cars began loading on July 31, and four more trains of about the same number of cars were loaded at intervals of a few days. These arrangements having been completed, Dr. Snively went to Coblenz, Germany, and awaited his trains, as also several hospital trains which he helped to forward through Germany to Poland.

By September 23 Dr. Snively was in Warsaw, Poland, where he found the situation "desperate," the typhus being constantly disseminated by vermin. Numerous houses and their inmates in Warsaw and other places in the Ukraine required cleansing and disinfecting. To accomplish this as expeditiously as possible, ten "flying columns" were sent out. Each column consisted of about thirty United States soldiers, some Polish interpreters, twenty-six motor vehicles, most of which were large trucks, a bathing machine, two or more sterilizers, and a few big ward tents. Each column had a capacity of 1,000 people a day. For three months Dr. Snively served as assistant to the director of health in Poland. He also conducted an expedition into Roumania to bring back 4,000 Polish refugees from the Russian front. He was present at the destruction of Denikin's army at Bendery, Bessarabia, and in May, 1920, while in charge of a supply train, entered the conquered territory with the victorious Polish army. In July he participated in th evacuation of Vilna and in removing 800 orphans from Bialystock to a camp near Posen.

In recognition of these notable services Dr. Snively was awarded the Polish Commemoration Cross, the Polish Silver Red Cross Medal, and a medal from the American Jewish Relief Committee. He was also cited for the United States Distinguished Service Cross.

Shortly after the termination of the siege of Warsaw Dr. Snively joined his wife and daughter in Paris and returned to the United States in September, 1920. He survived less than eleven years. His death occurred on July 20, 1931, in the 64th year of his age, and brought deep sadness to his innumerable friends and admirers in the United States and in foreign lands.

From the above very incomplete record it will be seen that the members of the Faculty and the graduates of the College of Medicine and its antecedent institutions rendered a noteworthy and honorable service in the war. Representatives of these groups were to be found in practically every line of medical work in the United States Army and Navy, as also in the Public Health Service and the American Red Cross. A number of the students and one instructor, Mr. R. A. Knouff of the Department of Anatomy, served as enlisted men. One student, Mr. Paul H. Charlton, became a commissioned officer in the Quartermaster Corps and was finally discharged with the rank of major.

CHAPTER XX

MEN OF THE COLLEGE OF PHARMACY IN MEDICAL, SANITARY, AND HOSPITAL UNITS

As soon as war was declared this college, in common with the others on the campus, placed its men and facilities at the disposal of the National Government. Both men and facilities were employed to a certain extent in solving various problems in the manufacture of medicinal compounds. Alumni, former students who had not completed their course, and undergraduates responded promptly and enthusiastically to the call to arms. At the time of the Armistice the College had about 175 men who were actively engaged in some branch of military service or training. While these men were to be found in practically every branch, the large majority were in the Medical, Sanitary, and Hospital Corps, for which their technical training fitted them and in which they were most needed. A number were also enrolled in the Navy. Not a few achieved promotion and officers' commissions, giving evidence of their ability and efficiency. All performed their duty with fidelity, courage, and cheerfulness, and several made the supreme sacrifice.

The following table shows the effect of the war on the enrollment of the college:

	1916-17	1917-18	1918-19
First Semester	94	78	62 (including 22 in S.A.T.C.
Second Semester	74	60	55
Summer Session	10	5	7
	178	143	124

During the days of May 10 to 14, 1917, when 170 students withdrew from all colleges on the campus to go into military service, seven of the pharmacy students left to assume military duties. This was only the beginning of the departures. Many who had expected to continue in the college could not find any satisfaction in doing so, and many young men who had intended to enter the pharmacy course failed to appear. Hence the decline in attendance shown in the above table.

Mustard-Gas Manufactory at Edgewood, designed and erected under the direction of Major Dana J. Demorest

Chemical Laboratory at Edgewood, for research and control work, presided over by Major W. L. Evans

Apparatus for the manufacture of carbon monoxide gas at Edgewood, designed in part by Major Dana J. Demorest

Tanks of phosgene gas ready for shipment

CHAPTER XXI

SERVICES OF THE COLLEGE OF VETERINARY MEDICINE

In 1914 the Faculty of the College of Veterinary Medicine increased the entrance requirements of the college so that only high-school graduates could be admitted and, at the same time, lengethened the veterinary curriculum from three to four years. The effect of this raising of standards should be taken into account, along with the war, in reducing the enrollment in the college. The changes in the curriculum did not make themselves fully felt until in the academic year 1917-18, when the college was left without the usual large senior class of previous years. In the fall of 1916 the enrollment was 121 and in the spring of 1917 it was 110. When the University Faculty excused students to devote the summer to farm work or go into military service, 46 veterinary students withdrew, two to enter the Army and the rest to go into agricultural service. In September, 1917, but 66 students enrolled.

In December of this year the War Department took steps to conserve the supply of medical men, including dentists and veterinarians, and to provide for the education during the war of young men who were preparing to practice these professions. This was done largely on the advice of representatives of the British Government, who had discovered early in the war that Great Britain was becoming rapidly depleted of men professionally and technically trained who had joined the combat units and were fighting in the trenches as common soldiers. The British War Office found it necessary, therefore, to call back from the front chemists, surgeons, veterinarians, engineers, and others who could render the country greater service in the rear or at home. In the light of this British experience and by virtue of the selective draft, which made possible the placing of individuals where they could perform the greatest service, the veterinary, dental, and medical colleges of the United States were put under the jurisdiction of the War Department, December 15, 1917. In certain respects the government of these institutions was directly administered through the Medical Department of the Army. By law the veterinary service in the Regular Army constituted a corps of this department. The surgeon general immediately issued regulations governing voluntary enlistment in the Medical Enlisted Reserve Corps of registrants who were medical students, hospital internes, dentists, dental students, veterinarians, and veterinary students.

Section 151(b) of the Selective Draft Regulations, December 15, 1917, provided that any veterinary student, who was physically fit and of draft age, might enlist in the reserve corps of the Medical Department upon receiving permission from the surgeon general of the Army. This placed him in the deferred classification, by making him a member of the Medical Enlisted Reserve Corps, and enabled him to continue his studies in college. The surgeon general's office required reports of each student's record at the end of each semester. Delinquent students were to be sent into active service. Full summer courses in veterinary medicine were to be offered by each college volunteering to do so. The College of Veterinary Medicine at Ohio State University offered such courses during the summer of 1918. The students taking these courses were included in the Medical Enlisted Reserve Corps.

Notwithstanding the arrangements thus made to keep veterinary students in college, the enrollment of such students at the University in the spring of 1918 was but 58, or eight less than before the M.E.R.C. was established. Attendance at the summer session of this year, however, was much larger than in the previous summers, being 43 as compared with three in the summer session of 1917 and with nine in that of 1916.

During the summer of 1918 the War Department organized the Committee on Education and Special Training under the General Staff. Through the efforts of this committee the Students' Army Training Corps was established simultaneously on October 1, 1918, at some six hundred authorized universities and colleges. Veterinary schools were included in this organization and notified that their eligible students would be transferred from the Medical Enlisted Reserve Corps to the Students' Army Training Corps. Meantime, the University had published a special bulletin, *The Veterinary Profession,* which was distributed to prospective students, and the college had sent out letters to its graduates and friends calling attention to the existing need for veterinarians. The Government had also given wide publicity to the advantages afforded to young men by enlisting in the S.A.T.C. The result of these endeavors was apparent in the greatly increased enrollment in the autumn of 1918. Instead of the 58 students of the previous spring, there were now 189 students, of whom 71 were cadets in the S.A.T.C.

These cadets were required not only to pursue their professional studies, but also to live in barracks, become subject to regular military discipline, and give a considerable amount of time to military drill. Opportunity for graduation was guaranteed to no cadet, for he might be transferred to an officers' training camp or a non-commissioned officers' school, or be sent to a cantonment for duty as a private. On the other hand, the cadet might be enrolled for further intensive training in a specified line for a limited time, or he might be assigned to the vocational section of the corps for technical training of military value. Obviously, the regular curriculum of the College of Veterinary Medicine had to be modified, in order to make room for the military requirements of the Students' Army Training Corps. But only the freshman veterinary courses were modified at Ohio State University. The Armistice was signed before the more advanced courses could be changed. As a matter of fact, not all of the students were formally transferred from the M.E.R.C. to the S.A.T.C., many of the upper classmen remaining in the former organization at the signing of the Armistice.

The principal differences between these two systems were that in the S.A.T.C. the curriculum of the college was fixed directly by the War Department and the cadets were required to drill, while in the M.E.R.C. the curriculum was determined by the Faculty of the college, subject to the approval of the War Department, and no military drill was required. Further, while the surgeon general approved all existing veterinary colleges admitting their students to the M.E.R.C., the committee administering the S.A.T.C. accredited only State veterinary schools. Students with full high-school training who had matriculated in schools not accredited by the committee were ordered to transfer to accredited veterinary colleges. As a result of this order our veterinary college admitted nine students from non-accredited veterinary schools. By December 20, 1918, the cadets in the S.A.T.C. were discharged from military service. The members of the M.E.R.C. who had been inducted into the other corps were not included in this order, and were still subject to military control "for the duration of the emergency." From the time of the demobilization of the S.A.T.C. the jurisdiction of the War Department over the College of Veterinary Medicine ceased. The reaction of the students after the cessation of hostilities and the discharge of the S.A.T.C. cadets is attested by the matriculation of only 87 men in the veterinary college in the spring of 1919, a loss of more than 100 students since the previous enrollment. Recovery began in September, 1919, with an attendance of 102 students.

From the spring of 1917 three members of the veterinary Faculty were absent in war service; another member was absent from March 1, 1918, and still another from June of that year. The absence of these teachers made necessary changes in the personnel conducting the courses in the theory and practice of veterinary medicine, physical diagnosis, veterinary anatomy, veterinary pathology, work in the clinics, and certain courses for the agricultural students. The teachers who remained in the college carried not only their own courses of instruction but also the added work of those who had gone. They deserve credit for having kept the college organization intact and for contributing in an inconspicuous way to the winning of the war. That the services of these men were valued is shown by the fact that the Government enabled such persons to be classified as "essential teachers," in July, 1918, thus preventing their enlistment in any branch of the service. In the absence of Dean White, Dr. Oscar V. Brumley was appointed acting dean, October 2, 1917, and served until Dr. White's return.

Including those on temporary, as well as those on permanent, appointment in the veterinary Faculty, six members of the staff received commissions in the United States Army. During June and July, 1917, Dean David S. White served as special examiner for the State of Ohio for the Veterinary Officers' Reserve Corps. About 200 candidates were examined, of whom 150 passed and were commissioned in the corps. Late in July Dean White was called to Washington to assist in the organization of a Veterinary Corps for the National Army. Ultimately an advisory board to the surgeon general, consisting of five members, was created, Dean White being appointed on this board. After a study of the veterinary organizations of the Great Powers, this board adopted, with some modification, the organization of the British Veterinary Service and compiled a manual for the new organization, which was adopted by the War Department and officially issued as *Special Regulations No. 70*. The advisory board also succeeded in obtaining the sanction of the War Department to an increase of the officer personnel of the Veterinary Corps. In the Regular Army there were not over 50 veterinary officers of experience, of whom only seven held field rank. Before the Armistice was signed more than 2,500 officers were commissioned in the Veterinary Corps, and a force of 32,000 enlisted men had been provided.

From August 1 to October 4, 1917, Dean White served as a contract surgeon with the rank of first lieutenant. He was then commissioned a major in the Veterinary Corps, National Army, and placed in charge of veterinary supplies and equipment, with headquarters at Washington, D. C. During the months that followed he devoted his efforts to the creation of combat equipment for veterinary units in the field, including veterinary hospitals. Nearly $5,000,000 were expended in a few months for equipment and supplies alone. Having completed this task to a point where its continuance became a matter of routine, Major White was sent to Camp Greenleaf, Georgia, to organize a veterinary school for commissioned officers who formed at that time one company of the 7th Battalion of the Medical Officers' Training Camp. This work occupied about one month.

On July 12, 1918, Major White's rank was raised to that of lieutenant colonel, and he was ordered to join the American Expeditionary Force in France. On arrival overseas he was made chief veterinarian of the American Army. This Army had been abroad for some fifteen months, but had failed to perfect any workable veterinary organization. Hospital units arriving at a base port were stripped of their equipment and supplies, dismemebered, and segments scattered here and there over France wherever there happened to be an accumulation of sick animals. Of the 160,000 animals of the American Army 72,000 were incapacitated through disease, injury, or inanition due to improper care and management. One of the first tasks was to perfect an organization that would place the veterinary service overseas where it was in the United States. After some delay this was finally accomplished. By order of General Pershing, the Veterinary Service was transferred from the Quartermaster Corps to the Medical Department of the Army. The organization was just beginning to bear fruit when the enemy signed the Armistice. The morbidity had been reduced from 75,000 to 42,000 sick, and the mortality greatly lessened. After the signing of the Armistice Dr. White, who had been promoted to the full rank of colonel, became the guest of the Royal British Veterinary Corps in England, being entertained at the home of Major General Blengenses, director general of that corps. By motor car and train he visited the principal veterinary units of the Southern Command in England, gaining much valuable information. On his return to his headquarters at Tours, France, he found orders awaiting him to return to the United States. On February 11, 1919, he received his discharge from the Army at Camp Dix, New Jersey. He was awarded several decorations.

Lieutenant Colonel Russel L. Mundhenk made a remarkable record as an officer of the line. He had served an enlistment in the Navy before entering the University as a student in 1913. In 1916 he had entered the Ohio National Guard as a private, had been made captain of Company G, 4th Infantry, a few weeks later, and from June, 1916, until March, 1917, was with his command on the Mexican Border. After resigning his commission in April, 1917, he was recommissioned first lieutenant, 4th Ohio Infantry, and assigned as battalion adjutant. In the following July he was given special duty as recruiting officer for western Ohio. He was soon promoted to the rank of major and in January, 1918, was transferred to the Signal Corps and assigned to command the 112th Field Signal Battalion, 37th Division, with which organization he left for overseas in June, 1918. On July 22 the 37th Division relieved the 77th Division in the Baccarat sector, Vosges. In this sector the division participated in numerous raids, being frequently shelled by the enemy's artillery and bombed by their aviators. In September the 37th Division moved to the Verdun front, took over the Avecourt sector and went over the top on the morning of September 26 at the start of the Argonne-Meuse offensive. In this drive the division captured Mentfausen, Iviery, Cierges, and other places, while suffering heavy casualties. It was relieved on October 2. At Mentfausen Major Mundhenk was gassed and had a horse shot under him. In October the 37th Division left with the 91st for Belgium and fought two phases of the Ypres-Lys offensive, capturing Cruyshautes, Wannegen-Lede, Huerne, and other places. At the signing of the Armistice the 37th was in active pursuit of the retreating Germans and suffering severe casualties. In this action Major Mundhenk and his men were subjected to an attack of mustard gas, and the major's helmet was penetrated by a machine gun bullet. After participating in King Albert's re-occupation of Brussels, the division was recalled.

Major Mundhenk received the Croix de Guerre at Ballon in February, 1919, citation in the orders of the Corps du Armée, and was promoted to the rank of lieutenant colonel, February 21, 1919, shortly afterward sailing for the United States. During Colonel Mundhenk's entire service overseas he remained in command of the same organization, without a single day's absence.

Dr. Fonsa A. Lambert entered the veterinary service as a second lieutneant, December 3, 1917. From March 15 to April 15, 1918, he was in active duty on the Horse Purchasing Board at Kansas City, Missouri. He was then transferred to Camp Greenleaf, Georgia, where his administrative ability was soon recognized. He was promoted to first lieutenant, then to captain, and from September 1, 1918, until January 15, 1919, he acted as battalion commander. He also served as a teacher in the School of Veterinary Instruction from July 20 until the close of the school, December 20, 1918. Some 1,300 officers, 68 of whom were from Ohio State University, came under his supervision. His record was such that he was granted a commission as captain in the Veterinary Reserve Corps, which he accepted. After receiving his discharge, Captain Lambert returned to the University, February 4, 1919.

Mr. William M. Weldishofer, who held a temporary appointment for the year 1917-18 in the College of Veterinary Medicine, was commissioned as second lieutenant and, at the expiration of his term of service in the University, placed on active duty. He was promoted to first lieutenant and sent overseas. He was there promoted to the rank of captain and saw service in Germany with the Army of Occupation.

Dr. Samuel J. Schilling and Dr. Russell E. Rebrassier were commissioned second lieutenants in the Veterinary Officers' Reserve Corps of the Army. At the request of the University authorities, however, they were placed on "inactive duty" in order to help carry on the work of necessary instruction in the college. Dr. James H. Snook, who was one of the best revolver shots in the United States, refused a majority in the United States Army to remain with the College of Veterinary Medicine during the period of the war. From May to September, 1918, while conducting his regular courses in the college, he served as an instructor in rifle and small arms practice, including machine guns of various types, in the School of Military Aeronautics on the University campus.

Like the three members of the veterinary staff just mentioned, Professor Septimus Sisson rendered civilian service, but in his case the service was performed in Canada. Professor Sisson was on leave of absence during the academic year 1917-18 at the Ontario Veterinary College in Toronto. A number of the Faculty of that institution had enlisted in the British Veterinary Corps, leaving the college without a sufficient number of teachers. Professor Sisson was therefore called to Toronto to assist his *Alma Mater* in the work of instruction and organization.

Of the 620 graduates of the College of Veterinary Medicine, 203 entered the Army and were in active service. Of these 203 graduates 187 received commissions as follows: colonel, one; lieutenant colonels, two; majors, eight; captains, 22; first lieutenants, 51; and second lieutenants, 103. Three of these officers, namely, Colonel David S. White, Lieutenant Colonel Reuben Hilty, and Major George R. Powell, each received the decoration *Officier de la Legion d'Honneur* from the French Government. The distinction of holding the highest rank ever given to a veterinary officer in the United States Army, namely, that of colonel, belongs to Dr. D. S. White, '90, former dean of the college. Two of our veterinary officers died in service, and one was severely wounded.

Sixteen graduates of the College of Veterinary Medicine did not receive commissions, but served as privates in the Army. Besides the privates and officers among the graduates of the college, twenty-one of its former students, who were not eligible to the Veterinary Corps because they had not completed their professional training, entered other branches of the service. Seven of these received commissions, and all of them rendered excellent service. One, who had graduated from another veterinary school, became a major in the Veterinary Corps, two became captains, and the others became lieutenants of the line.

As a memento of this splendid record, there hangs in the dean's office a service flag whose stars of blue and gold testify to the patriotism of the men who went out from the College of Veterinary Medicine. Whether in the training camps, the headquarters at Washington, the service of supply, or the front line trenches in France, wherever duty called them, graduates of this college were found. Had the war continued longer no doubt every alumnus who was physically fit would have joined the Army. Even after the Veterinary Officers' Reserve Corps was filled, many were striving to enter its ranks, each willing to make the supreme sacrifice for home and country.

CHAPTER XXII

THE AFTERMATH OF THE WAR IN THE UNIVERSITY

In various ways the Great War left its mark on the University. The signing of the Armistice and the subsequent discharge of our undergraduate and graduate students from the ranks enabled numbers of them to return to the campus for the purpose of completing their courses. The premium placed upon a college education by the Government during the time of hostilities encouraged them to do so and many other students to matriculate. The following table shows the effect of the war on enrollment both before and after the signing of the Armistice:

	Men	*Women*
First Half-Year, 1918-19	3,341	1,547
Second Half-Year, 1918-19	3,784	1,699
First Half-Year, 1919-20	4,997	1,611
Second Half-Year, 1919-20	5,272	1,751

The increase in the number of men in the second half-year of 1918-19 was 443, in the number of women, only 152; in the first half-year of 1919-20 the increase in the number of men was 1,213, in the number of women there was a loss of 88; in the second half-year the men increased 265 and the women 265. These figures speak for themselves.

The marked increase in student enrollment in September, 1919, made necessary an appeal by the Board of Trustees to the State Emergency Board for funds for the immediate employment of additional teachers in congested departments. This appeal was fully met.

The demand for the erection of Government buildings and others to accommodate essential industries during the war rendered it impossible for the University to proceed with the buildings for which the Legislature had appropriated the money. Instead, Military Barracks and an Aeronautical Laboratory, the latter being subsequently equipped as a mess hall for the Students' Army Training Corps, were constructed. The economic situation after the signing of the Armistice prevented the making of public contracts for building projects. The scarcity of labor and the high cost of materials contributed much to the difficulty, despite the fact that in the summer of 1920 nearly $400,000, appropriated for University buildings, remained unexpended. This money was to have been used for a woman's building, an addition to the Chemical Building, a field artillery barn, and two structures for live stock. The sums for these purposes, however, reverted to the State treasury, and all University building enterprises were deferred more than three years. Meanwhile, the need for new buildings became greater than ever.

Another effect of the war was the failure of teachers to return after the war service and the resignation of more than forty others in September, 1920, to accept more remunerative positions elsewhere. The large student enrollments in the universities after the war caused a demand for teachers that Ohio State University could not withstand, and the increased cost of living could not be ignored by the teachers themselves. In addition, there was the demand on the part of technical industries for men who had the requisite training, and who would receive from them better salaries than the University was able to pay. The experience of our technically trained teachers and some others who had accepted places in the industries was such that they preferred to continue in non-educational employment and hence did not return to the University.

In the *Fiftieth Report of the Board of Trustees to the Governor* (1920) President Thompson stated that the very rapid turnover in our teaching staff after the war was due to several factors: first, the demand for teachers arising out of the large enrollment of students in other institutions of higher learning; second, the unusual demand at increased salaries for teachers in the newer forms of education; and, third, the commercial demand for men with technical education. In that report he made it clear that the University was not paying adequate salaries to its teachers.

There can be little doubt that the educational ferment in the University during and after the war hastened, if it did not cause, the adoption of the four-quarter plan of instruction on the campus. It is true that the proposal to adopt the plan of operating the institution "practically a continuous year" had been under consideration for some time. The argument in favor of such action was the full-time utilization of an extensive plant at little additional cost beyond that for its operation during nine months. Further, the University of Chicago and several state universities were operating on the four-quarter basis. With some reluctance the Faculty adopted the plan in wartime and later reaffirmed its action, still with reluctance. Later the Board of Trustees approved the new educational policy, which was carried into effect in the summer of 1921.

On Thursday, November 8, 1918, the University, like the city of Columbus and the country at large, was deeply stirred by a cablegram sent from Paris by Roy W. Howard, president of the United Press, to the effect that an Armistice had been signed by the representatives of the belligerent Powers at 11 o'clock that morning, that hostilities had ceased at 2 o'clock, and that the Americans had taken Sedan the same morning. As a matter of fact the German white-flag delegation had not yet been received by General Foch when this message was cabled.

Despite the fact that the Department of State at Washington officially announced at 2:15 o'clock that the Germans had not signed the Armistice, the people of that city and other cities and towns all over the country began to celebrate. The populace of Columbus marched in throngs both afternoon and evening, with choruses singing, bands playing, whistles blowing, and claxtons rending the air. Among the paraders were members of the Red Cross canteen at the Union Station, among whom were some of the University women. Governor Cox addressed several hundred working men in the State House yard at 2:30. In the evening a gathering at the same place, called by the Chamber of Commerce, was addressed by Mayor Karb. Saloons had been ordered closed in the early afternoon. At 9 o'clock P. M., High Street was a seething flood of pedestrians. In this general outburst of enthusiasm the University had its unofficial share.

The news of the actual signing of the Armistice was received in Columbus in the early hours of Monday, November 11, and reached many people before daybreak. The celebration of the preceding week seemed only to stimulate appetites for a prolonged and unrestrained demonstration, which began forthwith by the blowing of whistles, the screeching of sirens, and the jubilations of early risers. All over the city factory wheels stood idle, store doors remained closed, and office chairs were vacant. Streams of people, including University students, hastened to the down-town section, and by 10 o'clock the crowd numbered thousands, who disported themselves up and down High Street from the Union Station to Main Street. The street-cars quickly returned to their barns, and the crowds held full sway in the thoroughfare and the side streets.

The Chamber of Commerce arranged an official celebration for 2:30 P. M. A parade was formed at the University, with the Columbus Reserve Guards, Company D of the Students' Army Training Corps under the command of Lieutenant Harold Hebbeler, and the Barracks Band as a nucleus. At the head rode President Thompson and Dean John J. Adams of our College of Law. The Faculty and students did not participate, except as spectators, chiefly on account of traffic difficulties. As the procession moved southward, units of paraders from the side streets fell into line. When it reached the memorial at Broad and High Streets, silence fell upon the marchers, their spirit of revelry was forgotten for the moment, and hats were removed, and heads bowed in tribute to those who had fallen. At the State House the parade, which took forty minutes to pass, was reviewed by Governor Cox and Maryor Karb. It now had a bicycle brigade as escort and was interspersed with shop bands, improvised floats with workmen pounding as though their lives depended on it on long iron pipes, boilers, or other resonant objects, and large marching groups from the various industrial plants, besides companies of Boy Scouts, Spanish-American War veterans, and women war workers.

Many of the celebrants were in grotesque costume, or rode in ridiculous conveyances and outlandish contraptions. Flags, American and Allied, were everywhere in evidence, and many placards and transparencies were carried bearing humerous, sarcastic, or vitupertive slogans on the abdicated Kaiser. He was carried in caskets, or shown beheaded or hanged in effigy. Despite the chill north wind, numbers of women marched, rode, or clung to unsightly conveyances.

The celebration was kept up all day with Chinese gongs, circular saws, cowbells, cymbals, anvils, horns, and guns. Tin cans were dragged rattling over the streets in lieu of anything else to make a discordant noise. At 1 o'clock a meeting of people from various churches was hastily planned to be held in the evening. In consequence more than 3,000 men and women assembled in Memorial Hall. Thence they marched down Broad Street singing "Onward Christian Soldiers" and the "Battle Hymn of the Republic" and displaying appropriate mottoes, until at High Street they were enveloped and divided by surging crowds of revelers. The din continued until midnight, when the people, tired and happy, dispersed to their homes, leaving the streets covered with confetti, colored paper ribbons, battered tin cans, and the burnt ends of Roman candles.

By the opening of January, 1919, the University was beginning to receive rehabilitation students. This was made possible by an act passed by Congress late in June of the previous year, which provided for the vocational rehabilitation and return to civil employment of disabled men who had been discharged from the military and naval service of the United

States. The act established a Federal Board for Vocational Education in Washington, D. C., to pass upon the eligibility of disabled men for educational aid, with central-district and branch-district officers. Ohio, Indiana, and Kentucky constituted one of the fourteen districts. The central officer for this district was located at Cincinnati and a branch officer at Columbus. There was also a coordinating officer at the University, with a rehabilitation committee. The act further provided for the payment of the tuition and expenses of the disabled soldiers and the cost of their books and other equipment. The branch officer received applications, made examinations, and questioned the applicants to discover their ability, previous training, and the occupations they desired to follow. Medical service was supplied either by the Federal Board or the United States Physical Health Service.

The Columbus branch officer began his work in October, 1918. Three months later three disabled soldiers were receiving special training in our College of Agriculture. Two of them took instruction in meat inspection and the third in animal husbandry. Their courses lasted a year. In March, 1919, there were six more, one studying horticulture and poultry-keeping, another electrical engineering, another meat inspection, and the others subjects preparatory to law and medicine. In the summer session of 1919 nearly 250 of these rehabilitation or Federal Board students entered the University, being distributed among the various colleges. Agriculture received over 150; Arts, Commerce and Journalism, and Engineering, more than 20 each; Law, 11; Education, 8; Veterinary Medicine, 3; and Dentistry, Pharmacy, and the Graduate School, 1 each. In the summer session of 1920 the number of rehabilitation students dropped to 133, distributed as follows: Agriculture, 79; Arts, and Engineering, 13 each; Commerce and Journalism, 12; Medicine, 9; Education, the Graduate School, and Veterinary Medicine, 2 each; and Pharmacy, 1. The departments in which these students were taking studies were required to send monthly reports of their marks to the coordinating officer. During the first- and second-half years of 1919-20 the enrollment of rehabilitation students in the University was on the average more than 180. These men remained in the University usually long enough to prepare them for the occupations they intended to enter.

During vacations they were in numerous instances placed by the Columbus branch officer in positions where they gained practical experience in their chosen vocation. Men in the short agricultural course were sent to poultry farms, stock farms, stock yards, or into factories and repair shops. Men preparing for the practice of the law were sent into law offices and those studying journalism to work on newspapers.

The scope and results of this rehabilitation work may be illustrated by the case of a veteran who had lost his hearing. The branch officer sent him first to the Ohio Institution for the Deaf and Dumb, where he learned lip-reading during the year 1918-19. He was next sent to the Biological Station at Winona Lake, Indiana, for courses in biology and zoology. At length, in September, 1919, he entered the University and carried on his work successfully.

In the early days of April, 1919, Columbus and the University welcomed home Ohio troops of the 37th Division from overseas service, including numbers of University men. On Friday morning, April 4, at 11:15 o'clock, the 112th Sanitary Train arrived at the Union Station. It comprised 423 officers and men and was welcomed by Mayor Karb and a committee of Columbus representatives and a mass of relatives and friends of the soldiers. In the sanitary train were the 146th Field Hospital, the 146th Ambulance Company, both Columbus units and known formerly as the Second Field Hospital and the Second Ambulance Company of the Ohio National Guard; the 147th Field Hospital and the 147th Ambulance Company of Delaware; the 145th Ambulance Company of Canton; and the Headquarters Company. Another unit of the 37th Division that was in line was the 62nd Artillery Brigade, including the 134th, 135th, and 136th Regiments, and the 112th Field Signal Battalion. These organizations together numbered 4,000 overseas soldiers. Major Harry Snively, Captain Howard Boucher, and Sergeant Leroy Bradford, all Ohio State University men, did not return with the 112th Sanitary Train. The Columbus papers announced that the above named organizations would parade on Saturday, April 5, at 9 A. M., and that other units were expected to arrive in the city in time to take part in the procession.

All classes at the University were excused and its administrative offices closed on Saturday morning by order of President Thompson. The members of the University Battalion of Cadets were to serve as a guard of honor for the troops, but instead were assigned to guard duty to help keep the crowds in order. One hundred and fifty women were chosen by the dean of women from various campus organizations to give flowers to the soldiers.

The procession moved a little after 9 o'clock from Naghten and High Streets, went south on High to Main, countermarched to Broad and so eastward to the reviewing stand, which was occupied by Governor Cox, other State officers, Mayor Karb, and other representatives of the city, besides a large group of war mothers and a hundred wounded soldiers from Camp Sherman. Cheering tens of thousands greeted the "doughboys," with whom 8,000 civilians and men in uniform marched. As they swung into Broad Street the girls' glee club of the Patriotic League from the University, under the direction of Miss Lillian Stocklin, sang "Smiles" and other songs. Store fronts and windows were bright with gay decorations, and upper story windows and the roofs of buildings along the line of march held many spectators.

The day's program ended with an entertainment for the returned soldiers in Memorial Hall on Saturday evening. It consisted of music by the regimental bands, songs by the girls of the Patriotic League, and dancing.

On Monday, April 7, the 146th Infantry was welcomed in Columbus. The men of this unit had seen hard fighting in the Baccarat sector, then in the Meuse-Argonne offensive where many Ohio soldiers fell in action, next in the St. Mihiel sector, and, finally, in two hard drives near Ypres and over

President Thompson and Ohio State men at Fort Benjamin Harrison, Indiana, on May 27, 1917.

The 166th Infantry, 42d (Rainbow) Division being received at the Union Station on Saturday, May 10, 1919.

The 166th Infantry marching on High Street.

the battle-torn fields of Belgium. The parade followed the same route as that of April 5. At the reviewing stand the men were addressed by Lieutenant Governor Clarence J. Brown. At 2 o'clock they left for Camp Sherman to receive their discharge.

On Thursday, April 12, the 112th Supply Train arrived in the Union Station at 10:45 A. M. and was greeted by a concourse of people with umbrellas and rain coats. Since many of the soldiers were residents of Columbus, they were set free to visit their families and friends, with orders to report back to the station at 9 o'clock the next morning for the parade scheduled for 11:30. During the afternoon the 148th Infantry, the 112th Engineers, and Batteries C, D, E, and F of the 134th Artillery arrived. The theatres were thrown open for the entertainment of the soldiers, both afternoon and evening, on account of the rainy weather. A dance was held in the rotunda of the State House on Thursday evening.

About three thousand men took part in the parade on Friday morning, which was witnessed by thousands along the line of march. Most of these troops had been in the hard fighting that caused the heavy losses of the 37th Division. The 148th Infantry (the old Third Ohio) had suffered as much as any other infantry unit of the division. Battery C, the Columbus unit of the 134th Field Artillery, attracted the most attention from the spectators. The parade was headed by a detachment of police, next came the Barracks Band, then the guard of honor of G.A.R. men and Spanish-American War veterans, the governor, mayor, and president of the Chamber of Commerce, and the returned organizations. Girls of the Patriotic League sang at various places along the line of march, the glee club from the University, under the direction of Miss Lillian Stocklin, being stationed in front of the McKinley monument. After passing the reviewing stand, the troops were served with dinner by the Red Cross canteen women, and later in the afternoon the soldiers entrained for Camp Sherman.

On Friday morning C. B. Layne, formerly a student at the State University, appeared at the troop train. He had previously belonged to Battery C of the 134th Artillery. Later he had joined the tanks. He was with the British Army in the 301st Heavy Tank Corps, which trained for four months in England with the monster 35-foot tanks and lost heavily in the advance of September 29, 1918, that broke the Hindenberg line. For its work in that advance the unit was twice decorated by the British Government.

In the closing days of the war the 37th Division was hurriedly sent by General Pershing to the aid of the Belgian Army and participated in the Ypres-Lys and Lys-Escaut offensives, crossing the Scheldt River on an improvised bridge formed with tree trunks floated across the river under heavy shell and machine-gun fire from the Germans. The ranks of the 37th advanced farther toward Brussels, the Belgian capital, than any other allied military organization.

In memory of the Ohioans who lost their lives in the offensives, a memorial bridge was dedicated at Eyne, Belgium, on September 26, 1929. It spans the Scheldt a few miles from the spot where they first crossed the river and was erected by the State of Ohio at a cost of nearly $100,000.

The last and greatest demonstration of welcome for a homecoming unit was that of Saturday, May 10, 1919, for the 166th Infantry (the old Fourth Ohio) of the Rainbow, or 42nd, Division, which contained many University men. The 166th was commanded by Colonel Benson W. Hough, Law, '99. Elaborate preparations were made, the city was bedecked with flags, a detachment of 11 wounded soldiers of the regiment was brought from Camp Sherman on Friday evening to witnes the parade, and on Saturday morning thousands of people poured into Columbus from the neighboring towns and counties, bringing their local bands with them. The 166th numbered about 1,700 enlisted men and 53 officers. They arrived in three trains Saturday afternoon. By that time the downtown section was filled with a mass of perhops 200,000 people. The local military organizations had been assembled at Buttles

Avenue and High Street and in the side streets of that neighborhood and had patiently waited for several hours. An immense throng was at the Union Station to greet the soldiers as they arrived from Camp Merritt, New Jersey. The concourse of people in the reviewing stands on Broad Street, including the war mothers, and in that part of the street between Third and High Streets was entertained while waiting by the Marion and London bands and by some 500 University students, who gave college yells and songs and performed stunts.

The great welcome to the Rainbow men was due to the notable part they had played in the war. The Rainbow, or 42nd, Division had been put into the line in the Luneville sector on February 22, 1918, and soon after had taken over the Baccarat sector, which they held 100 days, a longer continuous period than any other American division held a sector. The 166th Infantry was in the front line for approximately 60 days of that time. As part of the noted French Fourth Army, the division, including the 166th, broke the German offensive of July 15, in the neighborhood of Châlons, and, as Major General Flagler, commander of the division, wrote, permitted the Allied High Command to start the great offensive which finally brought the war to a close. The regiment and division were then rushed to the Marne front and took part in the French-Allied offensive at Chateau-Thierry. They were in savage fighting at Hill 284 and the town of Seringes-et-Nesles, crossed the Ouerq under a hail of fire from the front and flanks, and reached the southern border of Mareu-en-Dole, when they were relieved by elements from a fresh division. The regiment was next sent into the St. Mihiel attack and advanced into the enemy's lines. Thence it was moved to the Argonne, marching through mud and rain, and took part in the attack on one of the strongest points in the line, the *Krimholde Stellung*, on which the enemy relied to stop the Allied advance. It reconnoitered and opened the road to Sedan, being within rifle shot of that historic city when it was relieved from its place in the front line. Thence it started on its marches with the Rainbow Division into Germany. It remained as part of the American Army of Occupation until it returned to the United States.

In Columbus the men of the 166th Infantry and the local organizations marched from Buttles Avenue and High Street south on High to Mound, east on Mound to Third, north on Third to Main, east on Main to Grant Avenue, north on Grant to Broad Street, and west on Broad to the State House, where they were reviewed. Everywhere along the line of march Harold T. Powell, or "Dutch" Powell as he was familiarly called, the former football-star back and tackler of the University, was hailed. He had been rejected for military service on account of a minor ailment, but had followed the 166th to Long Island and had managed to enlist. Overseas he had rounded up several Germans in "no man's land" and marched them into the Allied lines.

After the disbanding of the marchers, they were served dinner by the Red Cross canteen women in the basement of the State House. These women had made ample preparations to feed a throng of hungry men by providing 3,700 sandwiches, 3,800 deviled eggs, a large quantity of boiled ham, 165 gallons of coffee, hundreds of pies, 300 dozen doughnuts, 140 gallons of ice cream, and some other eatables. That the soldiers appreciated all this hospitality and did full justice to the food goes without saying.

In April, 1919, the General Assembly passed an act requiring all teachers to take an oath of office as a condition of their service. This law seems to have been intended to protect students and the State from expressions of opinion on the part of injudicious teachers at variance with our political institutions, or against the policies of our Government in time of war. Instances of such expression of opinion had occurred even on our own campus early in the war, when certain alien teachers voiced their sympathy with the Central Powers. At any rate, the law was approved by the governor on June 5 and has remained in force ever since. The requirement to take the oath appeared to several members of the

Faculty a reflection on the loyalty of the teaching profession, if not of their own. President Thompson heard rumors that the oath was somewhat disagreeable to certain individuals, but asserted that the University was in no way responsible for the passing of the act and that its duty was to see that the law was complied with. For that reason, he added, only the names of those persons who took the oath would appear on the pay roll.

The experience with psychological tests in rating men in the camps and cantonments was not forgotten by members of the Faculty who had been in service. However, it was not until May 8, 1919, that the University Faculty adopted, by unanimous vote, a resolution providing for the giving of such tests to all students in the institution, the results for upper classmen to be correlated with their grades as soon as possible by the Department of Psychology and the comparisons reported to the Faculty. The resolution further provided that the results of tests in the case of freshmen be kept by the department until the end of the first half-year, when the tests should be correlated with the marks and a report made to the Faculty.

At the meeting of the Board of Trustees in the following September a communication from the Society for the Promotion of Engineering Education was read, which proposed for engineering students psychological tests extending over four or five years, with reports on their standing and progress. It was also suggested that a report be made on the professional standing and progress of these men for a brief period after gaduation. The Tustees approved these proposals and authorized the incidental expense involved. The resolution of the Faculty was carried into effect in due time. President Thompson took the test for his own satisfaction on September 13 and did so well that he was placed in Class A. He urged the other members of the teaching staff to take it as a beneficial experience. October 8 was assigned for the giving of the test to the Faculty. Two days later the students took their tests. Psychological tests have continued in use on the campus ever since. The rating made by each student is entered on his record card and is usually considered in connection with his marks and other pertinent items if his case comes before the dean and executive committee of his college.

With the return to the campus of hundeds of our men who had been in active service, the Ohio State University Post No. 150 of the American Legion was organized in September, 1919, by a group of 15 men. The post added members rapidly, including many of the Faculty who had seen service and some of the Army military instructors on the campus. By the latter part of February, 1920, it numbered nearly 700 members, but, wishing to have every ex-service man on its roll, it entered upon a six weeks' campaign for the purpose of adding 500 more members, not including the men who belonged to posts in their home communities. Already the University post was the largest organization of its kind in any institution of higher learning in the United States, as it was also the first of these to oganize. The officers of the post were: Lawrence G. Andrews, Arts senior, commander; Frederick E. Croxton, Arts senior, vice-commander; W. William Willing, Dentistry freshman, finance officer; and John F. Burgett, a special student in the College of Commerce and Journalism, adjutant.

The purposes of the American Legion are: patriotism; Americanism; the upholding of the Constitution of the United States; the maintenance of law and order; the inculcation of a sense of individual obligation to the community, the State, and the Nation; fair play; the promotion of peace and good will on the earth; the transmission to posterity of the principles of justice, freedom, and democracy; the preservation of the memories and incidents of the association in the war; and the consecration of their comradship by mutual helpfulness. Eligibility to membership in the legion consists of service in the United States Army, Navy, or Marine Corps during the period between April 6, 1917, and November 11, 1918. In the winter of 1920 the legion put forth its efforts in Washington, D. C., in favor of $50 compensation for each month of service for the men. The University post supported this request.

In November, 1919, the post adopted a resolution declaring the existing system of Army courts-martial unjust and cruel. In the same month it arranged the celebration of Armistice Day, which was very impressive. Classes were dismissed at 3 o'clock, and the University Brigade, consisting of two regiments of infantry and one of artillery, together with four provisional companies of our veterans, marched in review. George Ackley, formerly a sergeant in the 37th Division, and Jerome E. Wagner, who had been a corporal in the 42nd Division, both of them students and wearers of the Distinguished Service Cross for valor in capturing German machine-gun nests, occupied the reviewing stand with Lieutenant Colonel Charles F. Leonard, the commandant of cadets. Taps were sounded by 16 buglers in tribute to those who had lost their lives in the war, while the student body stood with bared heads. Then, while the band played "The Star Spangled Banner," the companies stood at present arms until the last strains died away. Colonel Leonard took command of the brigade and presented it to the two honored veterans, in exemplification of his lofty conception and his admonition to the students that honor is placed above rank.

Early in March, 1920, the University post took up the question of credits for privates and non-commissioned officers who had not been able to obtain them for their term of active service. Many of the ex-service men had complained that they had been refused credit in the University on the ground that they had not completed their course in an officers' training school. Joseph A. Park, Arts senior, made a report to the post in favor of asking the Faculty to allow at least part credit for the service of such men. Accordingly, a petition was adopted and transmitted to the Faculty requesting credit according to a graduated scale for all students who had been in the military or naval service of the United States between April 6, 1917, and September 1, 1919, according to length of service, the full credit of eight hours to be given to those who had had six months' service overseas or twelve months' service in the United States. It was pointed out in the petition that under the ruling of the Faculty a completed course in an officers' training camp was necessary for credit, and that some members of the post had enlisted and gone to France before the first officers' training camp had opened on May 12, 1917, while other members of the post who had not enlisted until late in 1918 had finished their course in training camp, returned to the University and received their credit. The University post thought such discrimination unjust. The petitioners affirmed that they were proud of the record of the Faculty in military service and its many correlated branches and that they realized the difficulty of properly adjusting war credits, but that they believed the Faculty would devise a method by which due credit would be granted to the enlisted men.

At its meeting early in March, 1920, the University post was addressed by Major George F. Arps, dean of the College of Education. He said the American Legion was the cream of our manhood, and that the hope of democracy rested in its membership. He thought that the legion was one of the greatest forces in America, and that it should exercise its influence for the betterment of social and political conditions. He looked to it to help bring about a new era in the industrial world, which should be accompanied by a reform in our public school system. In closing, Major Arps urged the University post to enroll all ex-service men on the campus.

At the end of June, 1920, the post held its first meeting of the summer to discuss activities for the season and urge all former soldiers, sailors, and members of the Army Nurses' Corps to become members. Acting Commander James M. Patchell presided at the meeting and appointed a committee to make arrangements for a picnic to be held at Glenmary Park during the last week in July. During the first week of August the posts of Franklin County, including the University post, celebrated American Legion Week at Olentangy Park, with the objects of getting acquainted, gaining new members, raising a relief fund for the benefit of needy men of other counties, and securing money for the local posts and the national organization. The celebration at Olentangy Park was in the nature of a "carnival," with a series of athletic events and a sideshow.

The time for signing the charter of the University post was extended to September 1, 1920, to enable all eligible members of the Faculty to become charter members. Already at the end of July 30 Faculty men belonged to the post, but the desire was that the other ex-service men in the teaching staff should join.

In the year 1919-20 certain courses, approved by the committee on instruction of the University Faculty, were courses for students in the Colleges of Arts and Education that were clearly due to the war. These were all history courses. One of them was entitled "The World War: Its Causes, Issues and Results." It was a three-hour course continuing throughout the year and drew students in such numbers as to require four sections for their accommodation. Another was designated "The Problems of the World War." It was a one-hour course for the year. In the summer session of 1919 two such courses were offered: one, a one-hour course called "Problems of World Peace and Reconstruction," and the other, a two-hour course entitled "Revisions of American History." All of these courses attracted large classes.

The fact that German had been discontinued in the high schools by the school boards of Ohio early in the war and was not restored in many of them until some years after its close, resulted in the necessity of many new students beginning the subject in the University. Before the war students were permitted to major in German only by electing a number of the advanced courses. In 1919-20, however, the Department of German found itself without a clientele for such courses and struck out of its announcements in the college catalogues the following preliminary statement: "A student beginning German at the University is advised not to take the subject as a major study."

That the depression through which the country, including the University, has been passing since 1929, is part of the aftermath of the war, has been asserted by many prominent writers. For the University these years have meant the reduction of salaries, the lessening of the number of teachers and office staffs, and the serving on part-time of some of the instructors who have remained on the campus. Purchases of new equipment and supplies for departments and of new books for the library have been necessarily much restricted.

The student enrollment kept up surprisingly well through the years 1930-31 and 1931-32, as compared with the figures for 1929-30. There was, however, a decided decline in the enrollment for 1932-33, which became more marked in 1933-34. This downward trend seems likely to disappear in 1934-35. The following table gives the figures for the years mentioned:

Summer Quarter	Autumn Quarter	Winter Quarter	Spring Quarter
	Year 1929-30		
3,871	10,655	9,951	9,472
	Year 1930-31		
4,487	10,852	10,388	9,872
	Year 1931-32		
4,845	10,795	10,157	9,636
	Year 1932-33		
4,448	10,166	9,394	8,853
	Year 1933-34		
3,382	9,449	8,730	8,551

INDEX

INDEX

A List of the Most Important Occupations and Employments in the Food Producing Industries under the Supervision of the United States Food Administration. (Prepared by the Labor Division), 177, 178
Ackley, George, reviews parade, 299
Academic Board, composition of, 17
Adams, C. S., at field station, 214, 215
Adams, J. J., in civilian service, 14; submits contract, 32; lectures, 252; acting president, 253; in celebration, 288
Administrative Division, loses members, 13, 14
Adriatic Sea, W. C. Sabine flies over, 167
Aerial observation, instruction in, 24
Aeronautical Laboratory, plans for, 10; cost, 11; training in, 19, 20; airplane work transferred to, 23; number of men in, 25; mess hall in, 34; constructed, 286
Aftermath, of the war, 285-302
Agler, A. K., death of, 126
Agricultural Extension Service, mentioned, 131; in drive, 132; circulates publications, 135; C. S. Wheeler signs contract, 137; places applicants, 138; publishes bulletin, 143
Agricultural Engineering Extension Service, loses member, 142

Agricultural Faculty, recommends excusing students, 6
Agricultural Publications Department, sends out printed matter, 140
Agricultural Student, The, difficulties of, 85; reports enlistments, etc., 90, 91; editorials of, 100, 105
Air Service, adopts tests, 192
Alexander, W. R., invents machine, 55, 238
Allen, E. M., death of, 129
Allen, F. E., in uniform, 14; in service, 146
Allen, I. G., death of, 127
Allen, T., in civilian service, 14
Allied Governments, W. C. Sabine brings papers of, 167
Allison, Catherine, on farm, 118
American Chemical Society, offers services, 199
American Legion, at University, 298-301
American Library Association, funds for, 47
American Protective League, J. S. Myers in, 174
American Red Cross (*see* Red Cross)
American University, experiment station at, 202, 213; Government takes over buildings, 203; research organization at, 209; University's chemistry teachers at, 233, 234

Andrews, C. E., in uniform, 14; service record of, 159; collects trench poetry, 164
Applied Aeronautics, published, 23
Arick, Ola M., in relief work, 64
Armistice, effects of, 15; bright prospects after, 111; cadets withdraw after, 148; men return after, 171; laboratory closes at, 206; invoicing after, 207; number of pharmacy men in service at, 273; officers in Veterinary Corps at, 279; 37th Division in pursuit at, 281, 282; economic situation after, 286; premature news of, 287; signing of, 288
Armistice Day, celebration, 299
Armstrong, A., in service, 14
Army, enlistments in, 182; medical teachers in, 258; medical graduates in, 268; D. S. White in, 280; veterinary graduates in, 283; promotes gas investigations, 200; gas program of, 210; metallurgy men in, 237
Army camps, men released from, 178
Army of Occupation, E. J. Jordan with 268; W. M. Weldishofer with, 282; 42d (Rainbow) Division part of, 296
Army Nurses' Corps, members urged to join American Legion, 300
Arnold, R. H., death of, 128
Arps, G. F., in uniform, 14; in service, 163; record of, 190, 191; addresses Legion post, 300
Arts College (*see* College of Arts, Philosophy, and Science)
Arts-education course, withdrawals from, 147; enrollment in, 148, 149, 155; decline of, 156
Athletic Association, buys bond, 44
Athletics, during the war, 107-111
Atkins, Rev. G. G., in France, 71
Aviation Laboratory (*see* Aeronautical Laboratory)
Axtell, W. J., Jr., in service, 146

Baker, Lt. Col. C. B., chief of Motor Transport Division, 217; in Washington, 222
Baker, Hon. N. D., message from, 59; articles by, 97, W. C. Sabine sends resignation to, 169
Baldwin, R. H., death of, 128
Bancroft, W. P., death of, 126, 182
Barnett, S. J., in Washington, 222
Barracks, begun, 10; cost, 11; location of, 34; used for sick, 80
Barrett, T. W., death of, 128
Barrington, A. R., chairman of music program, 47
Baseball, loses letter men, 109
Basinger, A. O., in service, 74
Bauer, W. W., at field station, 214-215
Baum, E. F., in service, 74
Baumgardner, H. K., in research, 216
Bayes, Cecil, in service, 146
Bayles, Leo, in service, 74
Beach, F. H., in service, 146
Beatty, H. G., in uniform, 14; serves base hospital, 266
Beekman, T., in service, 75
Belgian Army, aided by 37th Division, 294
Belgian refugees, sewing for, 54
Belgium, anti-war demonstrations in, 102; study of German in, 150; H. C. Haddox in, 161; Pres. W. O. Thompson in, 253; H. H. Snively in, 270; 37th Division in, 281, 282; 146th Infantry in, 292, 293; memorial bridge in, 294
Benjamin, B., in service, 75

Index 307

Benjamin, Vera, Red Cross nurse, 249
Bergman, B. A., in service, 75
Bessarabia, H. H. Snively in, 271, 272
Bevan, Arthur, helps prepare scenic battlefield, 153
Bingham, W. E., service record of, 159, 160
Birch, L. W., teaches gunnery, 23
Bird, O. C., teaches recreation, 19
Blake, F. C., in service, 14, 163; president, Academic Board, 18
Blakey, H. B., in uniform, 14; in service, 266
Blengenses, Maj. Gen. ——, D. S. White guest of, 280, 281
Bloor, W. F., in service, 14; in Washington, 182
Blum, M., in service, 75
Board of Trustees (*see* Trustees)
Bolling, G. M., in service, 162
Bolsheviki, sign peace with Germany, 55
Boord, C. E., in War Chemical Association, 201; in charge of field station, 213; investigates new gas, 214
Boothman, D. M., officer, 211
Bornhorst, A. H., death of, 129
Boucher, Howard, delayed return of, 291, 292
Bowen, B. L., gives address, 15
Bowler, Miss A. C., in Red Cross work, 192
Bowman, J. C., death of, 127
Bownocker, J. A., chairman of committee, 43, 44; on war chest committee, 45
Bownocker, Mrs. J. A., in relief unit, 60
Boyd, C. C., in service, 74
Boyd, J. F., in service, 239, 240
Boyland, Vernette, in France, 116

Bradford, Leroy, delayed return of, 292
Brehm, G. W., in uniform, 14
Brehm, Wayne, at Camp Greenleaf, 261
Bricker, J. W., in service, 74
Bridges, J. W., in service, 14; in Medical Department, 191, 192
British Army, C. B. Layne with, 294
British Government, decorates unit, 294
British Labor Conditions During the War, by M. B. Hammond, 176
British Veterinary Corps, D. S. White guest of, 280, 281; men in, 283
British Veterinary Service, model for United States, 279
British War Office, recalls medical men, 275
Britton, W. C., helps standardize trucks, 220
Brooks, C., in service, 14
Brown, A. T., instructor, 19
Brown, C. J. (Lieut.-Gov.), reviews returned troops, 293
Brown, Maynard, at Edgewood, 207
Brown, Raymond, at Edgewood, 207
Brown, R. A., in service, 14, 18; gives wireless course, 230, 237, 238
Brown, R. H. arranges meeting, 222; secretary, 223
Bruce, C. A., mentioned, 53; death of, 128; service record of, 161
Bruce, Mrs. C. A., president of club, 53
Brumberg, D., in service, 75
Bucher, Paul, in service, 224
Bundon, M. L., in research, 216
Bureau of Aircraft Production, W. C. Sabine with, 169

Bureau of Mines, promotes gas investigations, 200; research by, 203
Burrell, G. A., in charge of gas research, 200, 201, 208, 209; decorated, 209; responds, 223
Burrell, G. O., death of, 128, 268
Burrett, C. H., on committee, 248
Burt, W. I., at Edgewood, 207
Burtt, H. E., in service, 192
Bush, S. P., president of war chest committee, 44
Butterfield, Col. A. D., characterizes W. C. Sabine, 167

Caine, W. H., award to, 250
Caldwell, F. C., invents machine, 55, 238
Campbell, Hon. James E., gives address, 59
Campbell, Kenyon S., in service, 74
Campbell, Lois, Red Cross nurse, 249
Campbell, M. L., death of, 128
Camps:
  Boyd, Tex., school at, 221
  Custer, Mich., E. F. McCampbell at, 261
  Dix, N. J., D. S. White at, 281
  Greenleaf, Ga., medical training camp at, 261; D. S. White organizes school at, 280; F. A. Lambert at, 282
  Holabird, Md., school at, 220; Victor Darnell at, 221; A. A. Case at, 239
  Jesup, Ga., school at, 221
  Lee, Va., R. Pintner at, 191; J. W. Bridges at, 192
  McArthur, Tex., E. F. McCampbell at, 262
  Meigs, D. C., E. S. Manson, Jr., at, 224
  Merritt, N. J., troops from, 295
  Normoyle, Tex., school at, 221
  Pike, Ark., pneumonia at, 261
  Sheridan, visited by G. W. Rightmire, 253
  Sherman, O., girls sew for, 57; its team defeated, 108; C. A. Bruce at, 161; Dean Hagerty visits, 174; R. D. McKenzie at, 180; G. F. Arps at, 190; visited by G. W. Rightmire, 253; wounded soldiers from, 292; 146th Infantry goes to, 293; soldiers from, 294; E. S. Manson, Jr., at, 224; G. C. Seegar at, 228
  Zachary Taylor, Ky., J. W. Bridges at, 191, 192
Canada, Septimus Sisson in, 283
Canadian troops, resist, 198
Cannon, Nan, in France, 72
Caples, Mrs. M. J., instructor, 52
Carder, C. F., death of, 127
Carmack, G. R., at Baltimore, 215
Carman, J. E., in service, 14, 154
Carpenter, W. B., ln medical corps, 248
Case, A. A., in uniform, 14; standardizes trucks, 220; establishes schools, 220, 221; captain, 239
Castleman, F. R., instructor, 19; team captain, 47
Chambers, B., in service, 74
Chance, E. M., cooperates, 206 anticipates demand, 210
Chandler, A. R., in Red Cross work, 60-62; services, 159
Chandler, Grace, canteen worker, 58
Chaney, Maj. J. E., service of, 30
Charlton, D. H., death of, 127
Charlton, P. H., commissioned, 272
Chautauqua Bureau, sends food experts, 179

Chauncey, Rev. E. F., gives address, 15
Chemical Warfare Service, research section of, 200; J. R. Withrow has field station of, 202; creation of, 208; Wm. McPherson officer in, 209; agencies incorporated with, 212; publishes monograph, 213; University men in, 215, 224; chemistry teachers in, 233; advanced students in, 234
Cheny, S. L., in service, 74
Chlorine gas, used by Germans, 198
Christensen, E. O., in uniform, 14; service record of, 194
Chubb, C. St. J., prepares scenic battlefield, 24, 153
Chubb, Mrs. C. St. J., in relief unit, 60
Cicle, Grace, lecturer, 118
City Federation of Women's Clubs, aids sick, 64
Civilian Relief Department, students serve in, 174
Civilian service, Faculty members in, 14
Claxton, P. P., articles by, 97
Clinton, H. W., in service, 248
Cockins, Edith D., assigns classrooms, 30
Coddington, E. F., on committee, 34; in Washington, 239; acting dean, 240
Coe, Dana, in service, 74
Cohn, S., in service, 75
Cole, A. D., in service, 14; in Washington, 216; record of, 222; gives wireless course, 230
Cole, Mrs. A. D., organizes group, 58
Coleman, T. C., record of, 229
College of Agriculture, loses students, 7, 12; cadets in, 33; deals with food problem, 131-146; disabled soldiers in, 290
College of Arts, Philosophy, and Science, loses students, 7, 12; men in service, etc., 13; cadets in, 32; in wartime, 147-170; disabled soldiers in, 290
College of Commerce and Journalism, loses students, 7, 12; cadets in, 33; in wartime, 171-182; disabled soldiers in, 290
College of Dentistry, "recognized" list in, 13; cadets in, 33; in wartime, 183-188; disabled soldiers in, 290
College of Education, loses students, 7, 12, 13; cadets in, 33; in wartime, 189-195; disabled soldiers in, 290
College of Engineering, loses students, 12, 13; cadets in, 33; in wartime, 197-241; communicates with other bodies, 199, 200; disabled soldiers in, 290
College of Homeopathic Medicine, "recognized" list in, 13; cadets in, 33; in wartime, 247-250
College of Law, in wartime, 251-253; disabled soldiers in, 290
College of Medicine, seniors released from, 7; "recognized" list in, 12; cadets in, 33; in wartime, 255-272
College of Pharmacy, in wartime, 273-274; disabled soldiers in, 290
College of Veterinary Medicine, in wartime, 275-284; disabled soldiers in, 290
Columbus, welcomes returned troops, 291-296
Columbus Chapter of Red Cross, formed, 51; branches of, 53; aids sick, 64; home-service depart-

ment of, 117; work for, 144; J. E. Hagerty, chairman of committee, 173; promotes Home Service Institute, 174. (*See* also Red Cross)

Columbus people, prematurely celebrate, 287, 288; news of genuine Armistice celebrated, 288-289; welcome returned troops, 291-296

Columbus Reserve Guards, in celebration, 288

Columbus (*or* Community) War Chest, established, 44, 45, 46; publicity for, 100; campus campaign for, 174, 175

Committee on Classification of Personnel, Trade Test Division of, 191

Committee on Education and Special Training, established, 32; instructions to, 33; prescribes curricula, 35; J. W. Bridges serves, 192; organized, 277

Committee on Patriotic Education, C. E. Parry serves, 178

Congress, hears ideas of Messrs. Converse, Orton, and Thompson, 1; declares war, 4; passes law, 13; passes Liberty Loan Bill, 42; passes act for rehabilitation students, 289

Converse, Capt. (*or* Maj.) G. L., has part in National Defense Act, 1-4; helps prepare letter, 4, 5; in uniform, 14; commandant, 17; chairman, Red Cross committee, 51, 52; in service, 163; recommends Archibald C. Huston, 226

Converse, Mrs. G. L., in relief unit, 60

Cook, Capt. F. C., in command of unit, 263

Coon, S. J., in service, 14; investigator, 180

Cooper, C. P., installs telephones, 227-228

Cooperider, Luke, in service, 74

Copenhagen, J. R. Knipfing, translator at, 163

Corra, F., in service, 14

Corry, H. C., in uniform, 14; teaching military law, 19, 252; on leave, 253

Cottingham, K. C., teaches aerial observation, 19; helps prepare scenic battlefield, 153; in service, 154

Cottrell, E. A., in service, 14; reports to Faculty, 140

Cottrell, Mrs. E. A., canteen worker, 58

Council of National Defense, requests investigation, 176; receives communication, 199, 200

Coursault, J. H., gives address, 165

Courtney, H. J., dies at sea, 111, 128

Covert, S. J., death of, 128

Covert, Florence, secretary, 63

Cowle, H. H., death of, 130

Cowle, W. W., death of, 130

Cox, Gov. James M., orders students into industries, 7, 43; confers with Trustees, 10; confers with Pres. Thompson and others, 131; program adopted, 138; appoints Ohio Historical Commission, 245; reviews parade, 289, 292

Craft, F. M., installs telephones, 277-228

Crawfis, O. R., at Baltimore, 215

Credits, for service men, 299, 300

Crites, C. R., death of, 126

Crites, D. O., in Bureau of Mines, 225

INDEX 311

Croxton, F. C., in service, 74, in conference, 131; helps organize committee, 132; supervises employment offices, 138
Cunningham, Jay S., adjutant, 32
Dagger, G. N., in service, 146
Daily, Harriett, E., in charge of section, 56
Daily, Rena, Red Cross nurse, 249
Daniels, Hon. Josephus, message from, 59; appoints B. G. Lamme, 226
Darby, H. J., at Edgewood, 207
Davis, E. R., in service, 14
Davis, W. E., record of, 229
Day, Harriet A., in charge of section, 56
Dayton, N. A., award to, 250
Dechon, A. H., death of, 127
Decorations for, G. A. Burrell, 209; Edward Orton, Jr., 220; W. E. Davis, 229; W. H. Caine, 250; N. A. Dayton, 250; H. H. Snively, 272; D. S. White, 281; R. L. Mundhenk, 282; D. S. White, Reuben Hilty, G. R. Powell, 283
Deeds, E. A., W. C. Sabine gives information to, 167, 168
Deibel, Edmund, in service, 75
De Long, D. M., in uniform, 14
Demorest, Dana J., in uniform, 14; in gas research, 202; commissioned, 210, in charge of chemical plant, 210, 211; summoned as expert, 236, 237; absence of, 241; in service 246
Demorest, Don L., in France, 69, 70, 71, 75; letters from, 87
Demorest, F. M., in charge of materials, 210, 211
Denney, J. V., committeeman, 34; article by, 94, 164; on condition of Arts College, 157, 158

Denney, Mrs. J. V., forms relief unit, 60
Departments:
Agricultural Chemistry, staff instructs farmers, 135; arranges meetings, 141; members in military service, 146
Agricultural Engineering, members in military service, 146
American History, enrollment in, 149; growth of, 151; offers public lectures, 156
Anatomy, enrollment in, 257
Art, enrollment in, 189
Astronomy, in wartime, 231, 241
Architecture, enrollment in, 231
Bacteriology, enrollment in, 257
Botany, member in military service, 146
Ceramic Engineering, enrollment in, 231
Chemistry, sets graduate students at gas problems, 202; effect of war on, 231, 233-236
Civil Engineering, enrollment in, 231
Dairying, members in military service, 146
Electrical Engineering, in wartime, 231, 237-238
Engineering Drawing, enrollment in, 231
English, enrollment in, 149, 154, 155
European History, enrollment in, 149; gains students, 151; offers summer courses, 156
Federal Employment Service (see U. S. Employment Service)
Geology, enrollment in, 149; gains students, 153, 154
German, teachers debarred from campus, 9; enrollment in, 149, 150

History and Philosophy of Education, enrollment in, 189
Home Economics, supplies equipment, 144; attendance, 145
Horticulture and Forestry, members in military service, 146
Husbandry, member in military service, 146
Industrial Arts, in wartime, 231, 238-239
Industrial Education, enrollment in, 189
Latin, enrollment in, 149, 154
Mathematics, enrollment in, 1917-19, 231
Mechanics, in wartime, 231, 239-240
Medicine, enrollment in, 257
Metallurgy, in wartime, 231, 236-237
Military Science and Tactics, notified of School of Aeronautics, 17
Mine Engineering, in wartime, 231, 240-241
Obstetrics, enrollment in, 257
Pathology, enrollment in, 257
Philosophy, enrollment in, 149, 152, 153
Physics, enrollment in, 231
Physiology, enrollment in, 257
Political Science, enrollment in, 149, 152
Principles of Education, enrollment in, 189
Psychology, enrollment in, 189; effect of war on, 190
Romance Languages, enrollment in, 149; gains students, 150, 151
Rural Economics, effects of war on, 145
School Administration, enrollment in, 189

Surgery and Gynecology, enrollment in, 257
Zoology, effects of war on, 145
Depression, affects University, 302
Detroit Az-u-wer, G. F. Arps supervises, 191
Deutsch, E. A., in service, 75
Deutsche Verein, Der, presents play, 103
Dickson, Brig. Gen. Tracy C., and staff in charge of steel, 225
Diemer, Hugo, record of, 225
Dildine, S. C., at Baltimore, 215
District of Columbia, extended telephone system for, 227-228
Dodd, V. A., in uniform, 14; to report for duty, 258; service of, 262, 263, 264
Donaldson, M., in service, 75
Dorsey, F. A., in charge of development work, 208
Dougherty, W. A., in service, 75
Draffin, F. O., serves Shipping Board, 240
Drain, B. D., in uniform, 14; in service, 146
Drake, E. S., manager of Ohio Union, 78; serves hospital, 81
Druffin, J. O., takes class, 237
Drury, H. B., with Shipping Board, 182
Duffee, W. E., at Camp Greenleaf, 261
Duffy, T. J., in conference, 131
Duga, J. B., in service, 75
Dugan, J. C., death of, 127
Dunham, C. B., in service, 75
Dunbar, C. M., in service, 14
Dunn, Charlotte, instructor, 53
Dunn, Helen, instructor, 53
Dunn, Fay, instructor, 221
Dupre, Huntley, in Y.M.C.A., 67; in France, 69, 70, 71, 75; letters from, 87

INDEX 313

Durham, H. A., at Edgewood, 207
Dustman, Helen D., in charge of section, 56
Duvel, Dr. W. J. T., responds, 223
Dye, Mrs. C. A., in relief unit, 60
Dyer, J. N., death of, 127
Dyer, J. Ruskin, to France, 69, 71, 75

Eaton, Esther, in France, 64
Eberlein, Prof. R., article by, 91
Eckelberry, G. W., enters Air Service, 182
Edelman, S. D., in uniform, 14
Edgewood Arsenal, Md., poisonous gas plants at, 204, 205; closes, 206; chemical activities at, 210, 211; chlorpicrin plant at, 212; Ohio State Men at, 215, 223, 227
Eich, L. M., attempts to enter service, 161, 162
Eidelman, A., in service, 75
Eisele, Helen, in service, 117
Eisenlohr, B. A., in service, 14; record of, 160
Elden, W. S., teaches French, 154
Elden, Mrs. W. S., in relief unit, 60
Elder, C. M., death of, 129
Elwood, P. H., Jr., in uniform, 14; absent, 142; in service, 146
Employment Exchangees (*or* offices), increased, 131; M. B. Hammond organizes, 175
Engineer Enlisted Reserve Corps, students enlist in, 13, 230
England, submarine campaign against, 95; anti-war demonstrations in, 102; study of German in, 150; W. C. Sabine invited to, 166, 167; chemists at work in, 200; Wm. McPherson in, 209; Pres. Thompson in, 253; depletion of medical men in, 259; G. C. Shaeffer in, 265; D. S. White in, 280, 281; 301st Heavy Tank Corps trains in, 294

Ensign, Mabel, in France, 116
Enzor, Mrs. Kelly, in service, 118
Epstein, M., in service, 75
Erdman, H. E., assists milk commission, 140
Esper, E. A., record of, 162
Esprit de Corps, The, published, 93
Europe and Turkey, students attracted by course on, 151
Evans, C. R., death of, 126
Evans, L., in service, 75
Evans, M. B., in service, 162
Evans, W. L., in uniform, 14; in service, 163; member of War Chemical Association, 201; organizes laboratories, 204, 205, 206; invoices, 207; discharged, 208; responds, 223

Faculty, loses members, 13, 14; subscribes, 42, 43; releases students, 43, 230; contributes to war chest, 45; women in Red Cross work, 53; censured by *Lantern*, 99; interviews, 104; approves granting credits, 158; dismisses students, 172; summer work of, 185; votes late enrollment, 185; shortens holidays, 186; depleted by war, 232; members dislike teachers' oath, 296, 297; approves psychological tests, 297; members join American Legion, 298, 301; asked to adjust credits, 300
Fairfield Aviation School, airplane from, 46
Falconer, J. I., assists milk commission, 140
Far East, students attracted by course on, 15
Farmer, T. O., in Washington, 216; record of, 221

Fasig, E. W., at Edgewood, 206
Faulder, G. B., in uniform, 14; in service, 248; returns, 250
Federal Board for Vocational Education, passes on eligibility, 290
Federal Employment Service (see U. S. Employment Service)
Federal Food Administration in Ohio, Edna N. White on staff of, 134; in drive, 136; aided by press, 143; J. E. Hagerty's services to, 174; M. B. Hammond adviser to, 177; aids in carrying message, 179; C. F. Kelly serves, 193, 194; A. H. Tuttle serves, 252, 253
Federal Fuel Administration, F. A. Ray on advisory board to, 224
Federal Milk Commission for Ohio, appointed, 140
Felsman, H. H., in service, 75
Ferguson, Roy, in service, 75
Ferree, J. A., on medical staff, 248
Fieldner, A. C., in charge of research, 215
Fiftieth Report of Board of Trustees, Pres. Thompson's statements in, 286, 287
Fish, N. S., in service, 146
Fisher, Dorothy Canfield, in France, 113; writes book, 114
Fisher, Margaret E., in charge of section, 56; in Patriotic League, 118
Fitzgerald, Jean K., manager of *Lantern*, 84
Flagler, Maj. Gen. C. A. F., commands 42d (Rainbow) Division, 295
Flanagan, T. G., death of, 126
Fletcher, Fred, in uniform, 14; in service, 266, 267
Flickinger, L. C., at Edgewood, 207
Flowers, A. E., in uniform, 14; in Washington, 216, 221; in Signal Corps, 237; commissioned, 246
Foch, Gen. (*or* Marshal) ——
German delegation not yet received by, 287
Folk, S. B., teaches aids to flight, 19
Food, lectures on, 96
Food Control Act, establishes Federal Food Administration, 180
Food production, undergraduates mobilized for, 5-8
Forman, J., in uniform, 14; commissioned, 262
Fort McHenry, Md., G. C. Shaeffer at, 265
Fort Riley, Kan., medical training camp at, 261
Foulk, C. W., gives address, 164; secretary, 201
Four-quarter plan of instruction, in University, 287
Foureman, Mildred, at Wright field, 117
Foust, J. A., in uniform, 14; inspector, 239
France, supplies for, 53; photographs from, 59; W. T. Peirce in, 60; Esther Eaton in, 64; Pres. Woodrow Wilson and party in, 65; Huntley Dupre and Don L. Demorest in, 87; Margaret A. Knight in, 87; study of German in, 150; students attracted by history of, 151; H. C. Haddox in, 161; W. C. Sabine investigates tuberculosis in, 165; travels in, 166; chemists at work in, 200; Wm. McPherson in, 209; members of teaching staff in, 228, 229; Pres. Thompson in, 253; depletion of medical men in, 259; Faculty men on battle line in, 260; J. W. Means in, 264; G. C.

INDEX

Schaeffer in, 265; Faculty men in, 266; H. H. Snively in, 270, 271; D. S. White in, 280, 281; 37th and 77th Divisions in, 281
Frank, S. B., at Cleveland, 225
Franklin County, O., sum to be raised by, 46
Frary, F. C., to design phosgene plant, 210; technologist, 211
Fraternities, devote money to relief, 44; make merry, 106; in wartime, 113-130:
  Acacia, 121, 122, 124, 128;
  Alpha Gamma Rho, 119, 128;
  Alpha Kappa Kappa, 127;
  Alpha Mu Pi Omega, 129;
  Alpha Pi Upsilon, 129;
  Alpha Sigma Chi, 120;
  Alpha Sigma Phi, 128;
  Alpha Tau Omega, 122, 127;
  Alpha Zeta, 129;
  Beta Theta Pi. 119, 126, 127;
  Gamma Pi, 130;
  Delta Chi, 121, 129;
  Delta Sigma Rho, 129;
  Delta Tau Delta, 121, 127;
  Delta Theta Pi, 120;
  Delta Upsilon, 127;
  Eta Kappa Nu, 130;
  Kappa Sigma, 121, 127;
  Lambda Phi Omega, 120;
  Phi Alpha Gamma, 122;
  Phi Beta Kappa, 128;
  Phi Delta Theta, 121, 126;
  Phi Delta Kappa, 129;
  Phi Kappa, 129;
  Phi Kappa Psi, 119, 123, 126
  Phi Kappa Tau, 129;
  Phi Rho Sigma, 128;
  Phi Sigma Epsilon, 121, 129;
  Pi Kappa Alpha, 128;
  Psi Omega, 129;
  Sigma Alpha Epsilon, 121, 126, 127;
  Sigma Chi, 126;
  Sigma Delta Chi, 128;
  Sigma Xi, 128;
  Sigma Nu, 127;
  Sigma Pi, 120, 128;
  Xi Psi Phi, 119, 123;
  Zeta Beta Tau, 121
French, T. E., in service, 14
French, Walter, record of, 160
French Army, speaker from, 179
French refugees and orphans, sewing for, 54
French Government, cooperates to control tuberculosis, 165, 166; confers decorations, 283
French troops, flee, 198
Frick, C. E., at field station, 214
Friedman, M., in service, 75
Fritts, Minnette Y., chairman, 56; in service, 114
From the Front, trench poetry, 164
Fuller, M., in service, 75
Galicia, H. H. Snively in, 169
Gamper, Herman, power engineer 226
Garfield, H. A., fuel administrator, 170
Garland, Hamlin, poem by, 89
Gas masks, used by Allies, 198, 199; J. R. Withrow works on, 202; C. E. Frick works on, 214, 215; produced at Long Island City, 225
Geiger, C. A., death of, 182
General Assembly, requires teachers to take oath, 296
General Hospital No. 36, G. F. Arps at, 190
General Orders No. 62, affects Chemical Warfare Service, 208
Georgia School of Technology, school for officers at, 221
Gephart, G., in service, 14; in draft headquarters, 182

German, discontinued in high schools, 301
German Department, enrollment drops, 150
German Empire, J. R. Knipfing in, 163
German Government, declaration of war against, 4; warned, 150
Germans, use chlorine and other gases, 198, 199
Germany, Bolsheviki sign peace with, 55; Army of Occupation in, 65; C. F. O'Brien's article on, 94, 95; H. C. Haddox in, 161; H. H. Snively in, 271; 42d (Rainbow) Division in, 296
Gettys, W. E., in service, 182
Giesy, P. M., in charge of personnel, 214
Gilchrist, Col. H. L., importuned by Pres. Ignace Paderewski, 271
Gilliam, Florence, in France, 72
Gladman, M. D., death of, 127
Glenn, Alex, in service, 74
Goethals, Gen. G. W., H. L. Rietz serves under, 170
Gordon, E. J., in uniform, 14; in Ohio National Guard, 258; on battle front and in Germany, 268
Gorgas, Surgeon General, Wm. C., approves institutions, 13
Gorrel, Col. E. S., W. C. Sabine assistant to, 166
Government (see U. S. Government)
Government Research Laboratory, chemistry men in, 235
Graduate School, sustains loss, 12, 13; H. R. Spencer, acting dean, 160; students withdraw from, 243, 244; issues publications, 246; disabled soldiers in, 290
Graham, J. E., death of, 128

Graves-Walker, A. F., in service. 170
Great Britain, awards decoration to W. E. Davis, 229; depletion of professional men, 275. (See also England)
Greenburger, H., in service, 75
Groof, Paul, at Edgewood, 207
Gross, N., in service, 75
Gross, R., in service, 75
Gross, W. V., in service, 75
Grosvenor, F. B., in uniform, 14; absent, 250
Gunpowder Reservation (see Edgewood Arsenal, Md.)
Gun Range (see Machine-gun Range)
Gunnery, instruction in, 24
Gymnasium, for military use, 111

Haddox, H. C., service record of, 161
Hagerty, J. E., in service, 14, 163; in Red Cross work, 63, 64; chairman of committee, 173; adviser, 174
Haines, T. H., in service, 14
Hall, R. E., in charge of laboratory, 205; of division, 207
Hammond, C. K., death of, 129
Hammond, M. B., in service 14, 163; organizes employment offices, 138, 175; member of coal mining commission, 175, 176; writes monograph and attends conference, 176; member of War Labor Policies Board, 177; certifying officer, 178
Hammond, W. L., loses life, 109
Hampton Roads, Va., University medical unit at, 263
Hanger, W. E., obtains seed corn, 137
Hanson, L., in service, 74

INDEX 317

Harding, Hon. W. G., message from, 59
Harley, Charles, in uniform, 14; in service, 74
Harris, W. C., enters service, 161, 162
Harrison, Maj. G. R., succeeds commandant, 17
Harrop, C. B., at Bureau of Standards, 226
Hart, L. H., arranges meeting, 222
Hartford, F., in service, 14
Harvard University, W. C. Sabine teaching at, 168, 169
Hathaway, Maude C., instructor, 53; supervisor, 144
Hauer, A. M., in uniform, 14; commissioned, 262
Hayes Hall, headquarters at, 34
Hayhurst, E. R., teaching, 19, 256
Haynie, F. S., death of, 129
Hayward, Helen, canteen worker, 65
Hebbeler, H., in celebration, 288
Heifner, H. A., death of, 128
Hendrix, John, in service, 74
Helbig, Elmer, in service, 146
Helser, P. D., manufactures carbon dioxide, 211
Henderson, Mary, supervisor, 58
Henderson, W. E., in gas research, 201
Henniger, F. R., manufactures carbon dioxide, 211
Herman, Caroline, in service, 116
Heyde, Florence E., instructor, 53
Hills, T. M., in service, 14; teaches aerial observation, 19, 153, 154; helps construct ranges, 24
Hilty, Reuben, decorated, 283
Hindenburg Line, broken, 294
Hindman, S., in uniform, 14
Hinsdale, A. E., in medical corps, 248

Hinsdale, Mrs. A. E., chairman, 54
Hissem, H. L., death of, 128
Historical Commission of Ohio, endorsed, 105
History courses, due to the war, 301
Hixenbaugh, Mrs. E. R., visitor, 63
Hockett, H. C., in charge of course, 152; in service, 162
Hodges, W. H., serves in hospital, 266
Hodgman, A. W., teaches French, 154
Hoffman, Elizabeth (*see* Mrs. McManigal)
Hollingsworth, Marion, in gas research, 202
Holmes, W. M., teaches gunnery, 23
Holtcamp, Bertha, at Camp Jackson, 116
Home Economics Department, to conduct canning campaign, 132; supplies equipment, 144
Home Service Institute, organized, 63, 173, 174
Homeopathic Hospital Auxiliary, (Red Cross), 54
Hooper, O. C., in Red Cross work, 63; in service, 163; on committee, 173
Hoover, Hon. Herbert C., Dean Affred Vivian adviser to, 133; appoints milk commission, 140; requests service of M. B. Hammond, 176
Horse Purchasing Board, at Kansas City, Mo., 282
Hoskins, Don., in service, 74.
Hoskins, George, in service, 74
Hough, B. W., commands 166th. Infantry, 294
Houston, W. H., in service, 74
Howard, Ralph, in service, 74

Howard, R. W., sends false news of Armistice, 287
Hoyt, Roy, in service, 74
Hufford, G. H., at Edgewood, 207
Hugger, C. C., in uniform, 14; commissioned, 262
Hughes, D. G., in service, 146
Hughes, R. M., regional director, 35
Hugus, P. H., at Edgewood, 207
Humphrey, W. A., in medical corps, 248
Husband, H. A., death of, 126
Huston, A. C., record of, 226
Hutchinson, J. L., in service, 146; in gas laboratory, 205

Influenza epidemic, among cadets, 37, 64, 80, 144
Ingraham, Mrs. E. S., supervisor, 58
Inter-Allied Conference, on gas investigations, 209
Ireland, to be incited to revolution, 4
Isonzo (river), W. C. Sabine in offensive on, 166
Italian Army, speaker from, 179
Italy, A. R. Chandler in, 61, 62; R. C. Paterson in, 62, 63; H. R. Spencer departs for, 104; W. C. Sabine in, 166; tuberculosis unit in, 267

Jacoby, F. S., adviser, 133
Jaglinski, Peter, in service, 248
James, E. D., death of, 126
Japan, to join Germany, 4
Jewish Welfare Board, funds for, 47
Johns, L., death of, 128
Johnson, C. F., at Baltimore, 215
Johnson, Margaret, in Washington, 116
Johnson, Olga, Red Cross nurse, 249
Johnson, O. O., death of, 128
Johnston, T. P., death of, 129
Jones, A. H., death of, 129, 188
Jones, H. I., goes to Fort Benjamin Harrison, 107
Journal of Industrial and Engineering Chemistry, gas research in, 214
Judd, Horace, in service, 224

Karb, Mayor G. J., reviews parade, 289; welcomes troops, 291, 292
Kauffman, Mrs. G. B., supervisor, 57, 58
Keiser, J. G., commissioned, 246; returns, 250
Kelly, C. F., in service, 14, 193, 194
Kelly, Mary A., in Italy, 64, 65
Kennedy, C. L., in service, 74
Ketcham, V. A., attends committee, 48; in service, 163
Kettering, C. F., *Ohio State Engineer* dedicated to, 92
Key, Murriel, Red Cross nurse, 249
Kimmel, H., in service, 75
King, Enid, in Washington, 116
Kinkead, Mrs. E. B., instructor, 52
Kinley, David, invites M. B. Hammond to prepare study, 176
Kiplinger, Willard, responds, 223
Klein, Irving, in service, 75
Kleinmeyer, Jesse, in service, 75
Klingberg, F. J., gives course, 156
Knappenburger, C. W., in service, 248
Knight, G. W., on committee, 45; director of War Issues course, 152, 194
Knight, Mrs. G. W., Red Cross supervisor, 57; in relief unit, 60; criticizes University women, 98

INDEX 319

Knight, Margaret A., letter from, 87
Knight, W. A., in service, 14; attends Royal Aviation School, 17; heads instruction in gunnery and airplanes, 18, 23, 238, 239
Knights of Columbus, funds for, 47; at Camp Sherman, O., 190
Knipfing, J. R., article by, 94; translator, 163
Knouff, R. A., in uniform, 14; in service, 272
Koch, S., in service, 75
Komisaruk, L. B., in service, 75; at Edgewood, 207
Kotz, T. F., in uniform, 14; service record, 159
Kramer, M. Dorothy, chairman, 56
Krauss, Katherine, in service, 170
Krohngold, W., in service, 75
Kuertz, Jack, in service, 75

Laidler, H. W., speaks at University, 102
Lake Laboratory, classes reduced, 146
Lambert, F. A., in uniform, 14; service record of, 282
Lamme, B. G., record of, 226
Landacre, F. L., acting dean, 259
Lang, C., in service, 75
Lantern (see *Ohio State Lantern*)
Lantis, L. O , released from teaching, 138, 139
Laughlin, R. W., death of, 75, 129
Law School, teachers from, 152
Lawson, J. K., death of, 128
Laylin, C. D., instructor, 19; team captain, 47; lectures to adjutants, 253
Layne, C. B., record of, 294
Lazarus, R. L., at Baltimore, 215
Leighton, J. A., article by, 164
Leighton, M. M., teaching, 154

Lentz, Monobelle, in service, 114
Leonard, Col. C. F., reviews parade, 299
Levison, R., in service, 75
Lewis, W. K., assigns gas problems, 201
Liberty Loan campaigns: first, 42, 43; second, 43, 54; third, 45-46; fourth, 46-47; executive committee for, 174, 175
Lincoln, G., in service, 75
Lincoln, P. M., commissioned, 226
Linzell, S., with Canadian Army, 75
Lockhart, O. C., on leave, 182
Long, E., in service, 14
Long, Elizabeth, secretary, 63
Long, J., in service, 14
Lord, H. C., attends Royal Aviation School, 17; teaches aids to flight, 19, 241; builds apparatus, 21; gathers information, 22; work approved, 23
Lord, Mrs. H. C., member of relief unit, 60
Lord, N. W., G. A. Burrell student and chemist under, 200, 201
Loudermill, J. J., sent to University station, 215
Lowe, C. C., in service, 241
Ludwig, E. C., in uniform, 14; in service, 266
Lusitania, torpedoed, 4; effect on German Department, 150
Luttrell, John, in service, 75
Lutz, H. W., in service, 146.
Luxemburg, H. C. Haddox in, 161
Lyman, J. R., in gas research, 202
Lyons, Thelma L., in service, 170

McAdie, A. C., aids H. C. Lord, 22
McCampbell, E. F., on leave, 8; in uniform, 14; lectures, 56; in service, 163, 256; to report for duty,

258; given leave, 259; service of, 261

McClelland, C. E., death of, 129

McComb, K. S., death of, 130

McCormick, V. R., death of, 128

McCracken, W. C., on war chest committee, 44

McGaughey, W. J., in gas research, 202; takes class, 237; in Washington, 239

McKenzie, R. D., in service, 14; investigator, 180

McKinley, Helen, in service, 117

McManigal, Mrs. ———, in service, 113

McNaghten, Margaret, in service, 116

McNeal, E. H., chairman, 152; in service, 162

McNeal, Isabel, in France, 72

McNeil, C. P., at Long Island City, 225

McPherson, William, on leave, 8, 245; in uniform, 14; in service, 163; convenes University chemists, 201; in Washington, 202; commissioned, 203; enlists chemical plants, 204; promoted, 208, 209; to France and England, 209, 210; responds, 223

Machine-gun Range, plans for, 10; cost of, 11

Mack, C. E., at Edgewood, 207

Madden, J. W., teaches, 19; lectures to adjutants, 252

Magruder, T. M., sails for Bordeaux, 60

Magruder, W. T., in service, 14; attends Royal Aviation School, 17; instructor, 19

Magruder, Mrs. W. T., canteen worker, 58; in relief unit, 60

Maintenance Division, loses members, 13-14

Makio, The, effect of war on board of, 84; editors killed, 85; for 1917 shows little war influence, 89; for 1918 full of war items, 90

Mallon, Mrs. G. W., in France, 72

Maloney, D., aids in airplanes, 23

Manning, V. H., letter from 200, 201

Manson, E. S., Jr., in uniform, 14; record of, 224; leaves for camp, 241

Mansperger, M., in service, 75

Manual on Instruments, material in, 22, 23

Marino, A., called, 194

Mark, Mary L., statistical adviser, 180

Marquand, Carl, in service, 74

Marquis, F. W., in service, 14

Massachusetts Institute of Technology, school of aeronautics at, 192; men at Edgewood, 215

Masteller, Jessie F., chairman, 56

Matson, L. L., teaches gunnery, 23, 24

Matthews, B. B., death of, 127

Maxillo-facial surgery, Faculty members practice, 264-266

May, R. J., death of, 128

Means, J. W., in uniform, 14; released for service, 186; discharged, 187; to report for duty, 258; in maxillo-facial surgery, 264, 265

Medical Enlisted Reserve Corps, enrollment in. 255, 256; number in, 257; changed, 260; V. A. Dodd in, 262; regulations, 276; transfer of students from, 277; differences from Students' Army Training Corps, 278

Medical Faculty, leaves for, 8; members commissioned, 247; of-

INDEX

ficers in Army and Navy, 259; in naval unit, 262; in maxillofacial surgery, 264-626; serving in hospitals, 266-267; in tuberculosis unit in Italy, 267-268; on battle line, 268-272
Medical Reserve Corps (see Medical Enlisted Reserve Corps)
Medical Training Camps, organized, 260, 261
Mediterranean Sea. W. C. Sabine in dirigible over, 167
Mechanics of the Aeroplane, Duchene's, 22
Mellon, D. R., at Niagara Falls, 224, 225
Menorah Society, in drive, 49; men in service, 75
Men's Glee Club, reorganized, 106
Mershon, R. D., promotes National Defense Act, 1-4; record of, 225, 226
Mexican Border, trucks on, 217; Ohio National Guard on, 258; R. L. Mundhenk on, 281
Mexican Punitive Expedition, delays enforcement, 3; trucks in, 217
Mexico, southwestern States offered to, 4
Meyer, Florence, in service, 14
Military Airplanes, Loening's, 22
Military Barracks, constructed, 286
Military Department, supplies instructors, 256
Military Hospital, cost of, 11; too small, 37; location of, 80; influenza in, 144
Miller, F. A., vice-president, war chest committee, 44
Miller, H. C., enters Navy, 182
Miller, R. C., in service, 146
Miller, S. C., death of, 129

Miligan, L. H., at Edgewood, 207
Mitchell, Alton, at Edgewood, 207
Mix, S. E., record of, 162
Monnier, J. C., death of, 127
Moore, A. P., record of, 161
Morton, Mrs. T. A., chairman, 54
Motor Transport Corps, created, 219
Motor Transport Service, created and supplanted, 219
Motor Transport Training Schools, instruction for, 220
Mott, Dr. J. R., addresses student delegates, 47
Mueller, W. A., helps design plant, 210; manufactures mustard gas, 211
Mundhenk, R. L., in uniform, 14; record of, 281-282
Murray, Helen, in Washington, 117
Murray, Ruth, in service, 117
Myers, H. J, death of, 127
Myers, J. S., on war chest committee, 45; in Red Cross work, 63; chairman, 64; in war work, 174; fiinds nurses, 175

National Academy of Sciences, receives communication, 199, 200
National Defense Act, enactment and provisions of, 1-4
National Research Council, conducts gas investigations, 200
National War Labor Policies Board, M. B. Hammond serves on, 176, 177
Naval Unit, maintained, 36
Navin, C. A., death of, 127
Navy, enlistments in, 182; members of medical Faculty in, 259; medical unit of, 262-264; officers in, 260; medical graduates in, 268; pharmacy men in, 273; promotes gas investigations, 200

Navy Department, grants request, 264
Nevin, R. B., leaves truck squad, 107; loses life, 109
Nevin, Robert, in service, 74
New York Times, J. R. Knipfing's articles in, 163, 164
Nichol, Frances, Red Cross nurse, 249
Nichols, J. H., in uniform, 14; in service, 163
Nicholson, Meredith, editorials by, 89
Noble, Ellis, in service, 74
Nold, H. E., takes class, 237, 241
North, C. C., in service, 14; in war work, 180
Norton, F. W. (*or* Fred), death of, 111, 129

O'Brien, C. F., article by, 94
Ohio, erects bridge in Belgium, 294
Ohio Board of Agriculture, gives crop figures, 136
Ohio Branch, Council of National Defense, promotes drives, 41, 136; Edna N. White, chairman of Food Department of, 134, 135
Ohio Coal Mining Commission, M. B. Hammond a member of, 175, 176
Ohio Experiment Station, helps instruct farmers, 135
Ohio National Guard, at Camp Sheridan, 253; E. J. Gordon in, 258; H. H. Snively in, 269; R. L. Mundhenk in, 281; its former organizations return, 291, 293, 294
Ohio State Engineer, The, effects of war on, 85; war material in 92; urges need of engineers, 100
Ohio State Lantern, The, issues special, 45; loses men reporters, 84; changes appearance, 86; headlines in, 86, 87; features of, 87-89; war activities in, 95, 96; supports drives, 100; at Army camps, 101; editorials of, 102, 103, 105, 106; interviews in, 104; conducted largely by women, 172
Ohio State University, shapes National Defense Act, 1-4; Reserve Officers' Training Corps at, 3; mobilizes, 4-9; coal shortage at, 9; enrollment, 33; forms contract with Government, 33; Naval Unit at, 36; influenza at, 37; war drives at, 41-49; enlistment at, 73; supplies farm-hands, 132; students leave, 171; reduced enrollment in, 172; veterinary courses modified at, 277; officers from, 282; F. A. Lambert returns to, 282; students return to, 285; loses teachers after the war, 286; ferment in, 287; disabled soldiers in, 290; welcomes returned troops, 291-296; War Chemical Association of, 201; staff chosen from, 203; its reputation for training chemists, 236. (*See* also Colleges, and Departments)
Ohio State University Association, buys bond, 44
Ohio State University Monthly, The, makes changes, 86; chronicles services of Ohio State men, 93, 94; C. F. O'Brien's article in, 94, 05; J. V. Denney's article in, 164
Ohio State University Studies, issued, 246
Ohio Union, in wartime, 10, 77; additions to, 10, 11; mess hall at, 34, 77, 78, 79, 90; on war basis, 78; aids hospital, 80; its employees, 81

INDEX

Olin, H. L., in gas research, 202; at Edgewood, 206, 207
Oliver, N. S., commandant, 34
Olsen, H. C., teaches recreation, 19
Ontario Veterinary College, S. Sisson at, 283
Orr, A. H., at Edgewood, 207
Orton, Edward, Jr., promotes National Defense Act, 1-4; helps prepare letter, 4; on leave, 8; in uniform, 14; letter from, 95; in Washington, 216; record of, 217-220
Osburn, Mrs. R. C., instructor, 53; supervisor, 57; canteen worker, 58
Overholt, V., in service, 74, 146
Overturf, A. K., death of, 126

Paderewski, Madam Ignace, asks aid for Poland, 271
Paderewski, Pres. Ignace, asks for medical expedition, 271
Page Hall, barracks in, 34; supervised study in, 40
Palmer, W. R., in service, 74
Panhellenic Council, work of, 118; condition of, 122; housing plan of, 123
Park, J. A., on credit for service men, 299
Park, Joseph, in service, 74
Parry, C. E., in service, 14; secretary, 178; on leave, 179
Parsons, J. T., in gas laboratory, 205; at Edgewood, 207
Patchell, J. M., appoints committee, 300
Paterson, H. G., in tuberculosis unit, 267; promoted, 268
Paterson, R. G., in service, 14; in Red Cross work, 62, 63, 256
Paterson, Maj. Gen. R. U., invites H. H. Snively to Russia, 269

Patrick, J. E., at Baltimore, 215
Patriotic League, glee club of, 292, 293
Pavey, Eugenia C., instructor, 53
Payne, H. E., in service, 170
Peace Conference, W. T. Peirce translator for, 61
Peirce, W. T., in unfiorm, 14; in Red Cross service, 59-60; services of, 159
Perigord, Lieut. Paul, speaker, 179
Pershing, Gen. John J., W. T. Peirce interpreter at headquarters of, 60; transfers Veterinary Service, 280; sends 37th Division to aid Belgian Army, 294
Persia, H. H. Snively in, 269
Peterson, Dr. E. A., gives address, 15
Pettibone, F. G., in service, 248
Pettit, W., in service, 146
Phillips, T. D., in service, 14; adviser, 133; released from teaching, 138, 139
Phillips, T. G., in uniform, 14; in service, 146; in gas laboratory, 205
Pierce, J., in service, 74
Pilot squadrons, growth of, 24, 25
Pintner, Rudolph, in service, 14; at Camp Lee, 191
Poisonous gases, used by Germans, 198, 199; investigation of, 200; production of, 203, 204, 210; plant constructed, 204; mustard gas, 205; laboratory, 205, 206, 207; research work in, 208, 209; buildings for, 211; chlorpicrin and mustard gas plants, 212, 213, 214; selenium mustard gas, 213, 214; mustard gas produced at Niagara Falls, 225. (*See also* Edgewood Arsenel)
Poland, H. H. Snively in, 271

Pomerene, Hon. Atlee, message from, 59
Posonick, L., in service, 75
Powell, G. R., award to, 283
Powell, H. T. (or "Dutch"), hailed, 296
Preparedness League of Dental Surgeons, organized, 184
Princeton University, school of eronautics at, 192
Prinkey, J. W., instructor, 19.
Psychological tests, given to students, 297
Psychology, interest in applied, 193 (See also Department of Psychology)
Publications (campus), during the war, 83-111
Public Health Service, medical graduates in, 268
Publications of the Teaching Staff, issued, 246
Pugh, Edna H., in service, 72, 115

Quartermaster Corps, Veterinary Service detached from, 280

Radio Development Section, Signal Corps, 221
Ragsdale, Capt. E. J. W., Wm. McPherson adviser to, 202, 203
Ramsower, H. C. enrolling officer, 138; assumes duties, 142
Rankin, Allen, in service, 74
Ray, F. A., on leave, 9; in service, 224, 240, 241
Ray, Mrs. F. A. record of, 58; aids sick, 64
Raymond, Stockton, member of committee, 63
Recreation, as training, 25, 26
Rebrassier, R. E., on inactive duty, 282, 283
Red Cross, service with 13; members for, 41; activities, 51-65; student drive for, 67; rumors against, 97; campaign for, 98; supported, 100; classes, 144; promotes Home Service Institute, 174; J. S. Myers publicity agent for, 174; nurses sought by committee of, 175; at Camp Sherman, 190; R. G. Paterson in service of, 256; Faculty members in, 259; relief workers, 260; provides recreation center, 264; organizes tuberculosis unit, 267; H. H. Snively, director at Kiev for, 269
Reed, C. I., in uniform, 14; in gas research, 216
Reeder, C. W., in service, 14; instructor, 19
Reel, P. J., commissioned, 262
Rees, Col. ———, submits plan affecting colleges, 31
Reese, W. M., at Edgewood, 207
Rehabilitation students, in University, 289-291
Reichard, H. F., in uniform, 14
Reif, L., in uniform, 14; released for service, 186, 187
Reserve Officers' Training Corps, created, 2, 3
Reserve Officers' Training Camps, students leave for, 101
Richards, R. S., instructor, 221
Rietz, H. L., war work of, 170; responds, 223
Riggle, J. J., in service, 146
Rightmire, G. W., instructor, 19; lectures, 252; member of War Records Committee, 253
Roberts, A. R., death of, 127
Roberts, L. K., death of, 128
Rockefeller War Relief Commission, W. C. Sabine and wife serve, 165

Roehm, Ralph, in service, 74
Rogers, Joy N., in charge of section, 56
Ronan, W. C., in uniform, 14; instructor, 19
Rosselli, Bruno, speaker, 179
Royer, R. M., chairman of Liberty Loan committee, 46
Rowlen, Mary, in training, 114
Ruggles, C. O., in service, 14; on Shipping Board, 181
Russell, Rose W., in service, 116
Russell, Bertrand, review of publication by, 92
Russia, F. A. Ray in, 224; H. H. Snively in, 269
Russian Revolution, endangers democracy, 4
Ryder, Melvin, in service, 74

Sabine, W. C., death of, 127; war work of, 165-170
Sabine, Mrs. W. C., relief work, 165
Sage, H. M., in service, 248; returns, 250
St. John, L. W., on war chest committee, 45; director, 109
Sanborn, F. E., in uniform, 14; in Washington, 216; record of, 221, 239
Sanders P., in service, 75
Sanor, Mrs. D. G., chairman, 54
Sansculotte, The, contents of, 92
S. A. T. C. (see Students' Army Training Corps)
Sater, L. F., gives address, 59
Sater, Mrs. L. F., aids sick, 64.
Saunders, R. T., death of, 127
Schaeffer, G. B., in uniform, 14
Schaeffer, G. C., to report for duty, 258; in maxillo-facial surgery, 264, 265
Schilling, S. J., on inactive duty, 282, 283

Schleich, H. J., at Edgewood, 207
Schlesinger, A. M., in Red Cross work, 63; gives new course, 157, 158
Schneider, A. B., teaches, 250
School for Aero-Squadron Adjutants, account of, 27-28, 29;; closed, 77; J. J. Adams lectures to, 253
School for Aero-Squadron Engineer Officers, account of, 27; dates of, 29; added, 78
School for Balloon-Squadron Adjutants, account of, 28-30; started, 78, 79; referred to, 252
School of Military Aeronautics, housing and feeding of, 9-10; account of, 17-27, 29; established, 77; care of, 78; publishes *The Pilot*, 92, 93; dormitory for, 108; aerial observation for, 153; Engineering College supplies instructors for, 232; instruction in, 256; J. H. Snook instructor in, 293
School of Veterinary Instruction, at Camp Greenleaf, 282
Schumacher, W., in service, 162
Schuster, G., in service, 74
Scientific Monthly, The, J. A. Leighton's article in, 164
Seamans, H. M., examiner, 187
Searle, F. F., death of, 129
Sears, D., in service, 74
Sears, P. B., in uniform, 14; in service, 146
Sebrell, L. B., at field station, 214, 215
Seeds, Charme M., casualty searcher, 65
Seegar, G. C., record of, 228-229
Selective Draft Regulations, provisions of, 276
Selective Service Act (*or* Law),

326   HISTORY OF THE OHIO STATE UNIVERSITY

men enrolled under, 13; operation of, 230
Selenium mustard gas, produced, 213, 214
Service, J. H., instructor, 19, 22
Service flag, of University, 58, 59
Seymour, A. T., on war chest committee, 44
Shafer, M. O., at Edgewood, 207
Shapiro, A. S., in service, 75
Shaw, F., in service, 75
Sheetz, J. W., in uniform, 14; in service, 266
Shepperd, H. E., in draft headquarters, 182
Sherrard, Lieut. R. G., assists commandant, 3
Shick, Rhoda, service of, 118
Sibert, Maj. Gen. W. L., commander of Chemical Warfare Service, 208
Siebert, W. H., aids sick, 64; article by, 94; lectures, 164, 165; acting dean, 245; on War Records Committee, 245
Siebert, Mrs. W. H., uses machine, 55; supervisor, 57; in relief unit, 60; aids sick, 64
Sigerfoos, Edward, death of, 127
Signal Corps, issues manual, 22, 23; Radio Development Section of, 221; students enter, 230; A. E. Flowers in, 245, 246
Signal Enlisted Reserve Corps, men enroll in, 13
Sinks, F. L., at Edgewood, 207
Sisson, Septimus, in Canada, 283
Skinner, C. E., in charge of research, 225
Skinner, Evrett, death of, 126
Slavic Europe, course on, 151
Smart, George, approves letter, 5
Smith, C. C., death of, 129
Smith, E. C., in service, 14; record of, 225; expert, 236, 237
Smith, Gordon, in service, 75
Smith, L. I., sent to Washington, 216
Smith, R. H., at Edgewood, 207
Snively, H. H., mentioned, 51; record of, 268-272; delayed arrival of, 292
Snively, Mrs. H. H., conducts classes, 51; enrolls young women, 52
Snook, J. H., instructor, 19, 283
Society of Automotive Engineers, backs program, 218
Somermeier, E. E., G. A. Burrell student and chemist under, 200, 201
Sororities, devote money to relief, 44; prepare hospital supplies, 60; make merry, 106; in wartime, 113-118
Alpha Gamma Theta, 116, 117
Alpha Phi, 115
Alpha Xi Delta, 117
Chi Omega, 118
Delta Delta Delta, 116
Delta Zeta, 117
Kappa Alpha Theta, 114
Kappa Kappa Gamma, 114, 114
Phi Mu, 116
Pi Beta Phi, 115
Spanish-American War veterans, in parade, 289
Speakers' Bureau, carries message, 179
Special Regulations No. 70, for Veterinary Corps, 279
Spencer, H. R., in service, 14; in France, 69; supplies column in *Lantern*, 104; record of, 160, 161; acting dean, 245; on leave, 245
Sprague, P. E., in service, 75
Stack, H. G., in service, 248

INDEX 327

Stankard, L. T., instructor, 19; morale officer, 22
Starr, F. C., in uniform, 14; released for service, 186; in France, 187
State Emergency Board, Trustees appeal to, 285
Stauffer, George, in conference, 131
Stebbins, C. R., death of, 128
Steeb, C. E., in service, 9, 14; to have plans prepared, 10; chairman of war chest committee, 44; of Victory Loan committee, 48; record of, 170
Steinfeld, A. M., in uniform, 14; in orthopedic work, 266
Stephenson, B. D., at service-flag dedication; expert on pig iron, 221
Stinson, K. W., instructor, 19
Stocklin, Lillian, leader of glee club, 117, 292, 293
Stowe, G. T., record of, 211
Stratemeyer, Capt. George, commandant, 17
Students' Army Training Corps, students in, 32, 34; made separate school, 34; teachers for, 35; short life of, 36; demobilized, 38; discouraging features of, 40; girls sew for, 56; influenza among cadets of, 64; demobilized, 77; members advised to remain, 105; welcomed by *Lantern*, 96, 97; athletic activities of, 110; course on motor transports for, 142; increases enrollment in Arts College, 148; in geology, 154; requires many instructors, 157; students enter, 171; registration in, 189; J. W. Bridges supervisor in, 192; War Issues course required in, 194; men inducted into, 230; members elect chemistry, 234; causes drop in metallurgy, 237; emphasizes need of technicians, 238; cadets take shop work, 239; E. F. Coddington helps organize, 240; at selected institutions, 255, 277; teaching cadets in, 259; differs from Medical Enlisted Reserve Corps, 278; buildings for, 286; Company D of, in celebration, 288
Student Council, in Red Cross campaign, 51; only two members in college, 83
Summer session, enrollment in, 15, 155; patriotic rally of, 46; pharmacy men in, 273; veterinary students in, 276
Sun Dial, The, women on staff of, 84, 85; changes appearance, 89; sounds critical note, 98; on war gardens, 101; "Old Times Number" of, 106
Swain, L. C., in service, 75
Swartzel, K. D., in service, 224
Sweeny, O. R., in War Chemical Association, 201; in Washington, 203; in charge of plant, 212
Switzerland, W. C. Sabine's relief work in, 165

Taber, D. O., in service, 75
Taber, L. J., enlists granges, 139, 140
Taft, D. R., assistant, 181
Taylor, J. R., in service, 14, 162; writes inscription, 73
Taylor, W. N., in uniform, 14; in service, 266
Teachnor, Margaret, interpreter, 65
Teachers' oath, required, 296
Tenney, Gerald, in service, 75
Tenney, G. E., at Springfield Arsenal, 266

Terminal Charges at United States Posts, by C. O. Ruggles, 181

Teter, H. H., death of, 129; torpedoed, 268

Theiss, T. T., instructor, 19

Thomas, Ruby, instructor, 53

Thompson, Pres. W. O., shapes National Defense Act, 1-4; sends message, 5; on food situation, 5-6; in service, 9, 14; gives items, 11; conservative action of, 12; leaves for Washington, 17; president of Academic Board, 18; gives precedence to war schools, 29; accept service flag, 56; conducts dedication, 73; in conference, 131; gives address, 165; appoints War Records Committee, 245; makes trip for Federal Food Administration, 252, 253; his statements in *Fiftieth Report*, 286, 287; in celebration, 288; orders University closed, 292; takes test, 297; letter received by, 200; at meeting in Washington, 222, 223; returns from France, 223

Thompson, Mrs. W. O., does canteen work and supervises making of service flag, 58

Thorndike, E. L., work for, 191; psychology men cooperate with, 193

Thorpe, Lieut. T. D., at University, 2

Thrash, C. L., in service, 146; at Edgewood, 207

Thrift stamps (*see* War stamps)

Tilford, Capt. J. D., assists commandant, 3

Tobin, R. A., instructor, 23

Toulon (France), W. C. Sabine at, 166

Townshend, Vivian S., in charge of section, 56

Toxic gases (*see* Poisonous gases)

Trade Test Division, R. Pintner member of, 191; research for, 193

Trautman, G. W., in service, 14

Trench poetry, collected by C. E. Andrews, 164

Trench Warfare Section, plans laboratory, 204

Trentino, W. C. Sabine makes flights in, 166, 167

Troops:
37th Division, E. J. Gordon in, 268; H. H. Snively directs field hospitals of, 270; goes overseas, 281; units return, 291; heavy losses of, 293; aids Belgian Army, 294

42d. (Rainbow) Division, welcome to 166th Infantry of, 294; in France, 295

62d. Artillery Brigade, arrives, 291

77th. Division, in Baccarat sector, 281

112th. Engineers, arrives, 293

112th. Field Signal Battalion, arrives, 291

112th. Sanitary Train, arrives, 291, 292

112th. Supply Train, arrives, 293

134th. Artillery, arrives, 293

134th. Regiment, arrives, 291

135th. Regiment, arrives, 291

136th. Regiment, arrives, 291

146th. Ambulance Company, arrives, 291

146th. Field Hospital, arrives, 291

146th. Infantry, arrives, 292

147th. Ambulance Company, arrives, 291

147th. Field Hospital, arrives, 291

148th. Infantry, arrives, 293
166th. Infantry arrives, 294
Trucks, on Mexican Border, 217; types for Army, 217, 218; repair shops for, 218; standardized, 220
Trustees, provide for second officer, 2; approve letter, 5; authorize message, 5; remit diploma fees, 8; give Pres. Thompson power to arrange for leaves of absence, 8; in conference with Governor Cox, 10; order new buildings, 11; conservative action of, 12; approve action, 200; grant leave to Pres. Thompson, 252; grant other leaves, 258; appeal to State Emergency Board, 285; *Fiftieth Report* of, 286, 287; approve four-quarter plan, 287; approve psychological tests, 297
Tuberculosis unit, in Italy, 267-268
Tucker, W. M., teaching, 154
Tunell, Winifred, in France, 72
Tuttle, A. H., in service, 14; teaches military law, 19; to fraternities, 124; lectures, 252; services of, 253, 254

Ukraine, H. H. Snively in, 271
U. S. Army (*see* Army)
U. S. Department of Agriculture, supplies emergency sums, 132; Pres. Thompson makes trip for, 252
U. S. Employment Service, recruiting labor through, 177; examiners for, 178
U. S. Food Administration in Ohio, promotes drives, 41. (*See* also Federal Food Administration
U. S. Fuel Administration, established, 176
U. S. Government, getting college men into service, 5; war measures supported, 95; asks for lists of essential teachers, 258; 259; research for, 199, 200; builds gas-producing plants, 204-212; buys supply of helium gas, 209; difficulties with trucks, 217
U. S. Naval Medical College, seniors sent to, 7
U. S. Naval Reserve Force Unit, account of, 262-264
U. S. Naval Station Hospital No. 5, staff of, 262
U. S. Navy (*see* Navy)
U. S. Physical Health Service, supplies medical service, 290
U. S. Public Health Service, Faculty member in, 259
U. S. Shipping Board, C. O. Ruggles' services and report to, 181
University (*see* Ohio State University)
University Faculty, approves letter, 5; authorizes message, 5; adopts Gov. Cox's order, 7; empowers Pres. Thompson to excuse seniors, 8; authorizes special classes, 39. (*See* Faculty)
University of Chicago, four-quarter plan in, 287
University of Paris, W. C. Sabine lectures at, 165
University Women's Club, Red Cross division of, 53, 54
University Y.M.C.A., in drives, 41, 42, 44, 48. (*See* also Y.M.C.A.)
Upp, C. R., teaching, 23, 221
Usher, R. G., editorials by, 89
Usry, E. L., provides equipment, 55

Van Buskirk, L. H., remains, 256
Vander Werf, J. A., at American University and Edgewood, 216
Van Meter, Anna R., makes investigations, 143

330 HISTORY OF THE OHIO STATE UNIVERSITY

Van Orman, S. L., at Baltimore, 215
Veterinary Alumni Quarterly, The, difficulties of, 85; urges enlistment, 91; prints valuable articles, 92
Veterinary Corps, men not eligible to, 284
Veterinary Faculty, increases entrance requirements, 275; determines curriculum, 278; members absent, 278, 279
Veterinary Officers' Reserve Corps, D. S. White examiner for, 279; men striving to enter, 284
Veterinary Profession, The, bulletin, 277
Victory Loan, subscription to, 48
Vigor, L. E., in service, 14
Virtue, D. R., in gas laboratory, 205; at Edgewood, 207
Vivian, Alfred, on committee, 34; in conference, 131; makes addresses, 132; adviser, 133
Vivian, Mrs. Alfred, canteen worker, 58; in relief unit, 60
Vogel, Katherine A., leads team, 47

Wagner, J. E., reviews parade, 299
Walker, Mrs. G. G., instructor, 52, 53; in Red Cross work, 144
Walker, Col. W. H., commander of Edgewood and other toxic gas plants, 208
Walradt, H. F., in service, 14; in sugar division, 181
War Camp Service, funds for, 47
War College Committee on Education, frame bill, 2
War Department, creates Reserve Officers' Training Corps, 3; address list sent to, 5; contract with Trustees, 10; establishes schools, 17; receives replicas of H. C. Lord's apparatus, 21; on man power bill, 31; conserves supply of medical men, 275, 276; organizes committee, 277; jurisdiction over Veterinary College, 278; adopts regulations, 279; separates Chemical Warfare Service, 208
War Issues, Government requires course on, 151; taken by cadets, 152; teachers of, 253
War stamps, sale of, 46; sales featured, 100
Warren, J. H., in service, 266
Warrick, W. A., instructor, 19
Washburne, G. A., gives course, 157
Washington, D. C., W. C. Sabine in, 168, 169; group of Ohio State workers at, 170; F. E. Sanborn in, 223; F. M. Craft and C. P. Cooper in, 227-228; A. H. Tuttle in, 253; E. F. McCampbell in, 261; D. S. White in, 280; American Legion seeks compensation in, 298, 299; Wm. McPherson in, 202; O. R. Sweeney in, 203; J. R. Withrow in, 203; American University in, 203, 209, 213, 215, 216, 233; W. L. Evans and R. E. Hall in, 205; G. A. Burrell in, 208, 209; D. J. Demorest in, 210; chemists in, 212; Engineering College men in, 216, 223, 224; A. A. Case in, 220, 221; A. E. Flowers in, 221; F. E. Sanborn in, 221, 222; A. D. Cole and S. J. Barnett in, 222; gatherings of Ohio State men in, 222
Wasson, R. H., instructor, 19
Waters, Corinne, lectures, 118
Watson, Florence, in service, 117
Weaver, Galen, in service, 75
Weber, S. G., at Edgewood, 207
Webster, D. S., death of, 126
Weil, E. A., in service, 75

INDEX 331

Weiss, H., in service, 75
Welch, Margaret, chairman, 56
Weldishofer, W. M., commissioned, 282
Welling, Florence E., entertainer, 65
Western Conference, meets, 107
Whan, Lucille, conducts section, 56
Wheeler, C. S., in conference, 131; adviser, 133; gets contract signed, 137
Whitacre, Florence L., in charge of section, 56
White, D. S., on leave, 8; in uniform, 14; services of, 279-282; decoration of, 283; responds, 223
White, Edna N., in service, 14; urges girls to service, 52; director, 133; services of, 134
Whitehill, Juliann E., awaiting call as nurse, 114
Wilbur Wright Flying Field (see Wright Flying Field)
Wilce, J. W., in Medical Corps, 110
Wilkinson, J. A., on staff, 205; in charge of division, 207
Wilkoff, J., in service, 75
Williams, F. O., commissioned, 262
Williams, Ruth, in service, 117
Williams, T. R., in uniform, 14; serves in hospitals, 266
Willing, W., in service, 75
Wilson, Margaret, at Brest, 65
Wilson, P., in uniform, 14
Wilson, P. D., in service, 266; on battle front, 268
Wilson, President Woodrow, dismisses German ambassador, 4; urges declaration of war, 4; message to, 5; proclamation of, 8; requests cooperation, 47-48; at Brest, 65; war messages of, 97; W. H. Siebert lectures on, 164, 165; appeal of, 194

Wilson, Mrs. Woodrow, at Brest, 65
Wirth, W. A., death of, 129
Wise, L. W., in service, 146
Withrow, J. R., in service, 14, 163; works on gas masks, 202; consulting chemist, 203; departure of, 212
Withrow, S. S., in Ordnance Department, 225
Wolcott, R. C., in Medical Corps, 248
Wolf, Florence, chairman, 56
Wolfel, Evangeline, in relief work, 114
Wilman, B., in service, 75
Women's Council, in Red Cross campaign, 51; prepares supplies, 60; has supper, 106
Wood, Gen. Leonard, circulates Edward Orton, Jr.'s paper, 1
World War, course on, 151, 156
Wright, H. R., death of, 127, 188
Wright, J. D., at Edgewood, 207
Wright, W. E., in France, 69
Wright Flying Field, pilots at, 26; W. C. Sabine's trip to, 168

Yassenoff, L., in service, 75
Yassenoff, S., in service, 75
Yerges, L. C., death of, 125, 182
Y. M. C. A., service with, 13; in drives, 41, 44, 48, 51; funds for, 47; condition of, 67, 68; members in service, 71, 83; members abroad, 72; commemorates enlisted men, 73; supplies entertainment, 74; rumors adverse to, 97; at Camp Sherman, O., 190
Y. M. C. A. Cabinet, members in service, 83; drive of, 99; supported, 100; plans lectures, 105
Yost, Harold, in service, 75

Zimmerman Note, contents of, 4

CPSIA information can be obtained
at www.ICGtesting.com
Printed in the USA
BVOW08s0822060717
488317BV00017B/294/P

9 781331 621874